Regional Inequality in China

China's spectacular growth and poverty reduction has been accompanied by growing inequality which threatens the social compact and thus the political basis for economic growth. Chinese policy makers have realized the importance of the problem and have launched a series of investigations and policy initiatives to address the issues. The regional dimension of inequality – rural–urban and inland–coastal – dominates in a country as large as China, and especially with its particular history. Not surprisingly, regional inequality has come to loom large in the policy debate in China.

The policy debate has been informed by, and to some extent instigated by, a parallel analytical literature which has quantified the magnitude of the problem and identified recent trends, offered explanations based on rigorous analysis, and proposed policy interventions in light of the facts and understanding. Through a series of articles which have been published in leading journals, the editors have been involved in a systematic investigation into the nature and evolution of regional inequality in China for over a decade.

Bringing together a collection of research from leading development and inequality scholars, this book will be of interest to policy makers as well as to students and researchers in Chinese development and regional inequality.

Shenggen Fan is the Director of the Development Strategy and Governance Division at the International Food Policy Research Institute, USA.

Ravi Kanbur is T. H. Lee Professor of World Affairs, International Professor of Applied Economics and Management, and Professor of Economics at Cornell University, USA.

Xiaobo Zhang is a Senior Research Fellow in the Development Strategy and Governance Division at the International Food Policy Research Institute (IFPRI), Washington, USA and leader of IFPRI's China Program.

Routledge Studies in the Modern World Economy

Regional Inequality in China

Trends, explanations and
policy responses

**Edited by
Shenggen Fan, Ravi Kanbur,
and Xiaobo Zhang**

Routledge
Taylor & Francis Group

LONDON AND NEW YORK

First published 2009
by Routledge
2 Park Square, Milton Park, Abingdon, Oxon OX14 4RN

Simultaneously published in the USA and Canada
by Routledge
711 Third Avenue, New York, NY 10017

*Routledge is an imprint of the Taylor & Francis Group,
an informa business*

Typeset in Times New Roman by
RefineCatch Limited, Bungay, Suffolk

British Library Cataloguing in Publication Data
A catalogue record for this book is available from the British Library

Library of Congress Cataloging in Publication Data
A catalog record for this book has been requested

ISBN13: 978–0–415–74355–6 (pbk)
ISBN13: 978–0–415–77588–5 (hbk)
ISBN13: 978–0–203–88148–4 (ebk)

First issued in paperback in 2013

Contents

Editors and contributors

Editors

Shenggen Fan is the Director of the Development Strategy and Governance Division at the International Food Policy Research Institute, Washington DC. A Chinese citizen, Shenggen joined IFPRI in 1995. For the last 10 years, his major work includes technical change, institutional reforms, productivity measurement, and the effects of public investment on growth and poverty reduction in developing countries. Prior to IFPRI, he worked for the International Service for National Agricultural Research, and the University of Arkansas. He received his Ph.D in applied economics from the University of Minnesota. Both of his B.S. and M.S. are from Nanjing Agricultural University, China.

Ravi Kanbur is T. H. Lee Professor of World Affairs, International Professor of Applied Economics and Management, and Professor of Economics at Cornell University. He has a bachelor's degree from Cambridge and a doctorate from Oxford. He has served on the senior staff of the World Bank, including as Principal Adviser to the Chief Economist of the World Bank. The honors he has received include an Honorary Professorship at the University of Warwick, and the Quality of Research Discovery Award of the American Agricultural Economics Association. His vita shows over 160 publications, including in the leading economics journals.

Xiaobo Zhang is Senior Research Fellow at the International Food Policy Research Institute, Washington DC. A citizen of China, he earned a B.S. in mathematics from Nankai University, China; a M.S. in economics from Tianjin University of Economics and Finance, China; and an M.S. and Ph.D. in applied economics and management from Cornell University in January 2000. He joined IFPRI in 1998. He served as the president of the Chinese Economists Society (CES) from 2005 to 2006.

Contributors

Xinshen Diao is Senior Research Fellow, International Food Policy Research Institute, Washington DC, USA.

Cheng Fang is an Asia Officer/Economist, Food and Agricultural Organization, Rome, Italy.

Xiaopeng Luo is a Professor in Zhejiang University, China.

Li Xing is Associate Professor at the Chinese Academy of Agricultural Sciences (CAAS), Beijing, China.

Kevin H. Zhang is an Associate Professor, Department of Economics, Illinois State University, Normal, IL, USA.

Linxiu Zhang is Professor and Deputy Director, Center for Chinese Agricultural Policy of the Chinese Academy of Agricultural Sciences.

Acknowledgements

Thanks are due to our various co-authors – Xinshen Diao, Cheng Fang, Xiaopeng Luo, Li Xing, Kevin H. Zhang, and Linxiu Zhang. We have received excellent administrative support from Sue Snyder at Cornell and research support from the staff and students from the International Center for Agricultural and Rural Development (ICARD) in the Chinese Academy of Agricultural Sciences, which we acknowledge with appreciation. Funding support from the Natural Science Foundation of China (Approval numbers 70525003 and 70828002) is also gratefully acknowledged.

Shenggen Fan
Ravi Kanbur
Xiaobo Zhang

Permissions

Ravi Kanbur and Xiaobo Zhang, "Which regional inequality? The evolution of rural–urban and coastal–inland inequality in China from 1983 to 1995", 1999. *Journal of Comparative Economics*, 27: 686–701. Reprinted by permission of the publisher, Elsevier.

Ravi Kanbur and Xiaobo Zhang, "Fifty years of regional inequality in China: a journey through central planning, reform, and openness", 2005. *Review of Development Economics* 9(1): 87–106. Reprinted by permission of the publisher, Wiley-Blackwell.

Ravi Kanbur and Xiaobo Zhang, "Spatial inequality in education and health care in China", 2005. *China Economic Review*, 16: 189–204. Reprinted by permission of the publisher, China Economic Review.

Xiaobo Zhang, "Fiscal decentralization and political centralization in China: implications for growth and inequality", 2006. *Journal of Comparative Economics*, 34(4): 713–726. Reprinted by permission of the publisher, Elsevier.

Xiaobo Zhang and Shenggen Fan, "Public investment and regional inequality in rural China", 2004. *Agricultural Economics*, 30(2): 89–100. Reprinted by permission of the publisher, Wiley-Blackwell.

Xiaobo Zhang and Ravi Kanbur, "What difference do polarization measures make? An application to China", 2001. *Journal of Development Studies*, 37(3): 85–98. Reprinted by permission of the publisher, Taylor & Francis <www.informaworld.com>.

Xiaobo Zhang and Kevin H. Zhang, "How does globalization affect regional inequality within a developing country? Evidence from China", 2003. *Journal of Development Studies*, 39(4): 47–67. Reprinted by permission of the publisher, Taylor & Francis <www.informaworld.com>.

Xiaobo Zhang, Li Xing, Shenggen Fan, and Xiaopeng Luo, "Resource abundance and regional development in China", 2008. *Economics of Transition*, 16(1): 7–29. Reprinted by permission of the publisher, Wiley-Blackwell.

1 Regional inequality in China: an overview

Shenggen Fan, Ravi Kanbur, and Xiaobo Zhang

Abstract

China's spectacular growth and poverty reduction has been accompanied by growing inequality which threatens the social compact and thus the political basis for economic growth and social development. The regional dimension of inequality – rural–urban, inland–coastal and provincial – dominates in a country as large as China, and especially with its particular history. The three of us have been researching Chinese regional inequality for over a decade. In a series of papers which have been published in peer reviewed journals, we have been involved in a systematic investigation into the nature and evolution of regional inequality in China. The object of this volume is to bring together a selection of these papers by us and our co-authors, so that researchers and policy makers can have access to them in one place. This introduction provides an overview of the volume.

1.1 Introduction

China's spectacular growth and poverty reduction has been accompanied by growing inequality which threatens the social compact and thus the political basis for economic growth. Chinese policy makers have realized the importance of the problem and have launched a series of investigations and policy initiatives to address the issues. The regional dimension of inequality – rural–urban, inland–coastal and provincial – dominates in a country as large as China, and especially with its particular history. Not surprisingly, regional inequality has come to loom large in the policy debate in China.

The policy debate has been informed by, and to some extent instigated by, a parallel analytical literature which has quantified the magnitude of the problem and identified recent trends, offered explanations based on rigorous analysis, and proposed policy interventions in light of the facts and understanding. The three of us have been researching Chinese regional inequality for over a decade. In a series of papers which have been published in peer reviewed journals, we have been involved in a systematic investigation into the nature and evolution of regional inequality in China. Although by its very nature such a claim is difficult to substantiate, we like to think that our research, as part of the broader contribution from the research community, has had a policy impact. The policy discourse in China on regional inequality, and on inequality generally, is very different now than even a decade ago.

The object of this volume is to bring together a selection of these papers by us and our co-authors, so that researchers and policy makers can have access to them in one place. This introduction provides an overview of the volume. We begin in Section 1.2 with a brief conceptual consideration of spatial inequality, and report on what has been happening to it globally, to set the context for China's experience. Section 1.3 is devoted to trends in regional inequality in China as discussed in Part I of the volume, while Section 1.4 focuses on explanations and policy responses, and Section 1.5 concludes.

1.2 Spatial inequality: a global perspective [1]

Regional inequality – inequality between different regions – is now recognized to be a major issue for China's policy makers. But such inequality, or spatial inequality more generally – inequality between spatially distinct areas within a country – is equally a major issue for all countries and for their policy makers. Wars have been fought over the issue at one extreme, while the normal politics of a country is undoubtedly affected by spatial disparities in that country. But what exactly is this spatial inequality? How is it to be measured? What has been happening to it globally in the last two decades? What explains the patterns of evolution? And what can policy do about it? These are questions that face not just an analysis for China, but for any country. We begin by taking an abstract and a global perspective on the issue, to set the background for our China-specific discussion in the next two sections.

These questions were addressed for a global setting in Kanbur and Venables (2007), which reported on a major project documenting and analyzing trends in spatial inequality in the world. To take the first question, an economic approach to spatial inequality would quite naturally locate it in patterns of income inequality across individuals. Thus, for example, if individuals in a country can be assigned to mutually exclusive and exhaustive spatial groupings in that country ("regions"), then income inequality across individuals can be decomposed into that which can be accounted for by the fact that mean income differs across regions, and that which can be accounted for by the fact that even around the mean of any given region there is still variation in individual incomes. The former is known as the "between group" component of inequality, and the latter as the "within group" component of inequality. The between group component of inequality thus has some claim to be labeled as "spatial inequality."

However, this conceptualization effectively weights the mean income of a region by its population share, with the result that changes in the mean income of a small region do not have a big impact on overall spatial inequality. While this is a natural implication of the individualistic perspective in standard economic theory of inequality measurement, as Kanbur (2006) has argued, it may not be an accurate reflection of how spatial inequality is actually perceived and experienced on the ground, where group means may carry more significance. Thus for some purposes the evolution of unweighted means may be more appropriate, for example when comparing rural–urban disparities, or disparities in a country where the regional divide aligns with ethnic or religious divides. Both of these approaches are used in the papers represented in this volume.

However it is measured, what has been happening to spatial inequality within countries in the world? In the Kanbur and Venables (2007) project, a large number of authors wrote papers on different dimensions of spatial inequality, with data from different sources. Information was collected on spatial disparities (in income, primarily, but also on other measures of well-being like education and health) in 58 developing economies. For 26 of these countries, information was presented on dynamics of spatial inequality, across various periods over the last two decades. The conclusions are quite striking, and set the frame for our China discussion. Spatial disparities are high, and rising. Whether in Africa (for example, Sahn and Stifel, 2003), in Latin America (for example Escobal and Torero (2005) for Peru and Garcia-Verdu (2005) for Mexico), in Asia (Friedman (2005) for Indonesia), in the transition economies (for example, Anderson and Pomfret (2005) for Tajikistan or Forster, Jesuit, and Smeeding (2005) for the Czech Republic, Hungary, Poland and Russia), and for many other cases, the studies show that spatial inequalities are high, and they have been rising. China was indeed one of the countries studied (Chapter 4, this volume), and the results were similar – more on this in the next section.

What are the causes of high and rising spatial disparities? A major factor turns out to be public infrastructure, the location of which often strengthens (rather than mitigates) initial natural advantages and agglomeration economies. For example, Christiaensen, Demery, and Paternostro (2005) show the importance of transport connections in explaining regional poverty and its evolution in Africa. Lall and Chakravorty (2005) discuss lagging regions in India, and argue that there are strong pulls on firms to move away from these regions to regions already more advanced, thereby setting in motion a cycle of increasing spatial inequality in economic activity.

The second major factor that seems to be associated with growing spatial inequality is increasing openness to international trade. For example, for Mexico, Rodriguez-Pose and Sanchez-Reaza (2005), and Garcia-Verdu (2005) find that regional convergence was slower after NAFTA (the North American Free Trade Agreement) was introduced, and perhaps regional convergence even switched to divergence. For China, Kanbur and Zhang (Chapter 4, this volume) find that greater openness is associated with higher spatial inequality according to their measure – this will be discussed in the next sections. For Vietnam, Jensen and Tarp's (2005) simulation exercise also indicates an association between trade liberalization and rural–urban inequality. Again, these are themes that are present in China and are taken up later in this volume and in this overview.

Finally, the authors in the Kanbur and Venables (2007) global project on spatial inequality discuss possible policy responses. None of the authors support reducing openness to trade as a policy response. But two key policy responses with analytical support are: (i) development of economic and social infrastructure in lagging regions, and (ii) reducing barriers to migration between fast growing and lagging regions. For China, Ravallion (2005) finds support for poor-area development programs the government has been promoting, and some of the papers in this volume complement that finding. For Africa, Christiaensen, Demery, and Paternostro (2005) also argue for public infrastructure (roads in Ethiopia and electricity in Uganda) as key determinants of poverty reduction in remote locations. Similarly, for China (papers in this volume), for Brazil (Timmins, 2005) and for Chile (Soto and Torche, 2004), for example, impediments to migration are identified as key factors in maintaining spatial inequality.

Thus high and rising spatial inequality is a global phenomenon. China's experience in addressing this issue is thus not just of significance for China – it may also have lessons for the rest of the world.

1.3 Trends in Chinese regional inequality

Part I of this volume is devoted to a collection of our papers that measure regional inequality in China and establish its trends. The first three of these papers use a decomposition methodology to quantify spatial inequality as the between group components of interpersonal inequality.

Chapter 2 of the volume, "Which regional inequality? The evolution of rural–urban and inland–coastal inequality in China from 1983 to 1995," was the first paper to be published out of all the papers in this volume. It was worked on in the late 1990s and published in 1999 and contributed to the first wave of research on spatial disparities in China. It introduced the decomposition of the Theil index of inequality as a way of capturing different dimensions of spatial inequality. Since Chinese provincial data provide information on mean consumption for rural and urban areas by province, but no information on the distribution around these means, interpersonal inequality is calculated at the national level assuming that each population (rural and urban in each province) is clustered at its mean. The estimated inequality is thus a lower bound on the true interpersonal inequality. It is, in fact, the between group component of the true overall interpersonal inequality, and as such is a measure of spatial inequality in China. But the estimated inequality can in turn be decomposed by rural and urban groups across provinces, and by provinces in different clusters – given Chinese concerns we chose inland–coastal as the key provincial divide. This decomposition allows us to examine in greater depth the evolution of spatial inequality in China.

With this framework the paper presents the evolution of different components of inequality, specifically the inland–coastal dimension and the rural–urban dimension, for 1983–1995. It demonstrates the dramatic increase in spatial inequality in China during these years. It also shows that although the rural–urban component of spatial inequality is higher than the inland–coastal component, and both have been rising, the latter has been rising much faster over this period. It thus raises the question, without in any way diminishing the significance of the rural–urban gap within each of the provinces, of the growing disparities between the provinces themselves, especially between inland provinces on the one hand and coastal provinces on the other – a recognition that is quite widespread today in Chinese policy circles.

The next paper in the volume, Chapter 3, shows how the Chinese case was used to make a contribution to the general literature on inequality measurement. In the broader literature, concerns were expressed that standard measures of inequality would not capture "polarization", by which was meant the emergence of a bi-modal distribution – large numbers of people at the very top and at the very bottom, with a "disappearing middle class." In this paper, "What difference do polarisation measures make? an application to China," two advances were proposed. First, a different conceptualization of polarization was introduced, based on predetermined groups (in this case, regions). It was argued that the degree of polarization between groups in these settings could in fact be captured by the between-group component of overall inequality. Secondly, however, the paper posed an empirical question – did any of this make any difference? Would the trends in inequality be overturned by any of the polarization measures – those in the literature, and that proposed in the paper? It turned out that in the Chinese case, over this period, all measures moved in the same direction – inequality as well as polarization rose sharply in China during this period.

Chapter 4 of the volume, "Fifty years of regional inequality in China: a journey through central planning, reform and openness," extends the time period of investigation to a half century – stretching back to 1952 in the pre-reform period and forward to 2000. This allows a historical perspective on the evolution of regional inequality in China, and further permits time series econometrics on the determinants of the evolution. It is shown that there have been three peaks of inequality in the last fifty years, coinciding with the Great Famine of the 1950s, the Cultural Revolution of the 1960s, and the period of openness and global integration of the late 1990s. In the post-reform period there was a fall in inequality from the Cultural Revolution peak as the agrarian reforms of the late 1970s and early 1980s improved rural incomes. In fact, econometric analysis confirms that focus on agriculture (as measured by the inverse of the ratio of heavy industry to gross output) reduces spatial inequality. Interestingly, in the post-reform period, the degree of decentralization, as measured by the share of local government expenditure in total government expenditure, is associated positively with increasing inequality – the reasoning being that this allows the better performing provinces, especially those on the coast, to enter a virtuous cycle by using their higher revenues to invest in infrastructure, thereby attracting more investment and further increasing the revenue. Finally, the paper also establishes an association between a measure of openness and spatial inequality, in common with the global pattern identified in the previous section.

The next two papers in this part of the volume depart from the first three papers, which focused on the evolution of income inequality in a broad national context. Chapter 5 stays with income but focuses on poverty in urban areas, while Chapter 6 stays with regional inequality at the national level but turns the spotlight on non-income dimensions of wellbeing.

Chapter 5, "Emergence of urban poverty and inequality in China: evidence from household survey" uses a data set from an urban household survey for 28 provinces for 1992 and then each year from 1994 to 1998. In each province, one representative city with a sample size from 50 to 150 households is selected, giving a total sample size of around 3,600 households for each of the six years studied. It is shown that the incidence of urban poverty declined from 1992 to 1995, but increased from 1996 to 1998, when major urban reforms were launched. The western region has the highest concentration of urban poverty, and the income gap between the region and the rest of China has been widening over time. A further decomposition analysis shows that rapid economic growth has been the major force behind reduction in urban poverty, but the poverty reduction impact would have been even greater if worsening income distribution had been avoided. This paper also draws some policy conclusions. First, the current strategy of Western development should broaden its focus to include the urban poor in the region. Second, in addition to promoting growth, the government should also speed up the process of establishing a social safety net for the vulnerable groups. Third, since the urban reforms have led the poor to spend a higher proportion of their incomes on education, health care, and housing, expanding access to basic education and health care will enable the vulnerable to share the prosperity offered by market reforms.

Chapter 6, "Spatial inequality in education and health care in China," looks at regional inequalities in achievements in these key non-income indicators. In the pre-1978 period, basic education and health care were widely available, even though rural facilities were worse than in urban areas. Since 1978, however, the state has withdrawn considerably at the local and central level. What has been the impact? The paper looks at inequality in a number of education and health indicators for China. While the illiteracy rate has declined steadily between 1981 and 2000, there nevertheless exist large rural–urban and male–female gaps – the rural illiteracy rate was more than double the urban one, and female illiteracy was also more than double the male rate. The paper further calculates a measure of regional inequality in illiteracy using the Theil index. Regional inequality in education has increased across the rural–urban and the inland–coastal divide. Health inequality is analyzed using indicators like the infant mortality rate (IMR). While the IMR has declined for China as a whole, regional inequality increased from 1981 to 2000. The increasing inequality in this outcome variable is underpinned by increasing inequality in input variables like health care personnel or hospital beds per thousand persons. Overall, then, the story for non-income indicators is consistent with that for income – strong improvements in national averages accompanied by widening regional disparities.

1.4 Explanations and policy responses

The papers in Part I of this volume are devoted primarily to identifying and quantifying the trends in Chinese regional inequality. But elements of explanation and policy response are already present in these papers. Moreover, the global literature also suggests a number of key drivers of spatial inequality. The important issues, as identified in the global literature and in the papers in Part I of this volume are: (i) trade and openness, (ii) public infrastructure, and (iii) central and local social expenditures. The papers in Part II of the volume take up these themes.

Chapter 7 begins the second part of the volume by emphasizing the importance of the above three factors – it does so by showing that an obvious potential determinant of regional development – natural resource abundance in a region – does not in fact lead to better performance in that region. The paper, "Resource abundance and regional development in China," defines resource intensity as the ratio of resources production to total GDP, and uses a panel data set at the provincial level to show that provinces with abundant resources perform worse than their resource-poor counterparts in terms of per capita consumption growth. The rapid economic growth in the coastal region, coupled with increasing domestic market integration, has stimulated the demand for natural resources, which are mostly produced in the interior regions. In principle, the resource-rich regions should benefit from a higher resource price. However, because of the institutional arrangements on the property rights of natural resources, most gains from the booming resources have been captured either by the government, state-owned enterprises, or investors. The windfall of natural resources has more to do with government consumption than household consumption. Moreover, greater revenues accruing from natural resources bid up the price of non-tradable goods and hurt the competitiveness of the local economy. The resource curse thus appears to operate within China, and the institutional basis of rural poverty, in particular, is deep.

With this background, the next two chapters take up the issue of trade and regional inequality in China. Chapter 8, "How does globalization affect regional inequality within a developing country? Evidence from China," develops an empirical method for decomposing the contributions of trade and foreign direct investment to regional inequality in China and applies it to provincial data for the period 1986–1998. The basic story that emerges is that domestic and foreign investment has been increasingly concentrated in the coastal regions, and this is the driver of growing regional inequality. Even after controlling for other factors such as regional differences in education, the effect remains. Variations in the degree of globalization (foreign trade and foreign capital) account for almost a fifth of the increase in regional inequality. These findings are particularly important given China's accession to the World Trade Organization (WTO). If the results of Chapter 8 are any indication, then greater global integration will lead to widening regional disparity within China, requiring countervailing policy responses.

This point is developed in greater detail, but with a focus on agriculture, in Chapter 9, "China's WTO accession: impacts on regional agricultural income – a multi-region, general equilibrium analysis." The paper develops a regional computable general equilibrium (CGE) model with the 1997 Social Accounting Matrix (SAM) for China, disaggregated using the Global Trade Analysis Project (GTAP) database. The crop sector, for example, is split into nine sectors – wheat, rice, other cereals, vegetables, fruits, soybeans, other oilseeds, cotton, and other crops. Agriculture production data are disaggregated into seven regions using information in the *China Statistical Yearbook, China's Agricultural Statistical Materials*, and a number of other sources. With the model, a number of policy exercises are carried out. For example, the US–China agreement says China will reduce its tariff rate on agricultural imports from 22 percent to 17.5 percent. What would be the impact of such a policy shift? These and other exercises are carried out in the paper. The results show that total welfare will improve but regional income gaps will widen. The agricultural sector will suffer if only agricultural trade is liberalized. Lifting both agricultural and non-agricultural trade barriers will benefit farmers at the national level. However, rural income will increase less than urban income, implying that the rural–urban income gap will widen further. Among the regions, farmers in China's least-developed rural areas will benefit little or even suffer because agriculture, especially traditional agriculture, is still an important source of their livelihood.

Given that China has adopted a globalizing strategy for development, and that this has certainly delivered in terms of growth and overall poverty reduction, what can be done to address the growing regional imbalances that such openness seems to be associated with? One possible answer is investment in public infrastructure, which can be both an explanation for regional inequality and, therefore, part of a strategy of containing rising regional inequality. The next three chapters of the volume are devoted to this topic, focusing in particular on rural development.

Chapter 10, "Infrastructure and regional economic development in rural China," uses the 1996 Agricultural Census. This provides detailed data on rural infrastructure, education, and science and technology. Combining this with other official sources, it relies on a traditional source accounting approach to identify the role of rural infrastructure and other public expenditures in explaining productivity differences among regions. It is shown that rural infrastructure and education play an important role in explaining the difference in rural nonfarm productivity. Since the rural nonfarm economy is a major determinant of rural income, investing more in rural infrastructure is key to increasing the overall income of the rural population. Second, lower productivity in the western region is explained by its lower level of rural infrastructure, education, and science and technology. A different technique is used to address the same issue in Chapter 11, "Public investment and regional inequality in rural China." Using a provincial level data set for the period 1978–1995 in rural China, a model is estimated that enables the impacts on regional inequality of different types of public investments in each of three regions to be quantified. Regional variations in the impact of public investments on regional inequality are large. Increasing public investment in the less developed western region will lead to a decline in regional disparity. In contrast, if the government continues to favor the coastal region in its investment strategy, regional disparities will widen further. The paper also introduces a more disaggregated perspective on public investment. For example, investments in education and agricultural R&D in the western region are the two most powerful ways of reducing regional inequality.

Chapter 12 takes up the themes of the previous two chapters and develops a comprehensive analysis of the role of different types of government expenditure on rural growth and poverty. Using a wide range of provincial data over the past quarter century, it builds and estimates a simultaneous equations econometric model to calculate economic returns, poverty reduction, and impact on regional inequality of different categories of public expenditure. It is shown that productivity is enhanced and poverty is reduced by increased expenditures for research and development, irrigation, education, roads, electricity, and telecommunications. Moreover, while for the first decade of reforms the reforms themselves were more important for growth and poverty reduction, since the mid-1980s onwards public investment is shown to be the dominant factor explaining both growth and reductions in poverty. What is equally interesting, however, is that different categories of investments have different payoffs, which in turn differ across regions. Education has the biggest payoff for poverty reduction and growth in rural areas. The impact of rural telecommunications, electricity, and roads was also substantial, working through nonfarm employment and rural wages. Thus road investment, for example, had the second largest return to growth in the nonfarm economy and in the rural economy overall. The regional specifics confirm the results of the previous chapter – the poverty reduction effects of education, agricultural research and development, and infrastructure is particularly high for the western region of China. The policy implications of this analysis are direct and strong. If the government wishes to manage growing regional inequality in China, then investing in public infrastructure in the lagging regions will have to be an important policy priority.

The balance between central and local responsibilities in providing public goods services is a key policy issue for China. The final two chapters in the volume show that decentralization plays a central role as a determinant of regional inequality, as already suggested by the analysis in Chapter 4. Chapter 13, "Fiscal decentralization and political centralization in China: implications for growth and inequality," characterizes China's fiscal system as one that is largely decentralized but the governance structure is centralized with many top-down mandates. The paper uses a nationwide panel data set at the county level to analyze the impact of fiscal decentralization on spatial inequality. The county level public finance data are from 1993 to 2000 and come from the *China County Public Finance Statistical Yearbook*. Allowing for missing data, the analysis is based on a panel of 1,860 observations over this period. Due to large differences in initial economic structures and revenue bases, the implicit tax rate and fiscal burdens to support the functioning of local government vary significantly across jurisdictions. Regions initially endowed with a broader nonfarm tax base do not need to rely heavily on preexisting or new firms to finance public goods provision, thereby creating a healthy investment environment for the nonfarm sector to grow. In contrast, regions with agriculture as the major economic activity have little resources left for public investment after paying the expenses of bureaucracy. Consequently, differences in economic structures and fiscal burdens may translate into a widening regional gap.

Chapter 14, the final chapter in the volume, "Social entitlement exchange and balanced economic growth," further explores the implications of rigidities in local governance structures, where the size and functions at lower levels are closely related to those in the upper levels, with little relation to economic development. As a result, under fiscal decentralization, the regional fiscal burdens to carry out various central mandates and regulations have become increasingly uneven. This has led to the underprovision of public goods in less developed regions, thereby widening inequality. The paper argues that the large regional differences also imply opportunities for regions to trade social entitlements so as to increase both efficiency and equity. The latest innovations in land development right transfers in the coastal provinces and the use of police officers from the same regions as local migrants to fight crime in the coastal provinces show the feasibility of social entitlement exchanges. Institutional reform and innovation is thus identified as a key policy response to regional inequality. The particular reform measures can be heterodox and context specific.

1.5 Conclusion

The chapters in this volume have attempted to identify, quantify, and explain trends in Chinese regional inequality. Despite fast growth and falling poverty, regional disparities are increasing. If China wishes to continue along the current globalizing path to development, with the undoubted returns it has brought for growth and poverty reduction, and if at the same time it wishes to manage and mitigate widening regional disparity, a number of policy approaches are suggested by the papers in this volume. Prominent among these are public investment in the lagging regions, making migration easier to the fast growing regions, and institutional innovation to improve the performance of fiscal decentralization. Targeted social protection should also be used to help the poor in the short run to meet their immediate needs and to help them to participate in the growth process in the long run. Details on each of these dimensions are provided in the chapters. But this is the overall stance that will be needed to ensure that growing regional inequality does not end up as a break on Chinese development.

Note

1 This section draws on Kanbur and Venables (2007).

References

Anderson, Kathryn, and Richard Pomfret. 2005. "Spatial Inequality and Development in Central Asia." In Ravi Kanbur, Anthony J. Venables, and Guanghua Wan (editors), *Spatial Disparities in Human Development: Perspectives from Asia.*"

Christiaensen, Luc, Lionel Demery, and Stefano Paternostro. 2005. "Reforms, Remoteness and Risk in Africa: Understanding Inequality and Poverty During the 1990s." In Ravi Kanbur and Anthony J. Venables (editors), *Spatial Inequality and Development*. Oxford University Press. January.

Escobal, Javier, and Maximo Torero. 2005. "Adverse Geography and Differences in Welfare in Peru." In Ravi Kanbur and Anthony J. Venables (editors), *Spatial Inequality and Development*. Oxford University Press. January.

Forster, Michael, David Jesuit, and Timothy Smeeding. 2005. "Regional Poverty and Income Inequality in Central and Eastern Europe: Evidence from the Luxembourg Income Study." In Ravi Kanbur and Anthony J. Venables (editors), *Spatial Inequality and Development*. Oxford University Press. January.

Friedman, Jed. 2005. "How Responsive is Poverty to Growth? A Regional Analysis of Poverty, Inequality and Growth in Indonesia, 1984–99." In Ravi Kanbur and Anthony J. Venables (editors), *Spatial Inequality and Development*. Oxford University Press. January.

Garcia-Verdu, Rodrigo. 2005. "Income, Mortality, and Literacy Distribution Dynamics Across States in Mexico: 1940–2000." *Cuadernos de Economia*, Volume 42, Number 42, May pp. 165–192.

Jensen, Henning Tarp, and Finn Tarp. 2005. "Trade Liberalization and Spatial Inequality: A Methodological Innovation in a Vietnamese Perpsective." *Review of Development Economics*, Volume 9, Number 1, February, pp. 69–86.

Kanbur, Ravi. 2006. "The Policy Significance of Inequality Decompositions." *Journal of Economic Inequality*, Volume 4, Number 3, pp. 367–374.

Kanbur, Ravi, and Anthony J. Venables. 2007. "Spatial Disparities and Economic Development." In D. Held and A. Kaya (eds.), *Global Inequality*. Polity Press, 2007.

Lall, Somik Vinay, and Sanjoy Chakravorty. 2005. "Industrial Location and Spatial Inequality: Theory and Evidence from India." *Review of Development Economics*, Volume 9, Number 1, February, pp. 47–68.

Ravallion, Martin. 2005. "Externalities in Rural Development: Evidence for China."

In Ravi Kanbur and Anthony J. Venables (editors), *Spatial Inequality and Development*. Oxford University Press. January.

Rodriguez-Pose, Andres, and Javier Sanchez-Reaza. 2005. "Economic Polarization Through Trade: Trade Liberalization and Regional Inequality in Mexico." In Ravi Kanbur and Anthony J. Venables (editors), *Spatial Inequality and Development*. Oxford University Press. January.

Sahn, David, and David Stifel. 2003. "Urban–Rural Inequality in Living Standards in Africa." *Journal of African Economies*, Volume 12, Number 1, December, pp. 564–597.

Soto, Raimundo, and Aristides Torche. 2004. "Spatial Inequality, Migration and Growth in Chile." *Cuadernos de Economia*, Volume 41, Number 124, December, pp. 401–424.

Timmins, Christopher. 2005. "Estimable Equilibrium Models of Locational Sorting and Their Role in Development Economics." *Journal of Economic Geography*, Volume 5, Number 1, January, pp. 59–83.

Part I
Trends in regional inequality

2 Which regional inequality? The evolution of rural–urban and inland–coastal inequality in China from 1983 to 1995 [1]

Ravi Kanbur and Xiaobo Zhang

Abstract

This paper develops a unified empirical framework for describing the relative contribution of rural–urban and inland–coastal inequality to overall regional inequality in China during the 1980s and 1990s. The framework assesses rural–urban and inland–coastal inequalities from the same data set, presents results for a sufficiently long time period to transcend short-term fluctuations, allows for differential price changes and applies a consistent notion of the contribution to inequality using a decomposition analysis. While the contribution of rural–urban inequality is much higher than that of inland–coastal inequality in terms of levels, the trend is very different. The rural–urban contribution has not changed very much over time, but the inland–coastal contribution has increased several folds. The paper ends by investigating the role of labor migration in this outcome.

2.1 Introduction

The object of this paper is to contribute to the debate on growth and inequality in China by developing a coherent and unified empirical framework for describing the relative evolution of rural–urban and inland–coastal inequalities over a significant period of time. China is a country that has undergone phenomenal economic growth, but in which there are deep concerns about growing inequalities, coming from both inside and outside of the country. Inside China, commentators have expressed concerns on regional inequality. Thus Hu Angang (1996), an influential researcher in China, warned that further increases in regional disparities may lead to China's dissolution like the former Yugoslavia. Xue (1997, p. 46) noted that "further expansions of the differences may create serious social and political problems, generate nationalist conflicts and negatively influence China's economic and social stability." Commentators have stressed, in particular, rural–urban and inland–coastal differentials (Li, 1996; Li and Zhang, 1996; Huang, 1996; Hu, 1996; Yang, 1996; Ye, 1996; Yang, 1999).

Not surprisingly, there is a large academic literature that attempts to describe and explain the patterns of regional inequality in China. However, a number of different data sources, different time periods, and different methodologies are used to draw a range of conclusions. Thus, for example, Lyons (1991) shows a downward trend in inter-provincial inequality up to 1987, using nominal per capita national material product. In contrast, Tsui (1991) argues for an upward trend of provincial inequality up to 1985 using deflated per capita national income utilized. However, in a later paper (Tsui, 1996), he finds a U-shaped evolution of regional inequality in the post reform period using real per capita GDP from 1978 to 1989. On the other hand, Chen and Fleisher (1996) argue for a decline in inter-provincial inequality until the early 1990s, based on per capita real provincial GDP and national income when inequality is calculated without provincial population weights. Using the same method, they also find that the gap between inland and coastal provinces increased in the 1980s. Jian, Sachs, and Warner (1996) find growing divergence between inland and coastal province, but from 1990 to 1993 only. Using rural income only at the provincial level, Yao (1997) found a significant increase in regional inequality from 1986 to 1992.

Much attention has been devoted also to the rural–urban dimension of inequality. Xue (1997) uses aggregate time series data on nominal rural and urban consumption and demonstrates a dramatic increase in the ratio of these magnitudes (see also Yang, 1996 and Ye, 1996). Tsui (1993) conducts a detailed decomposition of rural–urban and inland–coastal inequality with county-level data. However, this is a snapshot for 1982 only. He finds that rural–urban inequality is the major component of county-level regional inequality in China. Similar decompositions are done, again for a single year (1986), by Hussain, Lanjouw, and Stern (1994) on the basis of a specially conducted survey. More recently, Yang (1999) observes a substantial increase in rural–urban disparity, using household level data in Jiangsu and Sichuan Provinces for the period from 1986 to 1994. The trend of within-rural or within-urban inequality is investigated using detailed household surveys, but coverage is limited to particular provinces. Aaberge and Li (1997) find that urban Gini coefficients increased slightly from 1986 to 1990 in two provinces; Chen and Ravallion (1996) conclude that rural inequality increased slightly from 1985 to 1990 in four southern provinces; Rozelle (1994) finds an increase in rural inequality during 1984 to 1989 in Jiangsu Province; Tsui (1998b) observes a modest increase in rural inequality in the second half of the 1980s.

Thus, while these different strands of analysis all point to the problem of increasing inequality by coming at it from different angles, we do not find a coherent analysis that treats the relative evolution of rural–urban and inland–coastal inequality in a unified empirical framework. Tsui's (1993) work comes closest to the spirit of our intentions, but his work is for a single year, and cannot speak to the relative evolution of the different dimensions of inequality over a significant time period. Our object is to develop a framework in which rural–urban and inland–coastal inequalities can be assessed from the same data set, there is a sufficient run of data to allow interesting intertemporal comparisons to be made that transcend possible short term fluctuations, price changes can be accommodated to the extent possible, and a consistent notion of contribution to inequality can be applied throughout. Such a framework is developed in Section 2.2. Section 2.3 presents the main results; to anticipate, we find that while the rural–urban gap is a more important contribution to overall regional inequality in China, the inland–coastal component has been growing very fast from a low level. Section 2.4 investigates the reasons for this marked contrast between the two dimensions of inequality.

2.2 Data and methodology

2.2.1 Data

Previous studies on regional inequality have used mainly Soviet type statistics such as gross value of industrial and agricultural output (GVIAO), e.g. Bramall and Jones (1993); Tsui (1993); Rozelle (1994); and Yao (1997), net material product (NMP), e.g. Lyons (1991) and Tsui (1991) and national income utilized (NIU), e.g. Lyons (1991) and Tsui (1991), in large part because there exist long term data series for these. All these measures are different from GDP in the sense that services are excluded. Also, GVIAO includes intermediate inputs, which may result in double counting in industrial sectors. Since the agricultural sector uses less intermediate input than the industrial sector, the double counting may exaggerate the degree of rural–urban inequality (Tsui, 1993). In addition, all of these measures are not designed for reflecting the living standards across different regions and differ from commonly used measures of income or expenditures. In the literature related to within-rural or within-urban inequalities, i.e. Hussain, Lanjouw, and Stern (1994); Khan et al. (1993); Chen and Ravallion (1996); and Aaberge and Li (1997), income and expenditures are more often used as measures of the standard of living. Generally speaking, expenditures are more appropriate than income for measuring the living standard because they are usually less subject to short-term fluctuations and proxy permanent income better than other measures (Grootaert, 1995).

Since 1983, both rural and urban per capita consumption expenditures at a provincial level have been published in *China Statistical Yearbook*. These average expenditures are compiled from annual rural and urban household survey data by the China State Statistical Bureau (SSB). Alongside the nominal expenditures, the annual growth rates of real expenditures for rural and urban residents at a provincial level are also published on the basis of separate rural and urban price indices.[2] China did not start radical price reform until October, 1984 when the central government lifted the control over all the prices of small commodities completely (Tang, 1987). Before that, prices were under strict control by state governments and allowed to fluctuate only within a 2 percent bound each year mainly for the purpose of keeping prices stable instead of allowing them to be market signals reflecting supply and demand (Tang, 1987). As a result, "in 1983, free prices covered only approximately 4 per cent of the items in domestic trade" (Guo, 1992, p. 43). On this basis, we assume that price levels were the same for all provinces in 1983, and that nominal expenditures are equivalent to real expenditures in that year. Under this assumption, the real expenditures for the whole period from 1983 to 1995, which is the latest available year, can be derived from the base year's nominal expenditures and the published annual growth rates of real expenditures.

In China, own production constitutes a large share of consumption for rural households (Chen and Ravallion, 1996). It is worth mentioning how rural consumption expenditures are estimated by the SSB. Prior to 1990, the consumption from self-production was valued at fixed state prices, which might be different from market prices. However, the sale of products and purchased inputs are all valued at market prices. As a result, using fixed state prices instead of market prices to value the consumption from self-production for the period from 1983 to 90 may lead to an underestimation of expenditures for rural residents (Chen and Ravallion, 1996). Also, the officially used sampling method and income (expenditure) definition may result in underestimation of the overall inequality (Bramall and Jones, 1993; Griffin and Zhao, 1993). In addition, there exist some non-comparability between rural and urban residents. For instance, urban residents enjoy housing and medical care subsidies while rural residents do not. In spite of these shortcomings of the consumption expenditure measure, it is the only summary measure at a provincial level that is readily available, consistently compiled, and covers both rural and urban populations in all the provinces for a reasonably long period.

We also need rural and urban population weights for each province. Prior to 1985, these data were published in *China Statistical Yearbook*. Thereafter, they can be found only from other data sources, such as *China Population Statistics*. Urban and rural residencies refer to the status registered in the household register system. Principally speaking, rural and urban residents are supposed to specialize in farm work and non-farm work in their registration areas, respectively. The strict household register system prevents the population from moving freely to a large extent. However, with the success of rural reform, many workers are freed up from agriculture activities and move to urban areas, especially to big cities, to seek opportunities without any entitlement to subsidies like urban residents. These floating migrants are not covered in the SSB sample that includes only the registered resident households. Hence, possible biases result from using the official registered numbers of rural and urban population. However, more than 80 percent of these floating migrants are laborers who work outside during the off-harvest season and send remittances back home to support their family (*China Development Report 1998*). In the rural expenditure survey, remittance is listed as one source of income (Tsui, 1998a), reducing some of the bias resulting from migration that is not captured by the official population statistics.

Tibet and Hainan Provinces are excluded from the analysis, due to the lack of consistent data on annual growth rates of per capita real expenditure. As a consequence, there are 28 provinces in our sample. With rural and urban components for each Province, we have 56 observations per year for each year from 1983 to 1995. Now, while the rural–urban classification is well developed and established in statistical sources, there is less guidance on how to determine the inland–coastal divide. One approach, found in the literature on inter-zone inequality in China, is to consider zones, which are at a level of aggregation above provinces. Two ways are used to classify these; see Yang (1997) for a detailed discussion. One way, following Tsui (1993), Huang (1996), and Yao (1997) is to divide China into three zones, i.e. east or coast, middle, and west. The other way, following Chen and Fleisher (1996), is to consider China as made up of only two zones, i.e. coast and inland. Under both, the east or coast zone includes the following provinces: Beijing, Liaoning, Tianjin, Hebei, Shandong, Jiangsu, Shanghai, Zhejiang, Fujian, Guangdong, and Guangxi. We adopt the second procedure and classify all the remaining provinces as inland for our study.

2.2.2 Decomposition methodology

Our assessment of the evolution of the relative contributions of rural–urban and inland–coastal gaps to overall regional inequality in China is based on a decomposition methodology explained in Cowell (1995) and used by Tsui (1993). We adopt the Generalized Entropy (GE) class of inequality measures (Shorrocks 1980, 1984), which can be written as:

$$
I(y) = \begin{cases}
\displaystyle\sum_{i=1}^{n} f(y_i) \left\{ \left(\frac{y_i}{\mu}\right)^c - 1 \right\} & c \neq 0, 1 \\[3mm]
\displaystyle\sum_{i=1}^{n} f(y_i) \left(\frac{y_i}{\mu}\right) \log\left(\frac{y_i}{\mu}\right) & c = 1 \\[3mm]
\displaystyle\sum_{i=1}^{n} f(y_i) \log\left(\frac{\mu}{y_i}\right) & c = 0.
\end{cases}
\tag{1}
$$

In the above equation, y_i is the ith individual's income measured as Chinese yuan, μ is the total sample mean, $f(y_i)$ is the population share of y_i in the total population and n is total population. The key feature of the GE measure is that it is additively decomposable. For K exogenously given groups indexed by g:

$$
I(y) = \sum_{g}^{K} w_g I_g + I(\mu_1 e_1, \ldots, \mu_K e_K).
\tag{2}
$$

$$\text{Where } w_g = \begin{cases} f_g \left(\dfrac{\mu_g}{\mu}\right)^c & c \neq 0, 1 \\[2ex] f_g \left(\dfrac{\mu_g}{\mu}\right) & c = 1 \\[2ex] f_g & c = 0 \end{cases}.$$

Where I_g is inequality in the gth group, μ_g is the mean of the gth group and e_g is a vector of 1's of length n_g, where n_g is the population of the gth group. If n is the total population of all groups, then $f_g = \dfrac{n_g}{n}$ represents the share of the gth group's population in the total population. The first term on the right side of (2) represents the within-group inequality. $\dfrac{w_g I_g}{I(y)} * 100$ is the gth group's contribution to total inequality. The second term is the between group, or inter-group, component of total inequality.

For all values of the parameter c, the GE measure is additively decomposable in the sense formalized by Shorrocks (1980, 1984). This property allows us to consider the contribution of different components to overall inequality. For values of c less than 2, the measure is transfer sensitive (Shorrocks and Foster, 1987), in the sense that it is more sensitive to transfers at the bottom end of the distribution than at the top. When c is 1 or 0, we have the measures of inequality made famous by Theil (see Cowell, 1995). For simplicity, we present results in this paper only for $c = 0$. The results for $c = 1$ are similar.

2.3 Empirical results

With a common data set and the decomposition methodology, we can assess the relative contributions over time of rural–urban and inland–coastal disparities to the evolution of regional inequality in China. Before the decomposition analysis, however, we consider the overall inequality. For each year we calculate several measures of inequality from the 56 observations in our data set, one rural and one urban observation with the population as weights for each of the 28 provinces. Apart from the GE measure with $c = 0$, we also present the standard Gini coefficients for the same data set. Table 2.1 reports the overall inequalities measured by the Gini coefficient and the GE index. Figure 2.1 presents the time path of inequality in real per capita expenditures from 1983 to 1995 relative to the 1983 values.

Three characterizations are immediately apparent from Table 2.1 and Figure 2.1. First, the overall trend has been one of sharply increasing regional inequality in China during this period of very fast growth. This result confirms the conclusion of earlier studies. Second, although there is an overall upward trend, it is not uniform as there have been short periods for which inequality has actually declined. This result emphasizes the importance of not

Table 2.1 Inequality measures, 1983 to 1995

Year	Gini	GE
1983	0.220	0.079
1984	0.217	0.076
1985	0.216	0.075
1986	0.225	0.080
1987	0.230	0.083
1988	0.239	0.089
1989	0.237	0.088
1990	0.241	0.091
1991	0.250	0.098
1992	0.263	0.108
1993	0.267	0.112
1994	0.273	0.117
1995	0.277	0.120

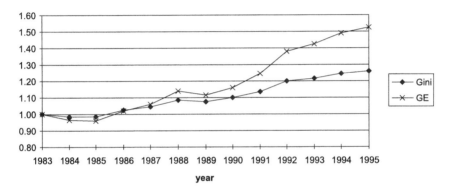

Figure 2.1 Inequality: evolution relative to 1983.

relying too heavily on a time series of only four or five years to draw overall conclusions. Third, the GE measure rises much faster than the Gini. This result indicates the different sensitivities of these two measures to changes in different parts of the distribution. The important point for us, however, is that the two measures agree concerning the trend over a significant length of time. To investigate this trend more fully, we focus on the GE measure because it, unlike the Gini, is additively decomposable across socio-economic groups.

Tables 2.2, 2.3, and 2.4 capture the key empirical results concerning the evolution of rural–urban and inland–coastal inequalities in China over the period from 1983 to 1995. Table 2.2 shows the evolution of the population weighted urban–rural and inland–coastal mean real expenditures. Two features are discernible from these mean ratios. First, the rural–urban gap is much higher than the inland–coastal gap for the entire period. Second, although the rural–urban gap shows a weak upward trend, it has remained more or less constant or, if anything, tended to decline in the 1980s but it has

Table 2.2 Real per capita mean expenditures and ratios

Year	Urban	Rural	Urban–Rural	Coastal	Inland	Inland–Coastal
1983	573	248	2.31	343	280	1.23
1984	622	278	2.24	383	313	1.22
1985	669	299	2.23	412	340	1.21
1986	709	316	2.25	440	359	1.22
1987	741	327	2.26	463	374	1.24
1988	775	335	2.32	486	382	1.27
1989	740	326	2.27	468	373	1.26
1990	761	327	2.33	476	376	1.27
1991	805	336	2.39	505	386	1.31
1992	871	354	2.46	556	404	1.38
1993	944	379	2.49	611	434	1.41
1994	1010	405	2.49	669	460	1.45
1995	1091	443	2.46	746	495	1.51

Notes

a The mean expenditures for urban, rural, coastal, and inland categories are aggregated from provincial level data by authors using populations as weights. The unit of the expenditure is Chinese Yuan.

b The provincial level real expenditures for the whole period are derived from the nominal expenditures in 1983 and the published annual growth rates of real expenditures. Both the expenditures and growth rates are from various issues of *China Statistical Yearbook*.

c The fourth and seventh columns are the ratios of urban to rural expenditures and coastal to inland expenditures, respectively.

Table 2.3 Inequality within groups: the GE index for rural, urban, coastal and inland

Year	Rural	Urban	Coastal	Inland
1983	0.019	0.009	0.068	0.077
1984	0.021	0.009	0.067	0.073
1985	0.020	0.008	0.064	0.076
1986	0.023	0.008	0.067	0.081
1987	0.024	0.008	0.070	0.083
1988	0.026	0.008	0.080	0.084
1989	0.027	0.010	0.080	0.082
1990	0.026	0.009	0.085	0.084
1991	0.028	0.010	0.088	0.090
1992	0.033	0.014	0.098	0.094
1993	0.032	0.014	0.100	0.095
1994	0.036	0.016	0.100	0.099
1995	0.040	0.020	0.099	0.099

risen in the 1990s by about 6 percent. However, the inland–coastal gap has increased sharply throughout the period by about 23 percent. Table 2.3 follows up by presenting results on GE inequality within each of the four groups, i.e. rural, urban, inland, and coastal. Inequality has increased on trend in each of these groups during the period.

Not only has the overall inequality increased, but also inequality in each of its components. Which components increased relatively faster, and which have contributed more to the overall increase in inequality? Table 2.4 presents the decomposition analyses for the overall inequality under two kinds of groupings. First, the 56 observations in each year are divided into rural and urban categories, i.e. 28 for each of them. Under this divide, the overall inequality is decomposed into three components according to formula (2): within-rural inequality, within-urban inequality, and inequality between rural and urban. Second, a similar decomposition is conducted across a inland-coastal divide. The coastal and inland groupings include 22 and 34 observations, respectively, in each year. The within-rural and within-urban contributions to overall inequality increased during this period, while the contributions of within-inland and within-coastal declined. At the same time, the between rural–urban contribution to total inequality was high but showed a weak downward trend over time. The between inland–coastal contribution was low but increased dramatically, although overall the contribution of the rural–urban gap to total inequality still dominates at the end of the period.

Thus, behind China's dramatic increase in regional inequality, disequal-izing forces have been at work within each of the four major categories of rural, urban, inland and coastal and also across the inland–coastal divide. On the other hand, these forces have not operated quite so strongly across the rural–urban divide. Considering the relative large contributions of within-rural inequality and within-inland inequality, we conduct further decom-position analyses for rural and inland areas.[3] Discussion of increasing inequalities within rural areas has focused on the role of nonagricultural

Table 2.4 GE inequality decomposition: contributions to overall inequality

Year	Rural–Urban			Inland–Coastal		
	Rural–Urban	Urban	Rural	Inland–Coastal	Coastal	Inland
1983	78.09	2.04	19.87	6.45	35.72	57.82
1984	75.76	2.10	22.14	6.55	36.57	56.88
1985	76.95	1.99	21.06	5.96	35.20	58.84
1986	74.50	2.04	23.45	6.26	34.33	59.41
1987	74.84	1.95	23.21	6.65	34.97	58.38
1988	74.70	1.89	23.41	8.02	36.55	55.43
1989	73.28	2.43	24.30	7.23	37.59	55.18
1990	74.88	2.17	22.95	7.49	38.42	54.09
1991	75.53	2.25	22.22	9.07	36.85	54.08
1992	73.54	2.86	23.60	11.60	37.25	51.15
1993	75.12	2.87	22.01	12.90	37.15	49.95
1994	73.25	3.12	23.63	14.74	35.13	50.13
1995	70.65	4.00	25.35	17.33	33.77	48.90
Growth(%)	−9.5	95.9	27.6	168.5	−5.5	−15.4

activities and the reform process (Rozelle, 1994; Chen and Ravallion, 1996; Tsui, 1998a). Our analysis reveals different relative dynamic roles for the inland–coastal gap and the rural–urban gap. The former is low relative to the latter but increasing fast, while the latter is large but stagnant. Table 2.5 considers only the rural areas and decomposes rural inequality across inland and coastal categories. Each province has one rural observation, so in total, there are 28 observations in each year, i.e. 17 for inland areas and 11 for coastal areas. The disequalizing forces behind the inland–coastal divide are apparent even when we restrict our attention to rural areas only. Correspondingly, Table 2.6 looks at 17 inland provinces only and considers the rural–urban decomposition within inland areas. There are 17 observations for both

Table 2.5 Coastal–inland inequality decomposition within rural areas

Year	Inland–Coastal	Coastal	Inland
1983	30.99	31.08	37.93
1984	26.52	33.39	40.09
1985	28.13	34.62	37.25
1986	26.06	31.75	42.19
1987	27.89	33.98	38.13
1988	28.83	38.19	32.98
1989	24.78	42.42	32.81
1990	25.39	43.06	31.55
1991	32.39	38.25	29.36
1992	38.10	39.68	22.22
1993	43.65	38.32	18.03
1994	46.47	33.95	19.59
1995	49.05	28.71	22.24

Table 2.6 Rural–urban inequality decomposition within inland areas

Year	Rural–Urban	Urban	Rural
1983	85.69	1.28	13.03
1984	83.21	1.18	15.61
1985	85.17	1.50	13.34
1986	81.82	1.53	16.66
1987	83.46	1.38	15.16
1988	85.05	1.02	13.93
1989	84.11	1.44	14.45
1990	85.52	1.09	13.39
1991	86.81	1.13	12.06
1992	88.67	1.08	10.25
1993	91.16	0.90	7.94
1994	89.60	1.17	9.23
1995	86.97	1.49	11.53

rural and urban groupings in each year. The relative contribution of the rural–urban divide is high but remains more or less constant. These empirical regularities confirm the very different evolving roles of the rural–urban and inland–coastal divides in income inequality in China.

2.4 The role of labor migration

The forces of growth and distribution seem to increase the inland–coastal gap dramatically while reducing modestly the rural–urban gap. There are several possible explanations for this. First, labor migration may occur more easily to an urban area from its rural hinterland than from an inland area to a coastal area. Second, the impact of reform in rural areas, especially in village enterprises, means that rural incomes in general have kept pace in general with their urban areas. Third, the dynamic growth in the coastal areas has been of an altogether different magnitude and nature; it has led to a widening gap with the inland areas. Indeed, the rural areas surrounding the coastal urban explosion have benefited, as some of the growth areas are spilling over into what were once, and perhaps still are, counted as rural areas. These forces are leading to a split in China along the inland–coastal divide, which is becoming increasingly more pronounced and will eventually dominate the traditional rural–urban divide if the rate of change continues.

To test the hypotheses that labor migration from an inland area to a coastal region is more difficult than from a rural area to a nearby urban region, data on rural–urban and inland–coastal migration are required. A growing literature on migration in China supports this claim. The *Hukou* system of household registration, established in the 1950s, confined people to the village or city of their birth (Chan, 1995; Solinger, 1993). After the success of the rural reform in the 1980s, which freed labor from agricultural production, an explicit policy was adopted to localize migration. To quote the Minister of Labor (Li, 1996, p. 2), the aim of the policy is to "limit the interregional movement of workers to the current level and the majority of redundant rural workers should leave agriculture for new jobs locally." Not surprisingly, local rural–urban migration increased, but cross-regional migration was deterred. Zhang and Chi (1996), in a study of six inland provinces, find that more than 96 percent of the rural-to-urban migration was intra-provincial. Meng (1994) shows that, in a survey of four counties, two coastal and two inland, less than 2.8 percent of workers in rural industries were from outside the provinces. Banister (1997) estimates that about 3.5 percent of the total rural population worked outside its province of origin. Although there is more mobility for educated workers (Zhang and Chi, 1996), the evidence seems to indicate that labor markets are still fragmented across provincial lines.

A more systematic investigation of the changes in aggregate labor force in rural, urban, inland, and coastal areas during the sample period confirms this point. We use aggregate labor force due to the lack of systematic labor migration data. Historical data for total, urban, and rural labor force at a provincial level, however, are available from various issues of *China Statistical Yearbook* and *China Agricultural Yearbook*. Based on these provincial level data, the total labor force for rural, urban, inland, and coastal areas for each year can be aggregated. The labor force data are supposed to contain more information on migration than the registered population data because they are not derived directly from the *Hukou* system. For example, the urban labor force includes not only the workers with urban resident status, but also the contract employees with rural resident status who are hired to work in urban areas. However, many floating labor migrants perform only temporary jobs and do not have any formal labor contract. Therefore, although better than the data from *Hukou* statistics, the labor force statistics used in this paper, may still underestimate the extent of true labor migration.

Table 2.7 provides information on the changes in labor force. The portion of the rural labor force to the total labor force decreases 4.2 percent, from 0.754 to 0.722, during the period from 1983 to 1995. In contrast, the ratio of the inland labor force relative to the total labor force increases slightly from 0.569 to 0.577 during the same period, in large part because of the higher birth rate in inland areas and less labor mobility across provincial boundaries.

As one referee points out, the inability of the SSB data to measure floating migratory workers may affect our estimates. The national migration data (*China Development Report 1998*, p. 245), derived from a 1 percent Population

Table 2.7 The changes in labor force and capital

Year	Total labor (million)	Rural/Total labor	Inland/Total labor	Capital (billion)	K/L ratio (Inland–Coastal)
1983	460.04	0.754	0.569	114.42	1.572
1984	478.57	0.752	0.567	130.32	1.470
1985	498.73	0.743	0.568	175.07	1.471
1986	509.60	0.744	0.572	241.76	1.488
1987	527.83	0.739	0.569	284.79	1.668
1988	543.35	0.737	0.571	349.95	1.819
1989	553.29	0.740	0.574	439.44	1.817
1990	566.49	0.742	0.576	479.31	1.783
1991	583.61	0.738	0.575	485.18	1.723
1992	594.31	0.737	0.576	542.37	1.786
1993	602.20	0.735	0.576	761.37	2.060
1994	614.70	0.726	0.576	1556.80	2.218
1995	623.87	0.722	0.577	2054.35	2.270

Notes
a The last column is the ratio of capital to labor in coastal regions relative to capital to labor in inland areas.
b Labor and capital are aggregated from 28 provinces, excluding Hainan, by the authors.
c From 1994, the capital accumulation variable has been adjusted to be consistent with western standards. Prior to 1989, the provincial capital data are from *China Fixed Assets and Investment Statistics*, while, for other years, the data are from *China Statistical Yearbook*.

Survey in 1995, provides us with a glimpse of the possible impact of including the floating labor migrants in the above analysis. According to the survey, there are 53.5 million floating population in 1995, of which 17.8 million are inter-provincial migrants. Furthermore, 86 percent of the floating population is in the age group between 15 and 65 and, thus, they can be regarded as part of the labor force. In other words, there are about 46.0 million floating labor migrants in China in 1995, of which 15.3 million are inter-provincial labor migrants. If we assume that all the inter-provincial labor movement is from inland to coastal regions and all the intra-provincial movement is from rural to urban areas, the labor ratios of rural/total and inland/total will become 0.648 and 0.552, indicating a 14 and a 3 percent decline from 1983, respectively. With the additional assumption that the natural growth rates of labor forces are the same across rural, urban, coastal, and inland areas, we estimate that 19.7 percent of the rural laborers migrated to urban areas while 14.5 percent of the inland laborers moved to coastal areas during the period from 1983 to 1995. Hence, incorporating the floating labor migrants in 1995 into our analysis confirms further our hypothesis that the rural to urban labor flow is faster than the inland to coastal flow.

In addition to labor mobility, capital flows may be an important determinant of economic growth and income distribution within and across regions. In contrast to a rather sluggish inter-provincial labor mobility, the change in the distribution of capital among regions is much more rapid. Table 2.7 indicates that the capital/labor ratio in coastal regions is 57 percent higher than that in inland areas in 1983, while the gap increases to 127 percent in 1995. Lack of detailed capital information for the rural–urban divide at a provincial level prevents us from drawing similar conclusions about rural–urban capital mobility.

This migration story, together with the changes in regional capital distribution, is broadly consistent with the rural–urban and inland–coastal inequality trends described in this paper (see also Jian, Sachs, and Warner, 1996). However, our findings may be subject to any limitations due to aggregate provincial data. For example, using micro data of individual households in two provinces, Yang (1999) shows a more substantial increase in rural–urban disparity than in this study and attributes part of the increasing disparity to the restrictions of rural–urban migration. However, because he only considered two provinces, his results are not directly comparable to ours. Furthermore, Yang does not contrast the contribution of the rural–urban divide to that of the inland–coastal divide, which would require, at a minimum, pooling his data for the two provinces.

2.5 Conclusions

This paper has developed a consistent and coherent empirical framework for assessing the evolution of regional inequalities for China. Our main conclusion is that, while the contribution of rural–urban disparities to regional inequality far exceed the contribution of inland–coastal disparities, the contribution of the latter has increased dramatically. The greater ease of rural-to-urban migration within provinces compared to the institutional and other difficulties of migrating from inland to coastal provinces provides a partial explanation for this phenomenon. Although fragmentary, the data seem to provide some preliminary support for our hypothesis. More analysis of the interaction at different points in time and in different parts of China is needed to explore further this hypothesis.

Notes

1 The views expressed here are those of the authors. We thank John. P. Bonin, Weifeng Weng, and two anonymous referees for helpful comments. An earlier version of this paper was presented in a session of the Western Economics Association International Conference in July 1998. Valuable suggestions from Lok Sang Ho, M.E. Jones, Hao Li, and other participants in the session are acknowledged.
2 According to the *China Statistical Yearbook* (1995, p. 54), rural and urban resident consumption refers to "total final consumption of goods and services by the resident units in a certain period of time; including the purchase of various kinds of goods for consumption and outlays of various kinds of services, such as rents, traffic, health care, cultural life and education, etc.; imputed value of consumption of owner-occupied dwelling and consumption goods in the form of physical wages obtained by residents, excluding outlays on the purchase of buildings and production." The annual growth rates of real consumption per capita of national, rural (agricultural), and urban (non-agricultural) residents are calculated based on separate comparable prices (SSB, 1995, p. 258) "to reflect accurately the change in real term(s)" (SSB, 1995, p. 52).
3 Decomposition is also conducted for urban and coastal areas and the results are consistent with the analyses for rural and inland areas.

References

Aaberge, Rolf, and Li, Xuezeng, "The Trend in Urban Income Inequality in Two Chinese Provinces, 1986–90." *Rev. of Income and Wealth*, **43**, 3:335–355, Sept. 1997.
Banister, Judith, "China: Internal and Regional Migration Trends." In Thomas Scharping Ed., *Floating Population and Migration in China: the Impact of Economic Reforms*, pp. 72–97. Hamburg: Institute für Asinkunde, 1997.
Bramall, Chris, and Jones, Marion E., "Rural Income Inequality in China since 1978". *J. Peasant Stud.*, **21**, 1:41–70, Oct. 1993.
Chan, Kam Wing, "Migration Controls and Urban Society in Post-Mao China." Seattle Population Research Center working paper, No. 95–2, 1995.
Chen, Jian, and Fleisher, Belton M., "Regional Income Inequality and Economic Growth in China." *J. Comp. Econom.*, **22**, 2:141–164, April 1996.
Chen, Shaohua, and Ravallion, Martin, "Data in Transition: Assessing Rural Living Standards in Southern China." *China Econom Rev.*, **7**, 1:23–56, Spring 1996.
China Agricultural Administration, *China Agricultural Yearbook*, various issues. Beijing: China Agricultural Press.
China State Statistics Bureau (SSB), *China Development Report*. Beijing: China Statistical Press, 1998.

China State Statistics Bureau (SSB), *China Fixed Assets and Investment Statistics*, various issues. Beijing: China Statistical Press.

China State Statistics Bureau (SSB), *China Population Statistics*, various issues. Beijing: China Statistical Press.

China State Statistics Bureau (SSB), *China Statistical Yearbook*, various issues. Beijing: China Statistical Press.

Cowell, Frank, *Measuring Inequality*, 2nd ed., London, New York: Prentice Hall/ Harvester Wheatsheaf, 1995.

Fleisher, Belton M., and Chen, Jian, "The Coast-Noncoast Income Gap, Productivity, and Regional Economic Policy in China." *J. Comp. Econom.*, **25**, 2:220–236, Oct. 1997.

Griffin, Keith, and Zhao, Renwei, *Distribution of Income in China*. London: Macmillan Press, 1993.

Grootaert, Christiaan, "Structural Change and Poverty in Africa: A Decomposition Analysis for Côte d'Ivoire." *J. Develop. Econom.*, **47**, 2:375–401, August 1995.

Guo, Jiann-Jong, *Price Reform in China, 1979–1986*. New York: St. Martin's Press, 1992.

Hu, Angang, "Excessively Large Regional Gaps Are Too 'Risky'." *Chinese Econom. Stud.*, **29**, 6:72–75, Nov.–Dec., 1996.

Huang, Shikang, "Control the Development Gap between the Seaboard and the Interior; Accelerate the Development of the Central and Western Regions." *Chinese Econom. Stud.*, **29**, 6:76–82, Nov.–Dec., 1996.

Hussain, Athar, Lanjouw, Peter, and Stern, Nicholas, "Income Inequalities in China: Evidence from Household Survey Data." *World Develop.*, **22**, 12:1947–1957, Dec. 1994.

Jian, T., Sachs, Jefferson, and Warner, Andrew, "Trends in Regional Inequality in China." National Bureau of Economic Research working paper, No. 5412, 1996.

Khan, Azizur R., Griffin, Keith, Riskin, Carl, and Zhao, Renwei, "Sources of Income Inequality in Post-reform China". *China Econom. Rev.*, **4**, 1:19–35, Spring 1993.

Li, Baiyong, "Objective of Labor Work in New Century." *Renmin Luntan (People's Forum)*, January 8, 1996.

Li, Peilin, "Has China Become Polarized?" *Chinese Econom. Stud.*, **29**, 3:73–76, May–June 1996.

Li, Qiang, and Zhang, Zhiying, "Lasting Political Stability Requires a Massive Middle-Income Stratum." *Chinese Econom. Stud.*, **29**, 6:68–71, Nov.–Dec. 1996.

Lyons, Thomas P., "Interprovincial Disparities in China: Output and Consumption, 1952–1987." *Econom. Develop. & Cult. Change*, **39**, 3:471–506, April 1991.

Meng, Xi, "Rural Labor Market and TVEs Development." In Qingsong Lin and William Byrd Ed., *China's Rural Industry: Structure, Development, and Reform* (Chinese version), pp. 410–438. Hong Kong: Oxford University Press, 1994.

Rozelle, Scott, "Rural Industrialization and Increasing Inequality: Emerging Patterns in China's Reforming Economy." *J. of Comp. Econom*, **19**, 3:362–391, Dec. 1994.

Shorrocks, Anthony F., "The Class of Additively Decomposable Inequality Measures." *Econometrica*, **48**, 3:613–625, April 1980.

Shorrocks, Anthony F., "Inequality Decomposition by Population Subgroups." *Econometrica*, **52**, 6:1369–1385, Nov. 1984.

Shorrocks, Anthony, and Foster, James E., "Transfer Sensitive Inequality Measures." *Rev. Econom. Stud.*, **54**, 3:485–497, July 1987.

Solinger, Dorothy, "China's Transients and the State: A Form of Civil Society?" *Politics & Society*, **21**, 1:98–103, Mar. 1993.

Tang, Xianguo, *The Reform of China's Pricing System*. Genaeve: Institut universitaire de hautes études internationales, 1987.

Tsui, Kai-yuen, "China's Regional Inequality, 1952–1985." *J. Comp. Econom.*, **15**, 1:1–21, April 1991.

Tsui, Kai-yuen, "Decomposition of China's Regional Inequalities." *J. Comp. Econom.*, **17**, 3:600–627, Sept. 1993.

Tsui, Kai-yuen, "Economic Reform and Interprovincial Inequalities in China." *J. Develop. Econom.*, **50**, 2:353–368, Aug. 1996.

Tsui, Kai-yuen, "Factor Decomposition of Chinese Rural Income Inequality: New Methodology, Empirical Findings, and Policy Implications." *J. Comp. Econom.*, **26**, 3:502–528, Sept. 1998a.

Tsui, Kai-yuen, "Trends and Inequalities of Rural Welfare in China: Evidence from Rural Households in Guangdong and Sichuan." *J. Comp. Econom.*, **26**, 4:783–804, Dec. 1998b.

Xue, Jinjun, "Urban–Rural Income Disparity and Its Significance in China." *Hitotsubashi J. Econom.*, **38**, 1:45–59, June 1997.

Yang, Dali, *Beyond Beijing: Liberalization and the Regions in China*. New York: Routledge, 1997.

Yang, Danis, "Urban-Biased Policies and Rising Income Inequality in China," *Amer. Econom. Rev.* (Paper and Proceedings), **89**, 2:306–310, May 1999.

Yang, Yihong, "Is 'Excessive Distribution' a Good Thing or a Bad Thing?" *Chinese Econom. Stud.*, **29**, 6:46–53, Nov.–Dec. 1996.

Yao, Shujie, "Industrialization and Spatial Income Inequality in Rural China, 1986–92." *Econom. of Transition*, **5**, 1:97–112, May 1997.

Ye, Fujin, "Since the Government Is the Referee, Why Does it Get Into the Game?" *Chinese Econom. Stud.*, **29**, 6:41–45, Nov.–Dec. 1996.

Zhang, Toni T., and Chi, Peter S., "Determinants of Rural–Urban Migration: a Study of Six Provinces in China, 1985–1990". Paper presented in the Annual Meeting of the Population Association of America, New Orleans, May 9–11, 1996.

3 What difference do polarization measures make?

An application to China

Xiaobo Zhang and Ravi Kanbur

Abstract

In recent years there has been much discussion of the difference between inequality and polarization. The vast literature on inequality is held to miss out key features of distributional change, which are better described as changes in polarization. Axioms have been proposed which capture some of these differences, and measures of polarization, as distinct from inequality, have been suggested. The theoretical distinctions proposed in this literature are indeed interesting. But do the newly proposed measures of polarization give different results in comparing societies over time? We address these questions for China, where dramatic increases in inequality and polarization have been much discussed in the literature. We find that, contrary to theoretical expectation, the new measures of polarization do not generate very different results from the standard measures of inequality. The paper ends by considering a different approach to polarization which might better conform to the policy concerns expressed in the specific context of China.

3.1 Introduction

In recent years there has been much discussion of the differences between inequality and polarization. It has been argued that these capture different features of distribution, and can move in opposite directions. At the same time, phenomena such as "the disappearing middle class" or "clustering around extremes" do not appear to be easily captured by standard measures of inequality such as the Gini coefficient. It is to characterize such phenomena that Esteban and Ray (1994), Wolfson (1994), and Tsui and Wang (1998) have proposed alternative indices of polarization. These indices seek evidence for clustering in the distribution of personal income at the lower and upper ends. It is claimed that, at least in theory, they represent a major departure from standard measures of inequality.

But would conclusions drawn from comparisons of inequality measures be reversed or significantly changed if we used the new polarization measures instead? Ravallion and Chen (1997) asked this question for a cross-country comparison of the Gini coefficient and the Wolfson index, and concluded "there is a surprisingly close correspondence between them for these data" (p. 369). In this paper we ask the same question for changes in inequality and polarization over time for one country. That country is China – where increasing inequality, and concerns about growing polarization, have been prominent in policy discussion ever since the start of reforms in the late 1970s, but increasingly so in the 1980s and the 1990s. Inland–coastal and rural–urban gaps have been particularly worrisome (Lyons, 1991; Tsui, 1991, 1996; Chen and Fleisher, 1996; Jian, Sachs, and Warner, 1996; Jalan and Ravallion, 1998; and Kanbur and Zhang, 1999). Li (1996) argues that China is becoming a polarized society in two dimensions – rural–urban and inland–coastal.

Can the new measures of polarization pick up and reflect these concerns in a manner which is different from standard inequality measures? Section 3.2 discusses the conceptual differences between the standard inequality and polarization measures. Section 3.3 sets out the data and presents the empirical comparisons for these measures. The results show that standard inequality and the polarization measures do not give us a very different picture of patterns and trends in China. Based on this finding, Section 3.4 proposes an alternative way to look at polarization measurement, which comes closer to capturing the spirit of many policy concerns. Section 3.5 concludes the paper.

3.2 Inequality vs. polarization

A standard measure of inequality is "a scalar numerical representation of the interpersonal difference in income within a given population" (p. 12, Cowell, 1995). An inequality index essentially measures the spread of an income distribution. It emphasizes the deviation from the global mean, ignoring clustering around local means. A key motivation behind inequality is the "Pigou-Dalton axiom" (PD axiom). That is, any transfer from rich to poor, other things remaining the same, always decreases inequality.

There are several standard measures of inequality. The Gini coefficient (Cowell, 1995) is defined as the ratio of the area between the Lorenz curve and the area under the 45§ line. It can be written as:

$$G = \left(\frac{1}{\mu}\right) \sum_{i=1}^{K} \sum_{j=1}^{K} f(y_i) f(y_j) |y_i - y_j| \tag{1}$$

where y_i is the income for each group, μ is the mean income for the whole sample, $f(y_i)$ represents the population share of the ith group, and K is the total number of groups.

The Generalized Entropy (GE) measure (Shorrocks, 1980 and 1984) can be written as:

$$I(y) = \begin{cases} \sum_{i=1}^{K} f(y_i) \left\{ \left(\frac{y_i}{\mu} \right)^c - 1 \right\} & c \neq 0,1 \\ \\ \sum_{i=1}^{K} f(y_i) \left(\frac{y_i}{\mu} \right) \log\left(\frac{y_i}{\mu} \right) & c = 1 \\ \\ \sum_{i=1}^{K} f(y_i) \log\left(\frac{\mu}{y_i} \right) & c = 0. \end{cases} \qquad (2)$$

In the above equation, y_i is i^{th} income, μ is the total sample mean, $f(y_i)$ is the population share of y_i in the total population and K is the number of groups.

Polarization places more emphasis on "clustering". Many phenomena, such as "the disappearing middle class," can be described as "polarization." The concept of polarization can run counter to the PD axiom underlying the conventional inequality measures. To illustrate, suppose there are four income levels, a, c, d, and f, as shown in Diagram 1a with equal population shares. Consider now an income redistribution between a and c, and between d and f, which leads to only two income levels b and e as shown in Diagram 1b. Clearly, overall inequality has decreased. However, comparing Diagrams 1a and 1b, it can bee seen the society is now "clustered" – the "middle class" has disappeared. In this sense, society is more polarised.

This is the intuitive difference between inequality and polarization which Esteban and Ray (1994), Wolfson (1994), and Tsui and Wang (1998) try to capture in different ways – all of them trying to capture "clustering" along the income dimension.

The Esteban-Ray index, which we refer to as the ER index, is built on

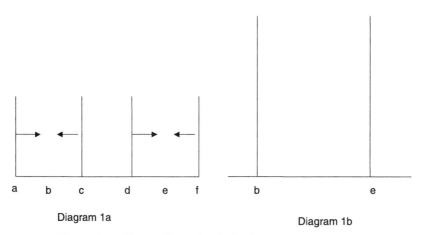

Diagram 1a

Diagram 1b

Diagram 1 Illustration of inequality and polarization.

Note: The horizontal line stands for income levels while the vertical lines correspond to distribution masses for each group.

the basis of two behavioral functions ("identification" and "alienation"). Identification is an increasing function of the number of individuals in the same income class of that individual. For any individual, the higher the number of people who have the same income level as him, the more sense of identification he feels. The alienation function characterizes the antagonism caused by the income difference. An individual feels alienated from others that are "far away" from him. Let y_i be the income of each individual in group i, and let y_j be the corresponding income for group j. If the identification function is represented by π_i^a, and the alienation function by $|y_i - y_j|$, then one way of capturing polarization is to use the product of these two for each individual and the sum across all individuals. This gives us:

$$ER = A\sum_{i=1}^{K}\sum_{j=1}^{K} \pi_i\pi_j\pi_i^a\,|y_i - y_j| \tag{3}$$

where K is the number of groups, and A is a normalization scalar. In fact, Esteban and Ray (1994) derive this specific form as satisfying certain reasonable axioms, and they show further that to satisfy these axioms, the "degree of polarization" sensitivity parameter a must lie between 0 and 1.6. The larger the value of a, the greater is the deviation of the ER index from the standard Gini coefficient. In our illustrative calculations, we set a to 1.5 to give a large weight to "polarization". It can been seen from (1) and (3) that ER is equal to the Gini coefficient if a is set to 0. Also, when $\pi_i = 1$ (each group has only one individual or has an identical number of members), the ER index collapses to the Gini. As the Gini is a special case of the ER index family, we may conjecture that the two indices behave closely when there are a large number of similar size groups.

The Wolfson (1994) index is derived from the Lorenz curve. It is twice the area between the Lorenz curve and the tangent line at the median point. It can be written as:

$$W = 2(2T\text{-Gini})/(m/\mu) = 2(\mu^* - \mu^L)/m, \tag{4}$$

where $T = 0.5 - L(0.5)$ and $L(0.5)$ denotes the income share of the bottom half of the population; m is the median income; μ is the mean income; μ^* is the distribution-corrected mean income which is given by the actual mean times (1-Gini); and μ^L is the mean income of the bottom half of the population. The maximum polarization occurs when half the population has zero income and the other half has twice the mean.

Wolfson (1994) shows that like the Gini index, this index lies between 0 and 1. Tsui and Wang (1998) generalize a new class of indices (*TW* index hereafter) based on the Wolfson index using the two partial ordering axioms of "increased bipolarity" and "increased spread." It can be expressed as follows:

$$TW = \frac{\theta}{N} \sum_{i=1}^{K} \pi_i \left| \frac{y_i - m}{m} \right|^r \tag{5}$$

where N is the number of total population, π_i is the number of population in group i, K is the number of groups, y_i is the mean value in group i, and m is the median income. θ is a positive constant scalar and $r \in (0,1)$. Here we set $r = 0.5$.

3.3 Data and empirical results

Data

Our focus is on patterns and trends of regional inequality and polarization in China from 1983 to 1995. Of the 30 provinces, Tibet and Hainan had to be excluded due to lack of consistent data. With rural and urban components in each province, we have 56 observations per year for each year from 1983 to 1995. For each component, we derive per capita real consumption expenditures from the *China Statistical Yearbook*, using a procedure described in Kanbur and Zhang (1999). Rural and urban population in each province is available from various issues of *China Population Statistics Yearbook*. It is the inequality of this per capita consumption that we are interested in (for a fuller discussion of this method versus others, see Kanbur and Zhang, 1999). The inland coastal divide is developed following the method of Tsui (1993), Huang (1996), Yao (1997), Chen and Fleisher (1996), and Yang (1997). The coastal zone is defined as being the following provinces: Beijing, Liaoning, Tianjin, Hebei, Shandong, Jiangsu, Shanghai, Zhejiang, Fujian, Guangdong and Guangxi. All remaining provinces are classified as inland.

Empirical results

For each year we calculated the two inequality measures and three polarization indices from 56 observations in our data set – one rural and one urban observation for each of 28 provinces. Table 3.1 reports the overall inequality and polarization measures over the period of 1983–1995. Figure 3.1 presents the evolution of these measures relative to their 1983 values.

Three features are immediately apparent. First, the overall trend for both inequality and polarization measures increases but at substantially different rates during this period of fast growth – this confirms earlier studies that there is indeed an issue to be investigated. Second, although there is an overall upward trend, this is not uniform, and there have been short periods for which inequality and polarization has actually declined. Third, the distinction between the three polarization measures is greater than that between the two inequality measures. The ER index gives very similar results to Gini although the parameter α in the ER formula has been set to 1.5, nearly the

Table 3.1 Inequality and polarization (all China)

Year	Gini	GE	ER	Wolfson	TW
1983	0.220	0.079	0.146	0.180	0.493
1984	0.217	0.076	0.142	0.180	0.504
1985	0.216	0.075	0.138	0.172	0.485
1986	0.225	0.080	0.144	0.189	0.506
1987	0.230	0.083	0.146	0.205	0.524
1988	0.239	0.089	0.147	0.221	0.541
1989	0.237	0.088	0.144	0.231	0.539
1990	0.241	0.091	0.147	0.237	0.548
1991	0.250	0.098	0.151	0.235	0.550
1992	0.263	0.108	0.157	0.261	0.570
1993	0.267	0.112	0.157	0.276	0.587
1994	0.273	0.117	0.157	0.286	0.599
1995	0.277	0.120	0.158	0.288	0.605

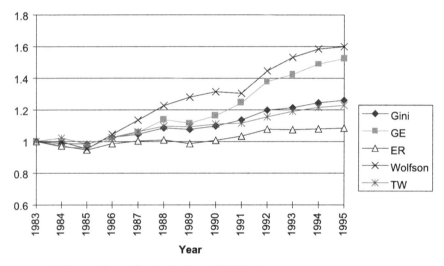

Figure 3.1 Inequality and polarization (all China).

largest value, to try and distinguish it from Gini (see the definition of the ER index in (3) in the last section). The Gini and the TW indices exhibit very similar patterns and magnitude. The increase in the Wolfson index is more rapid than all other measures. Moreover, the Wolfson index gives different results from other measures in 1988 and 1991.

Since the rural population accounts for more than 65 percent of total population, it is worthwhile to compare the measures of inequality and polarization for rural China (the comparison for urban China, not shown here, leads to similar results). Table 3.2 presents the evolution of these measures and Figure 3.2 graphs the results. Again, the ER index exhibits a similar

Table 3.2 Inequality and polarization (rural)

Year	Gini	GE	ER	Wolfson	TW
1983	0.107	0.019	0.140	0.105	0.364
1984	0.111	0.021	0.141	0.107	0.375
1985	0.108	0.020	0.134	0.109	0.379
1986	0.120	0.023	0.150	0.122	0.399
1987	0.123	0.024	0.154	0.115	0.391
1988	0.128	0.026	0.154	0.106	0.385
1989	0.129	0.027	0.152	0.102	0.371
1990	0.128	0.026	0.154	0.102	0.374
1991	0.131	0.028	0.159	0.104	0.382
1992	0.143	0.033	0.172	0.111	0.391
1993	0.139	0.032	0.165	0.110	0.370
1994	0.150	0.036	0.177	0.120	0.395
1995	0.157	0.040	0.187	0.119	0.407

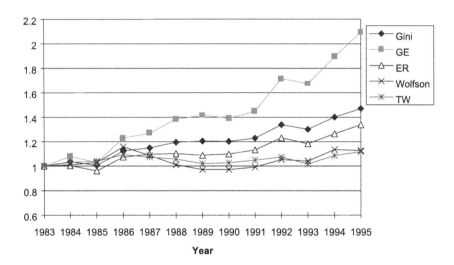

Figure 3.2 Inequality and polarization (rural).

pattern to the Gini. This time, the Wolfson index and the TW index have the lowest increase during the whole period and they show different patterns in 1986 and 1987 from other measures. The GE measure rises much faster than the Gini, suggesting the different sensitivities of these two measures to changes in different parts of the distribution. Because of its sensitivity to the median value, the Wolfson index may fluctuate more rapidly when the median value and its associated group change. But, the important point for us is that, overall, the polarization and the inequality measures agree on the trend over the sample period.

The measures of inequality and polarization for the four subgroups – rural, urban, inland, and coastal, in the initial year 1983 and the last year 1995 are presented in Table 3.3. These groupings are used because they are the most popularly discussed in daily political discourse. The results are also plotted in Figure 3.3a and Figure 3.3b. In 1995, all the five indices agree on the relative rankings of the four subgroups – the urban has the lowest and the coastal has the highest. In 1983, the five measures indicate consistent orderings for these four groupings except for the coastal by the ER index which, contrary to others, shows that the polarization in inland is lower than in coastal.

In summary, although the three polarization measures are theoretically different from standard inequality measures, empirically the new measures of polarization do not give us very different results from the standard measures

Table 3.3 Inequality and polarization

	Inequality		*Polarisation*		
	Gini	*GE*	*ER*	*Wolfson*	*TW*
1983					
Rural	0.107	0.019	0.140	0.105	0.364
Urban	0.074	0.009	0.073	0.084	0.316
Inland	0.213	0.077	0.309	0.173	0.477
Coastal	0.197	0.068	0.439	0.121	0.396
1995					
Rural	0.157	0.040	0.187	0.119	0.407
Urban	0.112	0.020	0.122	0.087	0.353
Inland	0.245	0.099	0.309	0.198	0.503
Coastal	0.251	0.099	0.506	0.222	0.539

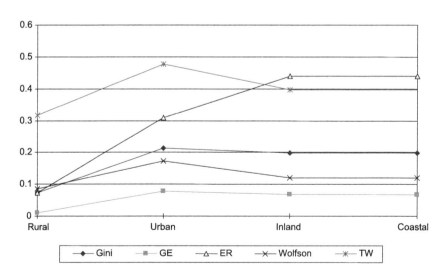

Figure 3.3a Inequality and polarization, 1983.

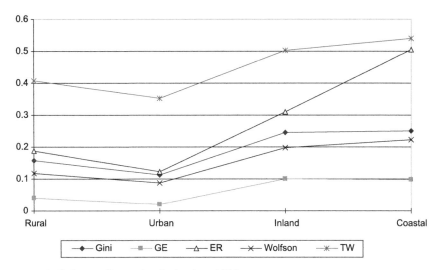

Figure 3.3b Inequality and polarization, 1995.

of inequality. Simply looking at the trends of these measures will not help us capture the distinctive concerns about polarization versus increasing inequality in China. In the next section, we consider an alternative approach, which derives directly from inequality measurement but which may capture better intuitive notions of polarization.

3.4 An alternative way of looking at polarization

The three polarization measures discussed so far aim to capture the "clustering" along the income dimension into high and low income groups. However, debates on polarization are often conducted in the framework of recognized and accepted non-income groupings. In the U.S., for example, clustering of black and white income levels is as much concern as "the disappearing middle class." In China, as discussed in the introduction, geographical clustering of income is a major policy concern. The "rural–urban" and "inland–coastal" divides in China are the analogs to the "black–white" divide in the U.S. These types of divergence or "polarization" cannot be captured by the polarization measures discussed so far.

With exogenously given groups defining the domains of the polarization discourse, one approach to measuring polarization is to simply look at the changes in mean income across the groups. Table 3.4 presents data for the urban–rural/inland–coastal divide. Two features are discernible from the table. First, the urban–rural gap is much higher than the inland–coastal gap for the entire period. Second, although the urban–rural gap shows a weak upward trend, it has remained more or less constant or, if anything, tended to decline in the 1980s but it has risen in the 1990s by about 6 percent. However,

Table 3.4 Real per capita mean expenditures and ratios

Year	Urban	Rural	Urban–Rural	Coastal	Inland	Inland–Coastal
1983	573	248	2.31	343	280	1.23
1984	622	278	2.24	383	313	1.22
1985	669	299	2.23	412	340	1.21
1986	709	316	2.25	440	359	1.22
1987	741	327	2.26	463	374	1.24
1988	775	335	2.32	486	382	1.27
1989	740	326	2.27	468	373	1.26
1990	761	327	2.33	476	376	1.27
1991	805	336	2.39	505	386	1.31
1992	871	354	2.46	556	404	1.38
1993	944	379	2.49	611	434	1.41
1994	1010	405	2.49	669	460	1.45
1995	1091	443	2.46	746	495	1.51

Note: The mean expenditures for urban, rural, coastal, and inland categories are aggregated from provincial level data by authors using populations as weights. The unit of the expenditure is Chinese Yuan. The provincial level real expenditures for the whole period are derived from the nominal expenditures in 1983 and the published annual growth rates of real expenditures. Both the expenditures and growth rates are from various issues of *China Statistical Yearbook*. The fourth and seventh columns are the ratios of urban to rural expenditures and coastal to inland expenditures, respectively.

the inland–coastal gap has increased sharply throughout the period by about 23 percent. Thus, according to mean differences, although rural–urban polarization is much greater than inland–coastal polarization, it is the latter which has been increasing dramatically during China's post-reform period.

While differences in mean present a readily understandable measure of the divide between groups, we have to bear in mind that there are within group inequalities as well. The richest in the low mean group could well be richer than the poorest in the high mean group. Such overlaps militate against the notion of "polarization" between the two groups. This is shown in Diagram 2, with significant overlaps. Group U has a higher mean than Group R but, because of inequality within each group, there are income overlaps between the two groups. The further apart are the two means, the greater, one can argue, is the polarization. For any given gap in means, however, the greater the spread within each of the groups, the greater the overlap between group members' incomes.

These two tendencies can be quantified using well-known concepts of "between group inequality" and "within group inequality" for decomposable inequality measures. Consider, for example, the GE index of inequality. For K exogenously given groups indexed by g:

$$I(y) = \sum_{g}^{K} w_g I_g + I(\mu_1 e_1, \ldots, \mu_K e_K) \tag{6}$$

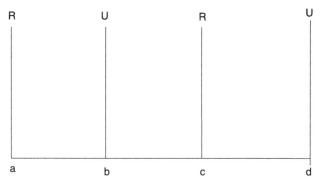

Diagram 2 Illustration of alternative polarization concept.

Note: R and U represent rural residents and urban residents, respectively. The horizontal line stands for income levels while the vertical lines correspond to population shares for each group.

$$
\text{where } w_g = \begin{cases} f_g \left(\dfrac{\mu_g}{\mu} \right)^c & c \neq 0, 1 \\[2ex] f_g \left(\dfrac{\mu_g}{\mu} \right) & c = 1 \\[2ex] f_g & c = 0 \end{cases}
$$

where I_g is inequality in the gth group, μ_g is the mean of the gth group and e_g is a vector of 1's of length n_g, where n_g is the population of the gth group. If n is the total population of all groups, then $f_g = \dfrac{n_g}{n}$ represents the share of the gth group's population in the total population. The first term on the right side of (6) represents the within-group inequality. $\dfrac{w_g I_g}{I(y)} * 100$ is the gth group's contribution to total inequality. The second term is the between-group (or inter-group) component of total inequality.

For all values of the parameter c, the GE measure is additively decomposable in the sense formalized by Shorrocks (1980, 1984), and this property allows us to talk about the "contribution" of different components to overall inequality. For values of c less than 2, the measure is transfer sensitive (Shorrocks and Foster, 1987), in the sense that it is more sensitive to transfers at the bottom end of the distribution than at the top. When c is 1 or 0, we have the measures of inequality made famous by Theil (see Cowell, 1995). For simplicity we only present results in this paper for $c = 0$. The results for $c = 1$ are similar.

The within-group inequality part in (6) represents the spread of the distributions in the subgroups; the between-group inequality is a measure of the distance between the group means. The ratio of between-group inequality to within-group inequality can thus be regarded as a scalar polarization index because it captures the average distance between the groups in relation to the income differences seen within groups. As income differences within groups diminish, i.e. as the groups become more homogeneous internally, differences across groups are, relatively speaking, magnified and "polarization" is higher. Similarly, for given within-group differences, as the groups means drift apart, polarization increases. Writing more formally, we can therefore define a polarization index as:

$$P = \text{between-group inequality/within-group inequality} \qquad (7)$$

where between-group inequality and within-group inequality are defined in (6).

Table 3.5 provides the GE inequality decomposition and the alternative polarization measure. The polarization measures for rural–urban and inland–coastal are also plotted in Figure 3.4. It can be seen from Figure 3.4 that the value of the alternative polarization measure calculated from the rural–urban dimension is much higher than that in the inland–coastal dimension. However, the inland–coastal polarization increases by 184 percent from 1983 to 1995, compared to the −32.5 percent decline in the rural–urban polarization. It does seem that the forces of growth and distribution are increasing inland–coastal polarization dramatically while modestly reducing the rural–urban polarization.

Kanbur and Zhang (1999) offered three hypotheses for the observed patterns. First, labor migration may occur more easily to an urban area from its rural hinterland than from an inland area to a coastal area. Second, the impact of reform in rural areas, especially in village enterprises, means that rural incomes have kept pace, in general, with those in urban areas. Third,

Table 3.5 GE inequality decomposition and the alternative polarization measure

| Year | Rural–Urban | | | Inland–Coastal | | |
	Between	*Within*	*B/W-RU*	*Between*	*Within*	*B/W-CI*
1983	78.09	21.91	3.56	6.45	93.54	0.07
1984	75.76	24.24	3.12	6.55	93.45	0.07
1985	76.95	23.05	3.34	5.96	94.04	0.06
1986	74.50	25.50	2.92	6.26	93.74	0.07
1987	74.84	25.16	2.98	6.65	93.35	0.07
1988	74.70	25.30	2.95	8.02	91.98	0.09
1989	73.28	26.72	2.74	7.23	92.77	0.08
1990	74.88	25.12	2.98	7.49	92.51	0.08
1991	75.53	24.47	3.09	9.07	90.93	0.10
1992	73.54	26.46	2.78	11.60	88.40	0.13
1993	75.12	24.88	3.02	12.90	87.10	0.15
1994	73.25	26.75	2.74	14.74	85.26	0.17
1995	70.65	29.35	2.41	17.33	82.67	0.21
Growth (%)	−9.5	33.9	−32.5	168.5	−11.6	203.8

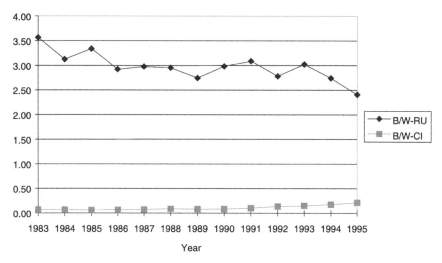

Figure 3.4 The ratios of between to within.

the dynamic growth in the coastal areas has been of an altogether different magnitude and nature; it has led to a widening gap with the inland areas. Indeed, the rural areas surrounding the coastal urban explosion have benefited, as some of the growth areas are spilling over into what were once, and perhaps still are, counted as rural areas. These forces are leading to a split in China along the inland–coastal divide, which is becoming increasingly pronounced.

3.5 Conclusion

The empirical behavior of three newly developed polarization indices has been tested against two standard measures of inequality using a complete data set at the provincial level in China over a long period. It is found that the polarization indices do not give distinctly different results from standard measures of inequality. An alternative polarization index, derived from inequality decomposition analysis, seems to offer more insight into changes in China's income distribution from two perspectives. It is found that in terms of levels, rural–urban polarization is more serious than inland–coastal while, in terms of trend, the inland–coastal polarization has increased much more dramatically than rural–urban. In our view, the analysis based on this alternative perspective on polarization reflects better current policy concerns than do the currently available measures of polarization.

References

Chen, Jian, and Belton M. Fleisher (1996), "Regional Income Inequality and Economic Growth in China." *Journal of Comparative Economics*, 22 (2): 141–164, April.

China State Statistics Bureau (SSB), *China Population Statistics*, various issues. Beijing: China Statistical Press.

China State Statistics Bureau (SSB), *China Statistical Yearbook*, various issues. Beijing: China Statistical Press.

Cowell, Frank (1995), *Measuring Inequality*, 2nd edition, London: Prentice Hall/Harvester Wheatsheaf.

Esteban, Joan-Maria, and Debraj Ray (1994), "On the Measurement of Polarisation." *Econometrica*, 62 (4): 819–851, July.

Huang, Shikang (1996), "Control the Development Gap Between the Seaboard and the Interior; Accelerate the Development of Central and Western Regions." *Chinese Economics Studies*, 29 (6): 76–82, Nov.–Dec.

Jalan, Jyotsna, and Martin Ravallion (1998), "Are There Dynamic Gains from a Poor-area Development Program?" *Journal of Public Economics*, 67 (1): 65–85, Jan.

Jian, Tianlun, Jeffery Sachs, and Andrew Warner (1996), "Trends in Regional Inequalities in China." National Bureau of Economic Research working paper, No. 5412.

Kanbur, Ravi, and Xiaobo Zhang (1999), "Which Regional Inequality? The Evolution of Rural–Urban and Inland–Coastal Inequality in China, 1983–1995." *Journal of Comparative Economics*, 27: 686–701.

Li, Peilin (1996), "Has China Become Polarized?" *Chinese Economics Studies*, 29 (3): 73–76, May–June.

Lyons, Thomas P. (1991), "Interprovincial Disparities in China: Output and Consumption, 1952–1987." *Economic, Development and Cultural Change*, 39 (3): 471–506, April.

Ravallion, Martin, and Shaohua Chen (1997), "What Can New Survey Data Tell Us about Recent Changes in Distribution and Poverty." *World Bank Economic Review*, 11 (2): 357–382, May.

Shorrocks, Anthony (1980), "The Class of Additively Decomposable Inequality Measures." *Econometrica*, 48: 613–625, April.

Shorrocks, Anthony (1984), "Inequality Decomposition by Population Subgroup." *Econometrica*, 52: 1369–1385, Nov.

Shorrocks, Anthony, and James E. Foster (1987), "Transfer Sensitive Inequality Measures." *Review of Economics Studies*, 54: 485–497, July.

Tsui, Kai-yuen (1991), "China's Regional Inequality, 1952–1985." *Journal of Comparative Economics*, 15 (1): 1–21, April.

Tsui, Kai-yuen (1993), "Decomposition of China's Regional Inequalities." *Journal of Comparative Economics*, 17 (3): 600–627, Sept.

Tsui, Kai-yuen (1996), "Economic Reform and Interprovincial Inequalities in China." *Journal of Development Economics*, 50 (2): 353–368, Aug.

Tsui, Kai-yuen, and Youqing Wang (1998), "Polarization Ordering and New Classes of Polarization Indices." Memo, the Chinese University of Hong Kong University.

Yang, Dali (1997), *Beyond Beijing: Liberalization and the Regions in China*. New York: Routledge.

Yao, Shujie (1997), "Industrialization and Spatial Income Inequality in Rural China, 1986–92." *Economics Transition*, 5 (1): 97–112, May.

Wolfson, Michael (1994), "When Inequalities Diverge?" *American Economic Review*, 84 (2): 353–358, May.

4 Fifty years of regional inequality in China

A journey through central planning, reform, and openness

Ravi Kanbur and Xiaobo Zhang

Abstract

This paper constructs and analyses a long run time series for regional inequality in China from the Communist Revolution to the present. There have been three peaks of inequality in the last fifty years, coinciding with the Great Famine of the late 1950s, the Cultural Revolution of the late 1960s and 1970s, and finally the period of openness and global integration in the late 1990s. Econometric analysis establishes that regional inequality is explained in the different phases by three key policy variables – the ratio of heavy industry to gross output value, the degree of decentralization, and the degree of openness.

4.1 Introduction

The second half of the 20th century has seen a tumultuous history unfold in China – the early years of communist rule in the 1950s culminating in the Great Famine, the Cultural Revolution and its aftermath in the late 1960s and the 1970s, the reform of agriculture in the late 1970s and the 1980s, and an explosion of trade and foreign direct investment in the late 1980s and the 1990s. All these events have affected the course of economic growth and income distribution. However, while a large literature has studied growth throughout these different phases of Chinese history (Lin, 1992; Fan, Zhang, and Robinson, 2003), few studies have matched the evolution of inequality over the long run with these different periods in Communist Chinese history over its entire course.

This paper presents and analyzes the evolution of Chinese regional inequality since the Communist revolution right up to the present. Most studies on China's inequality (Chen and Ravallion, 1996; Aaberge and Li, 1997; Tsui, 1998; Khan and Riskin, 2001) have focused on relatively short periods, mostly during the post-reform years, making use of the new household surveys that became available during this period. Of the studies which come closest to the spirit of our interest in Chinese inequality over the long run, Tsui (1991) stops in 1985 and Lyons (1991) stops in 1987, just as the increase in trade and foreign direct investment was beginning; Yang and Fang

(2000) go up to 1996, but focus only on the rural–urban gap at the national level; and Kanbur and Zhang (1999) disaggregate down to the rural–urban level within provinces to calculate a regional inequality index, and present a decomposition of regional inequality by its rural–urban and inland–coastal components, but their study is only for the post reform years of 1983–1995.

Using a dataset of provincial and national data covering the second half of the 20th century, we are able to construct a comprehensive time series of regional inequality in China, including its decompositions into rural–urban and inland–coastal components, from 1952 to 2000. We find that changes in regional inequality match the phases of Chinese history remarkably well, as do its rural–urban and inland–coastal components. The peaks of inequality in China have been associated with the Great Famine, the Cultural Revolution, and the current phase of openness and decentralization. We further use econometric analysis to establish that regional inequality is explained to different degrees in different phases by three key policy variables: the share of heavy industry in gross output value, the degree of decentralization, and the degree of openness.

4.2   Constructing a long run time series for regional inequality in China

Ideally, for an analysis of the evolution of inequality over Communist Chinese history we would have available representative national household surveys over the entire period. Unfortunately, while such surveys have been conducted throughout the last fifty years, they are available to researchers only for the post reform period, and in any case sporadically, for restricted years with varying but limited coverage. Thus, for example, Chen and Ravallion (1996) had access to official household survey data but only for four provinces between 1986 and 1990. Aaberge and Li (1997) analyze urban household surveys for Liaoning and Sichuan provinces for the same period, while Tsui (1998) analyzes rural surveys for 1985, 1988, and 1990, but only for Guangdong and Sichuan. Yang (1999) analyzes both rural and urban parts of the household survey for four years between 1986 and 1994, and for Guangdong and Sichuan. This different coverage across studies reflects the differential access to official data. Researchers have also conducted and analyzed independent surveys – for example, Rozelle (1994) did one for Township and Village Enterprises between 1984 and 1989 in Jiangsu province, and Khan and Riskin (2001) conducted household surveys for 1988 and 1995.

The inequality analysis that has been done on household surveys for the late 1980s and 1990s, has been extremely valuable in illuminating specific aspects of the distributional dimensions of Chinese development in the late 1980s and early 1990s. In general these analyses decompose inequality by income sources but few have aligned the patterns of inequality with national development policies. The bottom line is that researchers simply do not have comprehensive access to household surveys which are national and which cover the entire, or even a substantial part of, the half-century sweep of Chinese history that is of interest to us in this paper.

In the face of these data restrictions, we are forced to look for data availability at higher levels of aggregation than at the household level.[1] As it turns out certain types of data are indeed available at the province level, disaggregated by rural and urban areas, stretching back to 1952. This paper constructs a time series of inequality by building up information on real per capita consumption in the rural and urban areas of 28 of China's 30 provinces (unfortunately, data availability is not complete for Tibet and Hainan provinces).[2]

With these sub-provincial rural and urban per capita consumption figures, and population weights for these areas, a national distribution of real per capita consumption can be constructed, and its inequality calculated, for each year between 1952 and 2000, thus covering the vast bulk of the period from 1949 to the present. Of course what this means is that overall household-level inequality is being understated, since inequality within the rural and urban areas of each province is being suppressed. Moreover, we cannot say anything about the evolution of household-level inequality *within* these areas. Our measures do provide a lower bound on inequality over this entire period. But the fact remains that our study of inequality is essentially a study of regional inequality.[3]

Using the information available, we calculate the Gini coefficient of inequality using the standard formula. But the bulk of our analysis is done with a second inequality index, a member of the decomposable generalized entropy (GE) class of inequality measures as developed by Shorrocks (1984):[4]

$$I(y) = \sum_{i=1}^{n} f(y_i) \log\left(\frac{\mu}{y_i}\right) \tag{1}$$

In the above equation, y_i is the ith income measured as Chinese yuan, μ is the total sample mean, $f(y_i)$ is the population share of y_i in the total population and n is total population. A key feature of this measure is that it is additively decomposable. For K exogenously given, mutually exclusive and exhaustive, groups indexed by g:

$$I(y) = \sum_{g}^{k} f_g I_g + I(\mu_1 e_1, \ldots, \mu_K e_K) \tag{2}$$

In equation 2, I_g is inequality in the gth group, μ_g is the mean of the gth group and e_g is a vector of 1's of length n_g, where n_g is the population of the gth group. If n is the total population of all groups, then $f_g = \frac{n_g}{n}$ represents the share of the gth group's population in the total population. The first term on the right hand side of (2) represents the within-group inequality. The second term is the between group, or inter-group, component of total inequality. With our time series of inequality in China over the long term, we are now in a position to investigate dimensions of inequality in the different phases of Chinese development over the past half century.

4.3 Inequality change through the phases of Chinese history: a narrative

Following standard discussions, Communist Chinese history can be divided into several phases: 1949–56 (Revolution and Land Reform), 1957–61 (The Great Leap Forward and the Great Famine), 1962–65 (Post-Famine Recovery), 1966–78 (Cultural Revolution and Transition to Reform), 1979–84 (Rural Reform) and 1985 to present (Post Rural Reform, Decentralization and Opening up to Trade, and Foreign Direct Investment).

Table 4.1 presents economic indicators for China from 1952 to 2000. It includes three key indicators of economic policy – the share of heavy industry in gross value of total output (a measure of the bias against agriculture and China's comparative advantage), the ratio of trade volume to total GDP (a measure of the degree of openness), and the ratio of local government expenditure to total government expenditure (a measure of decentralization).[5] Figure 4.1 shows the evolution of real per capita GDP through the different phases identified above. Table 4.2 presents long-run inequality series, and Figure 4.2 plots the evolution of Chinese regional inequality, as measured by the Gini and the GE index, through the six phases of development

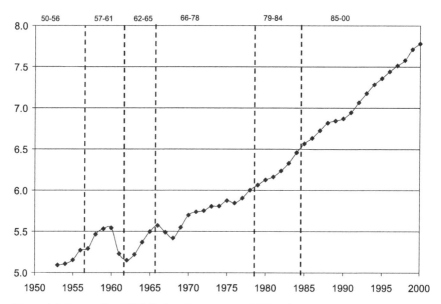

Figure 4.1 Per capita GDP (in logs) in constant 1980 prices.

Table 4.1 China: economic indicators, 1952–2000

Year	GDP (Billion)	Import (Billion)	Total expenditure (Billion)	GOV (Billion)	Tariff rate (%)	Trade ratio (%)	Decentralization (%)	Industrialization (%)
1952	67.9	3.8	17.2	81.0	12.8	9.5	25.9	15.3
1953	82.4	4.6	21.9	96.0	11.0	9.8	26.1	17.5
1954	85.9	4.5	24.4	105.0	9.2	9.9	24.7	18.9
1955	91.0	6.1	26.3	110.9	7.6	12.1	23.5	19.7
1956	102.8	5.3	29.9	125.2	10.2	10.6	29.6	21.7
1957	106.8	5.0	29.6	124.1	9.6	9.8	29.0	25.5
1958	130.7	6.2	40.0	164.9	10.4	9.8	55.7	35.2
1959	143.9	7.1	54.3	198.0	9.9	10.4	54.1	43.8
1960	145.7	6.5	64.4	209.4	9.2	8.8	56.7	52.1
1961	122.0	4.3	35.6	162.1	14.5	7.4	55.0	37.7
1962	114.9	3.4	29.5	150.4	14.3	7.0	38.4	32.3
1963	123.3	3.6	33.2	163.5	11.6	6.9	42.1	33.5
1964	145.4	4.2	39.4	188.4	10.4	6.7	42.9	34.4
1965	171.6	5.5	46.0	223.5	10.3	6.9	38.2	30.4
1966	186.8	6.1	53.8	253.4	10.6	6.8	36.9	32.7
1967	177.4	5.3	44.0	230.6	7.3	6.3	38.7	28.1
1968	172.3	5.1	35.8	221.3	12.4	6.3	38.7	26.9
1969	193.8	4.7	52.6	261.3	13.5	5.5	39.3	31.7
1970	225.3	5.6	64.9	313.8	12.5	5.0	41.1	36.4
1971	242.6	5.2	73.2	348.2	9.5	5.0	40.5	39.5
1972	251.8	6.4	76.6	364.0	7.8	5.8	43.7	40.2
1973	272.1	10.4	80.9	396.7	8.7	8.1	44.4	39.9
1974	279.0	15.3	79.0	400.7	9.2	10.5	49.7	38.7
1975	299.7	14.7	82.1	446.7	10.2	9.7	50.1	40.2
1976	274.4	12.9	80.6	453.6	11.6	9.6	53.2	40.3
1977	320.2	13.3	84.4	497.8	19.8	8.5	53.3	41.9
1978	362.4	18.7	112.2	563.4	15.3	9.8	52.6	42.8

(Continued overleaf)

Table 4.1 Continued

Year	GDP (Billion)	Import (Billion)	Total expenditure (Billion)	GOV (Billion)	Tariff rate (%)	Trade ratio (%)	Decentralization (%)	Industrialization (%)
1979	403.8	24.3	128.2	637.9	10.7	11.3	48.9	41.3
1980	451.8	29.9	122.9	707.7	11.2	12.6	45.7	38.5
1981	486.0	36.8	113.8	758.1	14.7	15.1	45.0	34.5
1982	530.2	35.8	123.0	829.4	13.3	14.5	47.0	34.9
1983	595.7	42.2	141.0	921.1	12.8	14.4	46.1	36.1
1984	720.7	62.1	170.1	1083.1	16.6	16.7	47.5	37.0
1985	898.9	125.8	200.4	1333.5	16.3	23.0	60.3	38.6
1986	1020.1	149.8	220.5	1520.7	10.1	25.3	62.1	38.6
1987	1195.5	161.4	226.2	1848.9	8.8	25.8	62.6	38.7
1988	1492.2	205.5	249.1	2408.9	7.5	25.6	66.1	38.4
1989	1691.8	220.0	282.4	2855.2	8.3	24.6	68.5	39.4
1990	1859.8	257.4	308.4	3158.6	6.2	29.9	67.4	38.3
1991	2166.3	339.9	338.7	3478.2	5.5	33.4	67.8	41.5
1992	2665.2	444.3	374.2	4368.4	4.8	34.2	68.7	44.8
1993	3456.1	598.6	464.2	5939.8	4.3	32.6	71.7	49.7
1994	4667.0	996.0	579.3	8592.7	2.7	43.7	69.7	35.5
1995	5749.5	1104.8	682.4	11223.5	2.6	40.9	70.8	33.1
1996	6685.1	1155.7	793.8	12195.3	2.6	36.1	72.9	30.0
1997	7314.3	1180.7	923.4	13749.7	2.7	36.9	72.6	29.2
1998	7801.8	1162.2	1079.8	14320.5	2.7	34.4	71.1	27.0
1999	8206.8	1373.7	1318.8	15063.0	4.1	36.4	68.5	23.6
2000	8940.4	1863.9	1588.7	n.a	4.0	43.9	65.3	n.a.

Note: The effective tariff rate is defined as the ratio of tariff revenue to total imports. Trade ratio is the share of trade (imports plus exports) in total GDP. Decentralization is defined as the share of local governments' expenditure in total government expenditure. The industrialization variable is defined as the ratio of the gross heavy industrial output value relative to the gross agricultural and industrial output value (GOV). GDP, government expenditures, and tariff data for the whole period are from *China Statistical Yearbook* (2001). Prior to 1999, the trade volume, gross agricultural output value, gross industrial output value, and gross heavy industrial output value are available from *Comprehensive Statistical Data and Materials on 50 Years of New China*. Information about the above variables in the years of 1999 and 2000 are from *China Statistical Yearbook* (2000 and 2001).

Table 4.2 Inequalities and decompositions: 1952–2000

Year	Gini (%)	GE (%)	Rural–Urban	Inland–Coastal
1952	22.4	9.0	6.9	0.6
1953	24.7	10.7	8.6	0.7
1954	23.2	9.4	7.9	0.6
1955	22.0	8.6	7.3	0.3
1956	22.9	9.4	8.2	0.2
1957	23.8	9.8	8.5	0.1
1958	24.4	10.2	8.8	0.2
1959	29.7	14.3	11.6	0.2
1960	32.2	16.6	13.5	0.3
1961	30.3	14.5	11.2	0.2
1962	28.5	13.1	10.7	0.2
1963	27.6	12.4	9.6	0.2
1964	28.2	12.8	9.5	0.2
1965	26.7	11.8	8.7	0.2
1966	26.6	11.7	9.1	0.2
1967	25.5	10.8	8.5	0.2
1968	26.3	11.3	8.7	0.3
1969	27.1	12.2	9.9	0.3
1970	27.0	12.1	9.8	0.3
1971	26.9	12.1	9.8	0.3
1972	28.1	12.8	9.8	0.3
1973	27.9	12.7	9.9	0.3
1974	28.8	13.5	10.3	0.3
1975	29.5	14.2	11.2	0.5
1976	30.9	15.5	12.1	0.5
1977	30.8	15.4	12.1	0.5
1978	29.3	14.0	11.0	0.4
1979	28.6	13.3	10.1	0.4
1980	28.2	13.1	9.9	0.5
1981	27.0	12.0	9.1	0.6
1982	25.6	10.6	7.2	0.5
1983	25.9	11.1	6.8	0.4
1984	25.6	10.9	6.3	0.4
1985	25.8	11.1	6.6	0.5
1986	26.8	11.9	6.9	0.5
1987	27.0	12.0	6.8	0.6
1988	28.2	13.1	7.7	0.8
1989	29.7	14.4	9.3	1.0
1990	30.1	14.9	9.5	1.0
1991	30.3	14.9	9.9	1.2
1992	31.4	16.0	10.2	1.5
1993	32.2	16.8	10.9	1.7
1994	32.6	17.2	10.8	2.0
1995	33.0	17.7	11.5	2.3
1996	33.4	18.2	11.7	2.6
1997	33.9	18.9	11.7	2.7
1998	34.4	19.6	12.2	2.9
1999	36.3	23.4	12.8	3.2
2000	37.2	24.8	13.9	3.8

Note: Calculated by authors.

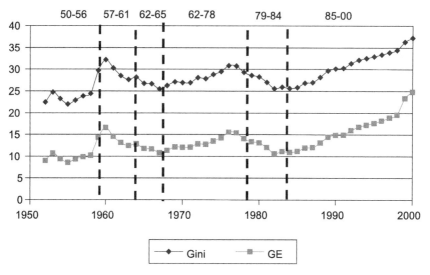

Figure 4.2 The trends of regional inequality.

Note: From Table 4.2.

identified above. The two indices move in close relation to each other, and match the different phases of Chinese development remarkably well.

Over the past fifty years inequality has peaked three times – during the Great Famine, at the end of the Cultural Revolution, and in the current period of global integration. Similarly, there are three major troughs in the overall evolution of inequality – in 1952, right at the beginning of the data series; in 1967, at the end of the recovery from the Great Famine and before the effects of the Cultural Revolution set in; and in 1984, at the end of the rural reform period and the start of the expansion based on global integration. Overall, inequality seems to have been low when policy was encouraging to agriculture and the rural sector generally, and high when this sector was relatively neglected.

These effects can be further investigated by decomposing overall inequality into sub-components and examining the evolution of these components. The 56 data points in each year from which the overall distribution is constructed, a rural and an urban observation for each of 28 provinces, can be divided into rural and urban observations across the provinces and, using equation (2) the GE index can be decomposed into a "within rural–urban" and a "between rural–urban" component (we will call the latter rural–urban inequality). The overall GE and the between rural–urban component are shown in Table 4.2. The within rural–urban component is the difference between the two.

A key dimension of inequality in China, especially in the post-reform period, is that between inland and coastal provinces (Chen and Fleisher, 1996; Zhang and Kanbur, 2001). We follow the practice of classifying the provinces of Beijing, Liaoning, Tianjin, Hebei, Shandong, Jiangsu, Shanghai,

Zhejiang, Fujian, Guangdong and Guangxi as coastal and the other provinces as inland. We therefore divide our 56 observations into 22 coastal and 34 inland observations and decompose the GE measure accordingly. The "between inland–coastal" component (we will call it inland–coastal inequality thereafter) is reported in Table 4.2.

Figures 4.3–4.5 go a long way in translating the above narrative into impacts on overall inequality and the rural–urban and inland–coastal inequalities, and provide some initial hypotheses for econometric testing in the next section. Under the central planning system, the central government had large powers to allocate and utilize financial revenues to achieve the goal of equity despite at the expense of efficiency. With economic reforms, the central government has granted local governments more autonomy in allocating their resources and bearing more responsibilities (Qian and Roland, 1998; Zhang and Zou, 1998). While Zhang and Zou (1998) have in particular analyzed the relationship between fiscal decentralization and economic growth for China, few studies have investigated the effect of decentralization on regional inequality. Tsui (1991) detected a positive relationship between decentralization and worsening regional inequality using a graph analysis based on data series up to 1985. This leads to the following hypothesis:

Hypothesis I. *Greater decentralization increases regional inequality during the economic transition from a planned economy to a market economy.*

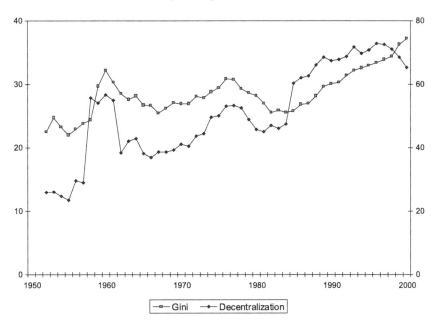

Figure 4.3 Decentralization and overall inequality (Gini coefficient).

Note: The left vertical axis represents Gini coefficient while the right refers to the degree of decentralization.

In order to accelerate the pace of industrialization after the initial period of land reform, the state extracted massive amounts of resources from agriculture mainly through the suppression of agricultural prices and restrictions on labor mobility (Lin, Cai, and Li, 1996). Almost all the scarce investment funds were allocated to heavy industry in neglect of light industry and agriculture. As shown in Figure 4.4, the share of heavy industry in gross output value rose from 0.22 in 1956 to 0.52 in 1960. The main enforcement mechanisms were a trinity of institutions, including the household registration system, the unified procurement and sale of agricultural commodities, and the people's communes. Consequently, the large rural–urban divide became a major feature of China's inequality (Yang, 1999; Yang and Fang, 2000), and the policies eventually led to the Great Famine. During the Famine, however, most urban residents were protected from starvation at the expense of about 30 million deaths in the rural areas (Lin and Yang, 2000). These developments are reflected in the sharp increases, up to 1960, in the rural–urban inequality in Table 4.2 and in Figure 4.4.

In reaction to the Great Famine, agriculture was once again given priority. The slogan, "Yi Liang Wei Gang, Gang Ju Mu Zhang" (Grain must be taken to be the core; once it is grasped, everything falls into place), reflects the spirit of this policy. In the years between 1961 and 1964, 20 million state workers and 17 million urban high school students were sent to the countryside for

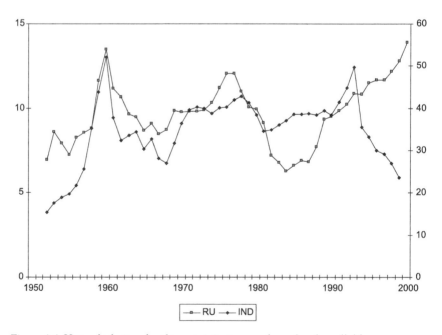

Figure 4.4 Heavy industry development strategy and rural–urban divides.

Note: The left vertical axis represents rural–urban disparity (RU) while the right refers to heavy industry output ratio (IND).

"re-education" by participating in agricultural production. Meanwhile, central planning was loosened a little, boosting agricultural productivity (Fan and Zhang, 2002). Not surprisingly, the share of heavy industry fell and the rural–urban divide narrowed. This is reflected in the declining rural–urban disparity during this period, which pulled down overall inequality to its next trough, just before the start of the Cultural Revolution.

With the outbreak of the Cultural Revolution in 1966, pro-Mao leftists came into the ascendancy. The combination of a lack of incentives in the agricultural sector and investment in military and heavy industry during the cold war atmosphere of the time, as reflected in the rise in the share of heavy industry in Figure 4.4, led to the rural–urban divide increasing to its peak at the end of the Cultural Revolution, on the eve of the 1979 reforms.

With the end of the Cultural Revolution, the Chinese economy was on the verge of collapse. In response to the agricultural crisis, the government started to give greater incentives to household producers. The "household responsibility" system spread from its origins in Anhui Province to cover 98 percent of all villages in China by 1983 (Lin, 1992). These and other market-oriented strategies led to a remarkable growth in agricultural output, and the share of heavy industry dropped. The first five years of the post-1979 reforms saw a sharp decline in rural–urban divide. Overall inequality fell as well, as shown in Figure 4.3. The above narrative leads to the second hypothesis:

Hypothesis II. *The heavy-industry development strategy, particularly in the pre-reform period, was a major contributing factor to the large rural–urban divide and to overall inequality.*

The latest phase in Chinese history begins in the mid-1980s. As is well known, this has been a period of accelerating integration into the global economy through greater openness in trade and especially in foreign direct investment. As seen in Figure 4.5, the trade ratio, after showing no trend for 35 years, began a steady increase since the mid-1980s both because of reductions in nominal tariffs and because of increases in import volumes. Between 1984 and 2000, the value of exports grew 11 percent per year. Changes in FDI flows are even more astonishing. We do not of course have long run time series for these, but from an almost isolated economy in the late 1970s, China has become the largest recipient of FDI among developing countries. In order to speed up the integration with the world markets, China has implemented a coastal-biased policy, such as establishing special economic zones in coastal cities and providing favorable tax breaks to coastal provinces. In other words, the opening process has inevitably had regional dimensions.

As is by now well appreciated, and as is shown in Figure 4.1, there has been spectacular growth in the past two decades largely due to the reforms and open-door policy. But the gains have not been evenly distributed across regions. Coastal provinces have attracted far more foreign direct investment

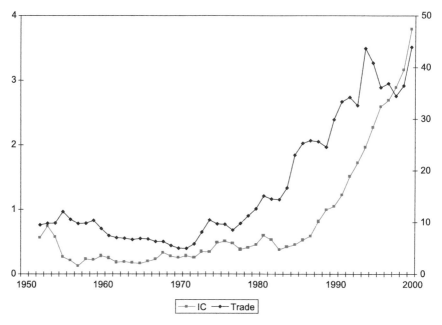

Figure 4.5 Openness and inland–coastal disparity.

Note: The left vertical axis represents inland–coastal disparity (IC) while the right refers to trade ratio (Trade).

and generated more trade volume than inland provinces during the liberalization process. In 2000, the three coastal provinces, Guangdong, Jiangsu, and Shanghai, were the top three, while the three inland provinces, Guizhou, Inner Mongolia, and Jilin, were the bottom three in terms of attracting FDI. The above three coastal provinces alone contribute to more than 60 percent of total foreign trade in 2000. The difference in the growth rates between the coastal and inland regions has been as high as three percentage points during the past two decades (Zhang and Zhang, 2003).

We can use Guangdong and Sichuan provinces to illustrate how internal geography affects the response to openness. In 1978, the coastal Guangdong Province ranked 14th in labor productivity, which was almost the same as the 15th rank of inland Sichuan province. In a closed economy, Guangdong did not enjoy any obviously better resource endowments than inland provinces. However, after China opened its door to the world, Guangdong has become one of the most favored places for foreign direct investment and international trade which is in large due to its proximity to Hong Kong. Meanwhile, the ranking of labor productivity in Sichuan has declined from 15th in 1978 to 23rd in 2000. Clearly, the relative comparative advantages between the two provinces have changed significantly and are associated with the opening up to the outside and the decentralization which facilitated this response.

The above story of Guangdong and Sichuan is reflected nationwide in the behavior of the inland–coastal component of inequality. The major change in the behavior of this component over the entire fifty-year period comes in the mid-1980s. After relative stability up to this point, inland–coastal inequality began to increase sharply. Although still quite small as a contributor to overall inequality, its contributions to *changes* in inequality increased dramatically. As shown in Figure 4.5, inland–coastal disparity has closely followed the path of the trade ratio.

When an economy opens up to world markets, theory suggests that there could well be affects on regional inequality, as argued recently by Fujita, Krugman, and Venables (1999). External trade liberalization can change internal comparative advantage and hence location patterns. Coupled with decentralization, opening up to world markets provides local governments an opportunity to better exploit comparative advantage. Trade liberalization could also lead to specialization and industry clustering.

Empirical evidence for the impact of globalization on income distribution in developing countries has been limited, and the findings of existing studies are at best mixed. The existing work for developing countries has been limited to the effects of trade liberalization on wage inequality (Wood, 1997; Hanson and Harrison, 1999), shedding little light on the effect on regional inequality. Jian, Sachs, and Warner (1996) have argued that China's regional inequality is associated with internal geography. China's rapid change from a closed economy to open economy provides a good testing ground for our third hypothesis:

> Hypothesis III. *Greater openness is associated with greater regional inequality.*

Our narrative of the phases of Chinese development, and of the evolution of inequality and its components, is suggestive of the forces behind the changes in inequality over this half century. We now turn to an econometric analysis of the correlates of inequality, to see if these hypotheses can be confirmed statistically.

4.4 The correlates of regional inequality: an econometric analysis

Our task is to test the association between inequality and its components on the one hand, and heavy industrialization, decentralization, and openness, on the other. Following several analyses on Chinese data (Lin, 1992), we use one-period lagged values of the independent variables as regressors to reduce potential endogeneity problems.[6] In the regressions, all the variables are in logarithms. We have compared regressions in levels and log levels and the latter gives a better fit based on R^2 and RESET misspecification test. In addition, the heteroscedasticity problem is greatly reduced after taking logarithms.

A central issue in this long run time series is that of structural breaks. It is common in the econometric literature on China (Li, 2000) to locate the break at the start of the reforms in the late 1970s. As shown in regression R1 in Tables 4.3–4.4 on overall inequality and rural–urban inequality, the Chow tests indicate a significant break in 1979. The Chow-test p-value is 0.105 in the regression on inland–coastal inequality (R1 in Table 4.5), indicating a marginally significant structural break.

There are two ways to handle this structural break. One way is to estimate the equations separately for the pre-reform period (1952–1978) and the post-reform period (1979–1999). However, in so doing, some degrees of freedom will be lost. Here, we adopt the second way by estimating the equations for the whole period but allowing coefficients to vary across the two periods. Regressions R2 in Tables 4.3–4.5 provide the estimation results under the varying-coefficient specifications. The Chow-test p-values indicate that structural break has been correctly captured in the new specification.

Because the three inequality series are not stationary, it is important to check whether regressing one or other policy variables produces stationary residuals, which means cointegration among variables. If the residuals are not stationary, the regressions with nonstationary data may give spurious results. Here we adopt two cointegration tests. The first one is the Phillips-Ouliaris test (1990, PO for short). The PO test is designed to detect the presence of a unit root in the residuals of regressions among the levels of time series. The null hypothesis is that the residuals have unit roots (no cointegration). The critical values for the PO test can be found in the appendix of Phillips and Ouliaris (1990). In addition to the Phillips-Ouliaris test, we also perform the KPSS test (Kwiatkowski et al., 1992) to check the cointegrated relationship. In contrast to the PO test, the KPSS test is to test the null hypothesis that the regression residuals are stationary (the variables are cointegrated).

Consider Table 4.3 first and start with the results for overall inequality. Regression R2 has better specification than R1 as it does not have structural breaks and passes both cointegration tests. The F-test indicates that the coefficients in the two periods are statistically different. In the pre-reform period, the heavy industry coefficient is significant and has the highest value (0.488), suggesting that the heavy industry development strategy implemented in the central planning era be a dominant force behind the overall inequality. Turning to the post-reform period, the coefficients for decentralization and trade ratio are significantly positive. In particular, trade ratio has the largest impact on overall inequality in this period. The coefficient for decentralization has changed from insignificant to significant, confirming the observation in Figure 4.3 that decentralization has a closer relationship with the overall inequality in the reform period. Despite the importance of heavy industry ratio in the pre-reform period, it has faded into insignificance in the reform period as China changes its development strategies.

As in Table 4.3, regression R2 with varying coefficients in Table 4.4 has a better specification than regression R1 with constant coefficients. The F-test

Table 4.3 Regressions results: total inequality

Variables	R1	R2	
	Whole period (1952–2000)	*Before reform (1952–1978)*	*Reform (1979–2000)*
Decentralization	0.279**	0.011	0.267**
	(0.072)	(0.068)	(0.056)
Trade ratio	0.295**	0.151**	0.455**
	(0.060)	(0.071)	(0.056)
Heavy industry ratio	0.003	0.488**	−0.161
	(0.111)	(0.113)	(0.128)
Chow-test p-value	0.000		0.997
F-test for coefficients (p-value)			0.001
Phillips-Ouliaris test	−3.350		−5.012
KPSS statistic	**0.116**		**0.054**
Adjusted R-square	0.675		0.817

Note: All the variables are in logarithmic forms and independent variables have one-year lag. Figures in parentheses are robust standard errors. * and ** indicate statistical significance at 10 percent and 5 percent, respectively. The null hypothesis of Chow-test is that there is no structural break in 1979. The F-test is for testing whether the coefficients are the same across the two periods. Phillips-Ouliaris Z_t test is for testing the null hypothesis of no cointegration. Phillips and Ouliaris (1990) report the critical values for regressions with independent variables only up to 5. The critical values to reject this null hypothesis with three and five independent variables at the 10 percent significant level are −3.833 and −4.431, respectively. The KPSS statistic is for testing the null hypothesis of cointegration. If the statistic is larger than 0.347, the null will be rejected at the 10 percent significance level.

Table 4.4 Regressions results: rural–urban inequality

Variables	R1	R2	
	Whole period (1952–2000)	*Before reform (1952–1978)*	*Reform (1979–2000)*
Decentralization	0.256**	−0.018	0.369**
	(0.078)	(0.060)	(0.079)
Trade ratio	0.128**	0.208**	0.406**
	(0.036)	(0.087)	(0.067)
Heavy industry ratio	−0.080	0.458**	0.121
	(0.108)	(0.102)	(0.159)
Chow-test p-value	0.000		0.993
F-test for coefficients			0.001
Phillips-Ouliaris test	−2.596		−4.529
KPSS statistic	**0.153**		**0.036**
Adjusted R-square	0.302		0.669

shows that there exists systematic difference in coefficients across the two periods. The results are similar to Table 4.3. In the pre-reform period, a greater favoring of heavy industry increases rural–urban spread. The impact of openness on rural–urban divide has almost doubled as China transforms from a closed economy to a more open economy. In the reform period, greater decentralization widens rural–urban disparity.

In Table 4.5 the two specifications on inland–coastal inequality produce similar results. The PO test and KPSS test indicate that the first regression R1 is cointegrated in levels. The coefficients for all the three policy variables are significant with signs inconsistent with our hypotheses. In particular, trade ratio has the largest impact on inland–coastal inequality, reflecting the dramatic changes in regional comparative advantage as a result of coastal-biased policy as well as the opening up to the world market. The negative coefficient for the heavy industry ratio tells the same story. In the planned era, most heavy industries were established in the interior regions, thereby reducing the inland–coastal disparity. As China opens up, the coastal region has found itself a pronounced comparative advantage in labor-intensive exporting sectors (usually light industries) in world markets. The faster growth in the coastal region has widened the inland–coastal gap. In the second regression R2, the coefficient for decentralization has increased by nearly 30 percent from the pre-reform period to the reform period, indicating that greater decentralization has played a larger detrimental effect on inland–coastal inequality.

Overall, these results represent broad support for the hypotheses advanced earlier on heavy industry, decentralization, and openness. Heavy industry increases inequality, especially its rural–urban component, and particularly in the pre-1979 period. Decentralization, when it is significant, increases overall inequality, rural–urban inequality, and inland–coastal inequality. The

Table 4.5 Regressions results: inland–coastal inequality

Variables	R1	R2	
	Whole period (1952–2000)	*Before reform (1952–1978)*	*Reform (1979–2000)*
Decentralization	0.564**	0.341*	0.440**
	(0.119)	(0.203)	(0.163)
Trade ratio	1.409**	1.070**	1.412**
	(0.072)	(0.280)	(0.133)
Heavy industry ratio	−0.611**	−0.260	−1.100**
	(0.293)	(0.421)	(0.363)
Chow-test p-value	0.105		0.242
F-test for coefficients			0.566
Phillips-Ouliaris test	−3.908		−3.895
KPSS statistic	**0.152**		**0.137**
Adjusted R-square	0.828		0.825

trade ratio is associated with greater overall inequality and, in particular, inland–coastal disparity in the reform period.

4.5 Conclusions

The tremendous growth in per capita GDP since the reform period, and its impact on poverty in China, has been much discussed and celebrated (Fan, Zhang, and Zhang, 2002). But this has not stopped a concern with growing inequality, for at least two reasons. First, as is well known, the poverty reducing effects of a given growth rate on poverty are lower at higher levels of inequality. Second, rising inequality may itself lead to tensions within a country and impede the prospects for future growth through a variety of social, political, and economic mechanisms (Kanbur and Lustig, 2000).

This study tries to comprehend the driving forces behind the changes in China's regional inequality over half a century. We find that the evolution of inequality matches different political-economic periods in Chinese history. In particular, we find that heavy-industry development strategy plays a key role in forming the enormous rural–urban gap in the pre-reform period, while openness and decentralization have contributed to the rapid increase in inland–coastal disparity in the reform period of the 1980s and the 1990s.

The empirical finding also has relevance to the ongoing debate on how globalization affects regional inequality in developing countries. Convergence or divergence of a nation's economy is dependent upon not only its domestic polices but also on its openness. With China joining WTO, the economy will become more liberalized, and open, likely resulting in more dramatic shifts in regional comparative advantages. If the government continues to favor the coastal region in its investment strategy, then regional disparity may widen even more. Further liberalizing and investing in the economy in the inland region is thus an important development strategy for the government, to both promote economic growth and reduce regional inequality.

Notes

1 Even when household data are available, regional inequality is still important because it accounts for a significant share of total income inequality in China and its rapid rise may be dangerous to social and political stability, in particular when aligned with political, religious, or ethnic tensions.
2 Data for Hainan Province since 1988 are incorporated into Guangdong Province, while data for Chongqing Province since 1997 are included in Sichuan Province.
3 Kanbur and Zhang (1999; 2001) provide detailed discussion about data sources. A number of studies (Lyons, 1991; Tsui, 1991) have used province level data to study regional inequality in the past, but they did not in general disaggregate by rural and urban areas within provinces. In the recent literature, Yang and Fang (2000) use the same data sources as we have used, but focus solely on the average rural–urban gap at the national level, and do not go into inequalities across provinces.
4 This is the so called "Theil's second measure." Results for the Theil index of inequality, also a member of this family, are similar.

5 See the footnote in Table 4.1 for data sources and definitions for the three indicators.
6 Given data restrictions it is impossible to find suitable alternative instruments covering the entire 50 year-period under consideration.

References

Aaberge, Rolf, and Xuezeng Li, "The Trend in Urban Income Inequality in Two Chinese Provinces, 1986–90," *Review of Income and Wealth*, 43 (1997): 335–355.

Chen, Jian, and Belton M. Fleisher, "Regional Income Inequality and Economic Growth in China," *Journal of Comparative Economics*, 22 (1996): 141–164.

Chen, Shaohua, and Martin Ravallion, "Data in Transition: Assessing Rural Living Standards in Southern China," *China Economic Review*, 7 (1996): 23–56.

Fan, Shenggen, and Xiaobo Zhang, "Production and Productivity Growth in Chinese Agriculture: New National and Regional Measures," *Economic Development and Cultural Change*, 50 (2002): 819–838.

Fan, Shenggen, Xiaobo Zhang, and Sherman Robinson, "Structural Change and Economic Growth in China," *Review of Development Economics*, 7 (2003): 360–377.

Fan, Shenggen, Linxiu Zhang, and Xiaobo Zhang, *Growth and Poverty in Rural China: The Role of Public Investment*, IFPRI Policy Report No. 125, 2002.

Fujita, Masahisa, Paul Krugman, and Anthony J. Venables, *The Spatial Economy*. The MIT Press: Cambridge, Massachusetts, 1999.

Hanson, G., and A. Harrison, "Trade Liberalization and Wage Inequality in Mexico," *Industrial and Labor Relations Review*, 52 (1999): 271–288.

Jian, T., Jeffrey Sachs, and Andrew Warner, "Trends in Regional Inequality in China." National Bureau of Economic Research working paper, No. 5412, 1996.

Kanbur, Ravi, and N. Lustig, "Why is Inequality Back on the Agenda?" *Proceedings of the Annual World Bank Conference in Development Economics*, World Bank, 2000.

Kanbur, Ravi, and Xiaobo Zhang, "Which Regional Inequality: Rural–Urban or Inland–Coastal? An Application to China," *Journal of Comparative Economics*, 27 (1999): 686–701.

Kanbur, Ravi, and Xiaobo Zhang, "Fifty Years of Regional Inequality in China: A Journey Through Revolution, Reform and Openness," London: Centre For Economic Policy Research (CEPR) Discussion Paper 2887, 2001.

Khan, Azizur Rahman, and Carl Riskin, *Inequality and Poverty in China in the Age of Globalization*, OUP, 2001.

Kwiatkowski, D., P.C.B Phillips, P. Schmidt, and Y. Shin, "Testing the Null Hypothesis of Stationarity Against the Alternative of a Unit Root: How Sure Are We That Economic Time Series Have a Unit Root?" *Journal of Econometrics*, 54 (1992): 159–178.

Li, Xiao-Ming, "The Great Leap Forward, Economic Reforms, and the Unit Root Hypothesis: Testing for Breaking Trend Functions in China's GDP Data." *Journal of Comparative Economics*, 27 (2000): 814–827.

Lin, Justin Yifu, "Rural Reforms and Agricultural Growth in China," *American Economic Review*, 82 (1992): 34–51.

Lin, Justin Yifu, and Dennis T. Yang, "Food Availability, Entitlement and the Chinese Famine of 1959–61," *Economic Journal*, 110 (2000): 136–158.

Lin, Justin Yifu, Fang Cai, and Zhou Li, *The China Miracle: Development Strategy and Economic Reform*. Hong Kong: The Chinese University Press, 1996.

Lyons, Thomas P., "Interprovincial Disparities in China: Output and Consumption, 1952–1987." *Economic Development and Cultural Change*, 39 (1991): 471–506.

Phillips, P.C.B., and S. Ouliaris, "Asymptotic Properties of Residual Based Tests for Cointegration." *Econometrica*, 58 (1990): 165–193.

Qian, Yingyi, and Gérard Roland, "Federalism and the Soft Budget Constraint," *American Economic Review*, 88 (1998): 1143–1162.

Rozelle, Scott, "Rural Industrialization and Increasing Inequality: Emerging Patterns in China's Reforming Economy." *Journal of Comparative Economics*, 19 (1994): 362–391.

Shorrocks, Anthony F., "Inequality Decomposition by Population Subgroups." *Econometrica*, 52 (1984): 1369–1385.

State Statistical Bureau (SSB), *Comprehensive Statistical Data and Materials on 50 Years of New China (Xin Zhongguo wushinian Tonji Ziliao Huibian)*. Beijing: China Statistical Publishing House, 1999.

——, *China Statistical Yearbook (Zhongguo Tongji Nianjian)*. Beijing: China Statistical Publishing House, various years.

Tsui, Kai-yuen, "China's Regional Inequality, 1952–1985," *Journal of Comparative Economics*, 15 (1991): 1–21.

——, "Factor Decomposition of Chinese Rural Income Inequality: New Methodology, Empirical Findings, and Policy Implications." *Journal of Comparative Economics*, 26 (1998): 502–528.

Wei, Shang-Jin and Yi Wu. "Globalization and Inequality: Evidence from China." Center for Economic Policy Research Discussion Paper, December 2001, No. 3088.

Wood, A., "Openness and Wage Inequality in Developing Countries: the Latin American Challenge to East Asian Conventional Wisdom." *World Bank Economic Review*, 11 (1997): 33–57.

Yang, Danis Tao, "Urban-Based Policies and Rising Income Inequality in China," *American Economic Review* (Paper and Proceedings) 89 (1999): 306–310.

Yang, Danis Tao, and Cai Fang, "The Political Economy of China's Rural–Urban Divide," Center for Research on Economic Development and Policy Reform Working Paper No. 62, Stanford University, 2000.

Zhang, Xiaobo, and Ravi Kanbur, "What Difference Do Polarization Measures Make? An Application to China." *Journal of Development Studies*, 37 (2001): 85–98.

Zhang, Xiaobo, and Kevin H. Zhang. "How Does Globalization Affect Regional Inequality within A Developing Country? Evidence from China," *Journal of Development Studies*, 39 (2003): 47–67.

Zhang, Tao, and Heng-fu Zou, "Fiscal Decentralization, Public Spending, and Economic Growth in China." *Journal of Public Economics*, 67 (1998): 221–240.

5 Emergence of urban poverty and inequality in China

Evidence from household survey

Cheng Fang, Xiaobo Zhang, and Shenggen Fan

Abstract

This paper investigates the poverty and inequality in urban China during the period of rapid urban reforms of 1992 to 1998 by using household survey data. The incidence of urban poverty has declined from 1992 to 1995 but increased from 1996 to 1998 when major urban reforms were launched. The western region has the highest concentration of urban poverty, and the income gap between the region and rest of China has been widening over time. The result suggests that the current strategy of Western development should broaden its focus to include the urban poor in the region. A further decomposition analysis shows that the rapid economic growth has been the major force behind reduction of urban poverty, but the poverty reduction impact would have been even greater if the worsening income distributions had been avoided. Therefore, in addition to promoting growth, the government should also speed up the process of establishing a social safety net for the vulnerable groups. In large because of the urban reforms, the poor spend an increasing share of expenditures on education, health care, and housing, leaving a smaller proportion to spend on food consumption. Expanding the access to basic education and health care will enable the vulnerable to share the prosperities offered by the market reforms.

5.1 Introduction

Although poverty in China was mostly confined to the countryside until very recently, there has been an increasing concern about worsening income distribution in cities in the wake of urban reforms in the 1990s (Cook, 2000; the *Economist*, 2001; Chen and Wang, 2001; Khan and Riskin, 2001). Until the 1980s, China implemented a strong urban-bias development policy through various implicit and explicit transfer programs in pursuit of industrial development strategy (Lin, Cai, and Li, 1996). The rationing system introduced in the 1950s enabled urban residents to have equal access to food and other necessities at much lower prices. Almost all urban residents in the working age group had guaranteed jobs in the state- or collective-owned sectors. Because these jobs were permanent (known as "iron rice bowl"), urban unemployment was virtually nonexistent. These jobs also provided urban residents with many benefits such as free or subsidized housing, and healthcare (Davis, 1989). As a result, income distribution was much more equal among urban residents than among rural residents. Also because of these welfare arrangements, many people's livelihoods were wrapped with the fate of state-sector jobs. Not surprisingly, poverty alleviation in urban areas was not on the policy agenda until recently, and China's anti-poverty program, first initiated in 1986, mainly focused on rural areas.

Since the late 1970s, China has carried out a transformation from a planned to a market economy with a series of reforms. One key element of the economic reforms is to allow private-, individual-, and foreign-owned enterprises to compete with SOEs (state-owned enterprises). After two decades of reforms, the share of gross domestic product produced by the non-state owned enterprises have swelled from almost zero to one third. The development of non-state sector greatly augments economic growth and provides enormous job opportunities. But it also poses fierce competitions to the SOEs, which has been plagued with heavy burdens of welfare provisions. To provide new impetus to the SOEs, the government launched an enterprise-restructuring plan in 1996. The central theme of the plan is to transfer welfare-provision obligations such as health care and housing from enterprises to social insurance agencies and individuals (China Development Report, 1997).

These reforms have provided workers with more freedom to choose jobs and achieve higher earning potentials. As shown in Figure 5.1, per capita urban income has grown quite dramatically with an annual growth rate of more than six percent in the 1990s. The urban reforms and severe competition from other sectors have resulted in soaring financial losses of state- and collective-owned enterprises and an increasing number of urban workers being laid off.[1] As a social safety net was largely not in place, the liberalization of the welfare system may have made some disadvantaged groups more susceptible to sudden shocks such as catastrophic illness. Increasing job opportunities in the non-state sectors and lack of protection for the vulnerable may have contributed to the worsening of urban income distribution from 1992 to 1998 as shown in Figure 5.1.

The trend of worsening income distribution in cities has caused policy makers a great concern recently because a widening gap between rich and poor poses a threat to social stability (The *Economist*, 2001). However, most previous studies on income distribution focused on the rural sector with a few exceptions on cities (e.g. Aaberge and Li, 1997; Chen and Wang, 2001; Khan and Riskin, 2001). Aaberge and Li found that the Gini coefficient increased slightly from 1986 to 1990 using household survey data from Liaoning and Sichuan Provinces. Using a sub-sample of the national household survey in 1988 and 1995 with some adjustments, Khan and Riskin observed an increase in both inequality and poverty. Based on grouped income distribution data at the national level, Chen and Wang found that from 1990 to 1999 urban inequality worsened but urban poverty incidence lacked a clear trend, varying

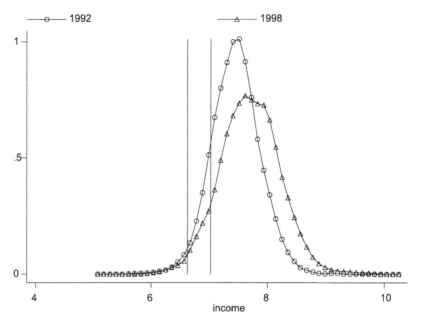

Figure 5.1 Income distributions in 1992 and 1998.

Note: The first and second vertical straight lines represent the poverty lines of $1.0 a day and $1.5 a day. The horizontal axis is in log scale.

from period to period. However, these studies are limited either to household level data in particular provinces and years, which are prior to the most recent major urban reforms, or to grouped distribution data, which are less accurate and lack regional focus. This study uses a unique data set from an official urban household survey to investigate both urban poverty and inequality during the period of rapid urban reforms. We attempt to answer the following questions: What are the levels and dynamic changes in urban poverty and inequality? What is the regional difference in poverty? How have growth and income distribution affected poverty reduction? What are the major driving forces behind the observed patterns?

The plan of the paper is as follows. Section 5.2 describes the data used in the study. Section 5.3 presents the trends of urban poverty and inequality at both national and regional levels. Section 5.4 examines causes for the observed trends, highlighting the effect of urban reforms. Section 5.5 concludes the paper. The appendix presents methodologies in poverty measures and decomposition in details.

5.2 Data

In this paper, we use a unique and comprehensive data set from the urban household survey (UHS) across 28 provinces in 1992, 1994, 1995, 1996, 1997, and 1998. The coverage period of the data set largely corresponds to the major steps of recent urban reforms, thus providing us a unique opportunity to evaluate the impact of urban reforms on poverty and inequality. The year of 1993 was excluded due to data unavailability.

The Chinese UHS began in 1956, was suspended during the Cultural Revolution from 1966 to 1976 and resumed in 1980. The UHS has been administered directly by the State Statistic Bureau (SSB), through its provincial and local survey network. The survey covers 30 provinces, 146 sample cities, and more than 80 counties (Han, Wailes, and Cramer, 1995). The sample is drawn based on several stratifications. The first step is to determine the sample size in each of the six large regions with the sample size being proportional to that region's population. Then, within each region, all the provincial capitals are chosen to represent large cities while the mid-size cities and county towns are randomly selected. Next, within the selected cities and towns, the neighborhood committees and finally households are chosen by a further random selection. Sampled households maintain a daily diary and transaction books that record all expenses and consumption in the households.

The data to which we have access includes households from 28 provinces.[2] In each province, we select one representative city with a sample size varying from 50 to 150 households. The total sample size is about 3,600 households each year. The biggest problem of the data set is that the "floating population" (rural migrants working in the city) is not included. Had they been in the estimation, the incidence of urban poverty might be higher. Nonetheless, our analysis may serve as a lower bound of the real pictures of China's urban poverty and inequality. Despite its limitations, this is the only data that is available to us and consistently compiled for the period of rapid urban reforms.

Table 5.1 compares real expenditure per capita calculated from the sample by three regions and for China as a whole.[3] The national average per capita

Table 5.1 Real expenditures per capita

Year	East	Central	West	China	China (SSB)
1992	2,122	1,478	1,404	1,883	1,907
1994	2,641	1,711	1,532	2,261	2,280
1995	2,770	1,836	1,792	2,412	2,423
1996	2,825	1,902	1,601	2,445	2,488
1997	2,953	1,865	1,594	2,527	2,593
1998	2,977	2,016	1,647	2,620	2,696
Annual Growth Rate					
1992–95 (%)	9.29	7.50	8.47	8.60	8.31
1996–98 (%)	2.66	2.95	1.43	3.52	4.10
1992–98 (%)	5.80	5.31	2.70	5.66	5.94

Note: Figures are calculated by the authors and are expressed as 1992 price. The last column is real expenditures per capita reported by the State Statistical Bureau (SSB).

expenditure and growth rates calculated from our sample are very similar to the published figures by the State Statistical Bureau, showing that the sub-sample used here is rather representative of the whole sample. For China as a whole, the annual growth rate was high at nearly six percent. Apparently, both the level and growth rate in the eastern region were higher than in the central and western regions, indicating a widening regional disparity.

5.3 The trend of poverty and inequality

5.3.1 Poverty and inequality measures

Poverty can be measured by both absolute and relative poverty lines. Absolute poverty line is more widely used for developing countries, while relative poverty line is more often used for developed countries. The absolute poverty line is usually determined by the minimum adequate calorie levels and estimated Engel curve. Yet, the minimum adequate calorie levels are themselves subject to uncertainty and controversy (Deaton, 1997). The most critical issue is that the tradeoffs between food and other goods are not taken into account in setting the line.

The World Bank (1992) has used 2,150 calories per day as the minimal energy intake to calculate the poverty lines in rural and urban China. It found urban poverty incidence far less than one percent up to 1990. A recent World Bank publication (2000) claimed urban poverty was still less than one percent but had an increase during the 1990s. However, using the same calorie requirement, Khan and Riskin (2001) came up with a much higher figure of urban poverty. The headcount index is 8.8 percent in 1988 and 8.0 percent in 1995. Even with a lower threshold at 2,100 calories per day, the incidence of urban poverty was reported as at 2.7 percent and 4.1 percent for the two years, much higher than the World Bank figures.

An alternative to the calorie-based absolute poverty line is the $1.0 per day initiated by the World Bank. Using 1985 purchasing power parity and price indexes, the poverty line can be converted into country-specific poverty lines measured in domestic currency and current prices. Poverty measures of $1.0 per day have been regularly reported by the World Bank and widely used in cross-country studies (Buhmann et al., 1988; Ravallion, Datt, and Van de Walle, 1991). Under the poverty line of $1.0 per day, Chen and Wang (2001) reported that the urban poverty incidence was one percent in 1998 for China as a whole.

In the case of China, the $1.0 per day measure has been used to evaluate rural living conditions. There are many reasons to believe that a higher poverty line should be used in urban China in the 1990s. One of the prominent reasons is the much higher cost of living of urban residents than their rural cohorts. Therefore, apart from $1.0 per day, this study also reports poverty measures of $1.5 per day.[4] Considering that $1.5 per day in cities is more comparable to $1.0 per day in rural areas, we put more emphasis and weight on this measure. Because of the essential arbitrariness of the poverty lines, we should focus more on changes in poverty. But the use of multiple poverty lines offers a broader picture of China's poverty levels at any particular time.

We use the following procedure to calculate each year's poverty line in each province. We first calculate China's national poverty line in 1985 using $1.0 and $1.5 per day multiplied by the PPP (purchasing power parity) exchange rate between US dollar and Chinese yuan. We then use the provincial urban consumer price index with 1981 as a base year to inflate the poverty line at the current price at each province for the years after 1985. China did not start price reform until 1983, prior to which prices were under strict controls by state governments. On this basis, we assume price levels were the same for all provinces in 1981. Previous studies have used similar methods to partially eliminate the problem of spatial price variations (Kanbur and Zhang, 1999; Yang and Cai, 2000).

In addition to the poverty lines of $1.0 and $1.5 per day, we also use the provincial-specific official poverty lines for comparison. Since 1997, China has begun to publish poverty lines for more than three hundred cities in *China Development Report*. For 1997 and 1998, we use the official figures, while for the years prior to 1997 we derive the poverty lines based on each province's urban consumer price index. In this study, we use the standard poverty measure, P_α. When the values of α are 0, 1, and 2, P_α corresponds to the head count (P_0), the poverty gap ratio (P_1), and the Foster-Geer-Thorbecke (P_2) index, respectively. For more details, refer to the appendix.

5.3.2 The trend of urban poverty and inequality

Table 5.2 reports the poverty measures in the sample period for urban China as a whole. It is apparent from the table that poverty incidence has declined from 1992 to 1998. There is a significant difference between two different poverty lines – $1.0 per day and $1.5 per day. In general, poverty incidence first declined dramatically from 1992 to 1995 and then increased when major urban reforms were implemented.

Based on the poverty line of $1.0 per day, about two percent of urban residents were poor in 1998, barely changed from 1992. The incidence of poverty based on the official poverty lines is comparable to our calculations based on $1 per day. Compared to the six percent of average growth rate of real expenditure per capita, the rate of reduction for the number of people living under $1.0 a day is astonishingly low, indicating the rapid economic growth has not trickled down to the people in the bottom. The indexes of P1 and P2, which measure income gaps between the income of the poor and the poverty line, show more rapid reductions, suggesting an improvement in income distribution among the absolute poor.

When the $1.5 per day line is used, the poverty incidence is much higher. In 1992, nearly 14 percent of urban population had consumption less than $1.5 per day. By 1998, the percentage dropped to about nine percent.

Table 5.2 Urban poverty for China as a whole

Year	$1.0 per day			$1.5 per day			Official poverty line			World Bank
	P0	P1	P2	P0	P1	P2	P0	P1	P2	P0
1992	2.09	0.45	0.17	13.74	2.60	0.82	2.48	0.51	0.18	0.83
1994	2.73	0.47	0.16	13.18	2.77	0.91	2.90	0.53	0.17	0.86
1995	1.65	0.36	0.12	10.27	1.98	0.64	1.68	0.29	0.08	0.61
1996	1.69	0.27	0.07	8.41	1.67	0.53	1.76	0.27	0.07	0.46
1997	2.00	0.42	0.14	9.21	2.06	0.71	2.44	0.45	0.14	0.53
1998	2.06	0.30	0.08	8.86	1.88	0.60	2.13	0.32	0.08	0.98
Annual Growth Rate										
1992–95	-7.58	-7.17	-10.96	-9.25	-8.68	-7.93	-12.17	-17.15	-23.69	-9.76
1996–98	10.41	5.41	6.90	2.64	6.10	6.40	10.01	8.87	6.90	45.96
1992–98	-0.24	-6.53	-11.81	-7.05	-5.26	-5.07	-2.50	-7.47	-12.80	2.81

Note: Except for the last column, all figures are calculated by the authors. The city-specific official poverty lines are from *China Development Report* (1998). The poverty line of the World Bank measure is $32.74 per month. The figures are available from http://www.worldbank.org/research/povmonitor/countrydetails/China.htm.

However, during the intensive urban reform period of 1996 to 1998, all the measures show an increase in poverty despite a modest growth in real income. In terms of trend, our results are similar to those in Chen and Wang (2001).[5] Interestingly, no matter whether we use the official poverty line or the $1 and $1.5 per day as a threshold, all the calculated rates of poverty incidence are higher than those reported by the World Bank.[6]

To gain a broader picture of spatial patterns of poverty and inequality, we group China into three regions: coastal, central and western. Table 5.3 presents the head count indexes (P0) by three regions based on three different poverty lines. Two features are of particular interest. First, the level of poverty in the coastal region was much lower than in the central and western regions. Under the poverty line of $1.5 per day, about one out of five people in western cities were poor during the sample period compared to less than eight percent in the coastal cities, indicating the problem of poverty incidence is the deepest in the western region. The western region is home to many of the country's worst performing state-owned heavy industries. Factory closures and layoffs may have taken a toll to the high incidence of urban poverty there. Second, the rate of poverty reduction in the central and western regions was slower than the eastern region. When using the $1.0 per day line or the official poverty line, poverty incidence increased in the central region from

Table 5.3 Urban poverty by regions: head count index

	$ 1.0 per day	$1.5 per day	Official poverty line
Coastal region			
1992	2.20	7.15	1.61
1994	4.95	7.89	1.50
1995	1.75	5.54	0.77
1996	4.14	4.42	0.65
1997	2.22	3.04	0.63
1998	1.07	3.48	0.70
Central region			
1992	2.22	19.36	1.89
1994	3.49	16.04	3.00
1995	1.53	13.89	1.48
1996	1.73	8.53	2.13
1997	2.10	12.27	3.02
1998	2.49	11.69	2.79
Western region			
1992	6.71	20.46	5.91
1994	7.38	22.23	6.50
1995	5.86	16.39	4.52
1996	5.07	18.98	4.10
1997	6.63	20.21	6.27
1998	6.32	17.70	4.65

Note: Calculated by the authors.

1992 to 1998; in the western region, all the measures show that the rate of poverty reduction was stagnant. The results suggest that the government should adopt more proactive measures to target the poor in the central and western regions.

Table 5.4 further reports the inequality measure by regions and for China as a whole. Evidently, both the Gini coefficient and Generalized Entropy (GE) measure show that inequality increased from 1992 to 1998 for entire China and three regions. For China as a whole, the Gini coefficient rose from 0.244 to 0.312 in this period. Both the magnitude and trend of the inequality measures are comparable to those calculated by Chen and Wang (2001), in which the Gini coefficient went up from 0.242 to 0.299 during the same time. The widening regional inequality might have prevented the gains of economic growth from trickling down to the people at the bottom.

5.4 Driving forces behind the observed pattern

5.4.1 The role of growth and distribution on poverty

In order to quantify the contributions of growth and distribution to the changes in poverty, we estimate the Lorenz curves using the ordinary least square (OLS) following the method by Datt and Ravallion (1992, see the appendix for details). Similar to previous studies, the estimated Lorenz curve fits the data very well with a R-square of 0.995.

Table 5.5 presents the decomposition analysis for three different poverty measures. Change in poverty is decomposed into increments in percentage points with 1992 as a base year. The growth component is defined as the change in poverty due to a change in the mean expenditure while holding the Lorenz curve constant at the 1992 level. The distribution component refers to the change in poverty due to a change in the Lorenz curve while holding the mean expenditure constant at the 1992 level.

For the head count index (P0), poverty declined by 35.52 percent from 1992 to 1998. The growth in expenditure led to a 57.52 percent decline. However,

Table 5.4 Inequality measures

Year	Gini				GE			
	China	Eastern	Central	Western	China	Eastern	Central	Western
1992	0.244	0.230	0.224	0.249	0.100	0.105	0.067	0.091
1994	0.300	0.276	0.300	0.290	0.149	0.151	0.117	0.120
1995	0.302	0.290	0.264	0.303	0.156	0.175	0.096	0.127
1996	0.298	0.282	0.270	0.285	0.150	0.162	0.100	0.112
1997	0.303	0.277	0.270	0.331	0.162	0.161	0.105	0.159
1998	0.312	0.296	0.291	0.298	0.178	0.188	0.129	0.133

Note: Calculated by the authors.

Table 5.5 Decomposition of poverty changes, 1992–1998 (based on the $1.5 poverty line)

	Total poverty reduction	*Growth component*	*Redistribution component*
P0	−35.52	−57.52	32.07
P1	−27.69	−50.06	35.77
P2	−26.83	−42.28	26.81

Note: A negative figure indicates a poverty reduction while a positive number means a poverty increase.

part of the growth effect was offset by the worsening income distribution, which resulted in a 32.07 percent increase in the head count index.

Similar to the head count index, the growth component reduced the poverty gap (P1) by 50.06 percent but worsening distribution caused an increase in poverty gap by 35.77 percent. The net change of the gap index fell by 27.69 percent from 1992 to 1998. The P2 index fell by 26.83 percent. The increase in mean expenditure resulted in a 42.28 percent reduction, while deteriorated distribution contributed to a 26.81 percent increase in the P2 index.

In short, there were rapid reductions in urban poverty from 1992 to 1995 but the incidence of poverty leveled off or increased later on when urban reform was deepened. Growth has been the dominant force behind the reduction in poverty. However, the rate of poverty reduction would have been much higher if income distribution was not worsened. Therefore, a comprehensive poverty-reduction strategy should focus on not only growth-enhancing but also inequality-reducing measures.

5.4.2 The effect of urban reform

The economic reforms have increasingly made an individual be paid according to his ability. Because one's ability may be largely related to one's education level, we expect that poverty incidence is lower among the more educated population. In order to quantitatively test this hypothesis, we decompose the population into two groups based on the years of schooling of the head of a household: those who have less than six years of schooling, or otherwise. Table 5.6 compares the poverty incidences between the two groups based on the $1.5 poverty line. Clearly, the proportion of the poor among the more educated group was much lower than their counterparts. Similarly, we can also compare the rate of poverty between the white-collar workers and blue-collar workers. In general, the white-collar worker's education level is higher than the blue-collar workers. The results show a similar finding that poverty incidence was higher among the blue-collar workers than among the white-collar workers.

Recently, China has transformed its basic education system from a virtually

Table 5.6 Poverty incidence by education and occupation (based on the $1.5 poverty line)

Year	Years of schooling		Occupation	
	<6	>=6	White collar	Blue collar
1992	18.91	9.22	8.65	18.06
1994	18.42	8.87	10.18	15.78
1995	14.63	6.98	8.17	12.62
1996	13.79	4.62	6.53	10.35
1997	13.65	5.88	6.89	11.20
1998	14.12	5.78	5.70	11.31

Note: Calculated by the authors. Based on the SSB household survey form, we define the following occupations as white collars: technical professionals, government employees, and managers. All the rest are classified as blue collars.

free service to a largely fee-based system. From 1992 to 1998, the share of education expenditure for poor in the bottom ten percentile increased by more than 25 percent from 8.2 percent to 10.4 percent, reflecting the effect of displacement of the old welfare system. Given the trend of decentralization in the education system, the government should pay more attention to the increasing unequal access to basic education.

Similarly, expenditures on health and housing also saw a rise, especially for the poor. The expenditure shares of housing and health care for the bottom ten-percentile population increased by 68 percent and 77 percent, respectively from 1992 to 1998. Compared to the average of the general population, the bottom decile spent a larger share of expenditures on health care and housing. This might be a consequence of increasing out-of-pocket expenses due to the reform of the welfare system. Therefore, the urban welfare reform may have made the population at the bottom more vulnerable despite rapid increase in income levels for population as a whole.

Education and health provide people with better capability to cope with the social costs of adjustment and to capitalize the new economic opportunities. The widespread access to basic education and health care might be one of the major reasons behind the rapid reduction in China's poverty in the process of economic reforms, as the well-educated and healthy labor force was well prepared "to have widely shared economic expansion and to make use of the opportunities of globalization" (Sen, p. 185, 2001). On this basis, Cook (2000) calls for investment in education and health care as part of a broader approach to social protection of the poor.

With reductions in protection from the SOEs and in the absence of an alternative social security system in place, the poor became more vulnerable to sudden shocks such as illness. This might be a reason why income distribution has worsened and the rate of poverty reduction has become stagnant in the late 1990s. Establishing an effective social safety net to protect some of the most vulnerable groups from falling into the poverty trap is an urgent and crucial task for China in the near future.

5.5 Conclusion

Microdata of urban household surveys from 1992 to 1998 was used to estimate the poverty and inequality and to analyze the contribution of growth and redistribution components to poverty reduction. While many have benefited from new economic opportunities and higher incomes as a result of urban reforms, some groups are facing new forms of risks and vulnerability. There is still a considerable number of poor in urban China. Using the $1.5 per day poverty line, the poverty incidence declined dramatically from 13.74 percent in 1992 to 8.41 percent in 1996, then increased to 9.21 percent in 1997 and 8.86 percent in 1998 as the urban reforms continued and unemployment increased. Most of the poor people were located in western China where state-owned industries remained the major job providers. Therefore it is crucial for the lagging western region to speed the development of non-state enterprises to absorb jobs lost from SOEs.

The changes in poverty are the net consequence of positive effect of rapid economic growth and adverse effect of worsening income distribution. Since economic growth has the largest impact on poverty reduction, the government should continue its reforms to enhance growth and augment employment. However, the widening gap between the poor and rich has prevented the gains of growth from trickling down to the poor. Future policies to reduce poverty should operate in tandem on a broader front with other broad-based development strategies such as reducing inequality and establishing safety nets. In the wake of China's integration with the global market, the state-sector enterprises will have to further adjust their production structures to China's comparative advantage, which may lead to more layoffs in the short run. Therefore, establishing an effective social safety net for the potentially vulnerable population in the urban areas emerges as an imperative agenda for policy makers. It is a great challenge for the Chinese government to extend the benefits of growth to all members of society, including the urban poor.

The abolition of the old welfare system has caused an increase in expenditures on education, health care and housing, leaving less on food consumption. This makes the poor more vulnerable to sudden shocks and malnutrition, reducing their capability to catch up. In the long run, the government should broaden access to basic education and health care through increasing investment so that all the people can share the opportunities offered by the economic expansion. Investment in human capital is key to long-term improvements in welfare for all.

Appendix: poverty measures and decompositions

There are a number of alternative poverty measures. One of the most popular generalizations of poverty measures comes from Foster, Greer, and Thorbecke (1984). For certain α:

$$FGT = \frac{1}{N} \sum_{i=1}^{N} \left(1 - \frac{x_i}{z}\right)^{a} 1(x_i \leq z). \tag{1}$$

The head count index (P0) and poverty gap index (P1) are special cases to values for α of 0 and 1. The larger the value of α, the more the measure penalizes the poverty gap. Following most previous studies, we set α = 2 in this paper, which is sensitive to the distribution among the poor.

Changes in poverty can be decomposed into a growth and redistribution component. Following Datt and Ravallion (1992), we express the poverty measure as a function of mean income and distribution at time t, $P(z/\mu_t, L_t)$. Where z defines poverty line; μ_t is mean consumption; and L_t is the Lorenz curve, representing income distribution at time t. Changes in poverty can be written as:

$$\Delta P(z/\mu_t, L_t) = [P(z/\mu_t, L_{t-1}) - P(z/\mu_{t-1}, L_{t-1})] + [P(z/\mu_{t-1}, L_t) - P(z/\mu_{t-1}, L_{t-1})] + \text{residual} \tag{2}$$

The first term on the right hand side represents the growth component assuming income distribution constant, while the second term stands for the redistribution component holding mean consumption constant.

Notes

1 The number of layoff workers is reported to be 11.57 million in 1997 (China Development Report, 1998).
2 Jilin and Tibet are excluded due to lack of systematic data.
3 The coastal region includes Liaoning, Beijing, Tianjin, Hebei, Shandong, Jiangsu, Shanghai, Zhejiang, Fujian, Guangdong, Hainan, and Guangxi. The central region covers Jilin, Heilongjiang, Inner Mongolia, Shanxi, Henan, Hubei, Anhui, Hunan, and Jiangxi. The remaining provinces are classified as the western region, including Ningxia, Gansu, Shaanxi, Sichuan, Guizhou, Yunan, Tibet, Qinghai, and Xinjiang.
4 In a recent Asia Development Bank study, $2.0 per day is used as the poverty line.
5 In Chen and Wang (2001), the urban poverty incidence was 2.6, 2.7, and 3.4, respectively, from 1996 to 1998. Their figures are much lower than ours for two reasons. First, unlike us, they used per capita income instead of per capita consumption as a measure of living standard. Because income is generally higher than consumption, using income tends to give a lower rate of poverty incidence. Second, they deduced poverty figures using grouped data, which may incur large estimation errors for the absolute poor due to lack of detailed data for the bottom decile.
6 The World Bank's calculations are based on income instead of expenditure. That might be a reason for the relatively lower figures.

References

Aaberge, Rolf, and Xuezeng, Li,1997. "The Trend in Urban Income Inequality in Two Chinese Provinces, 1986–90." *Review of Income and Wealth*, 43, 3: 335–355.

Buhmann Brigitte, Lee Rainwater, Guenther Schmaus, and Timothy M. Smeeding, 1988, "Equivalence Scales, Well-Being, Inequality and Poverty: Sensitivity Estimates across Ten Countries Using the Luxemboug Income Study (LIS) Database." *Review of Income and Wealth*, 94 (1988): 115–142.

Chen, Shaohua, and Yan Wang, 2001. "China's Growth and Poverty Reduction: Recent Trends between 1990 and 1999." Paper presented at a WBI-PIDS Seminar on "Strengthening Poverty Data Collection and Analysis" held in Manila, Philippines, April 30–May 4, 2001.

Cook, Sarah, 2000. "After the Iron Rice Bowl: Extending the Safety Net in China," Institute of Development Studies Discussion Paper # 377, University of Sussex.

Datt, Gaurav, and Martin Ravallion, 1992. "Growth and redistribution components of changes in poverty measures: A decomposition with applications to Brazil and India in the 1980s." *Journal of Development Economics*, 38: 275–295. North-Holland.

Deaton, Angus, 1997, *The Analysis of Household Surveys: A Microeconometric Approach to Development Policy*. The World Bank, Washington, D.C.

Davis, Deborah, 1989. "China social welfare: policies and outcomes." *The China Quarterly*, No. 119: 577–597.

The *Economist*, "Income Distribution in China: To Each According to His Abilities," p. 39. June 2nd 2001.

Foster, James, J. Greer, and Eric Thorbecke, 1984, "A class of decomposable poverty measures." *Econometrica*, 52, 761–765.

Han, Tong, Eric J. Wailes, and Gail L. Cramer, 1995. "Rural and Urban Data Collection in the People's Republic of China." In the *China Market Data and Information Systems*. Proceedings of WCC-101 Symposium, Washington, D.C.

Kanbur, Ravi, and Xiaobo Zhang, 1999, "Which Regional Inequality? The Evolution of Rural–Urban and Inland–Coastal Inequality in China, 1983–1995." *Journal of Comparative Economics*, 27: 686–701.

Khan, Azizur Rahman, and Carl Riskin, 2001. *Inequality and Poverty in China in the Age of Globalization*. New York: Oxford University Press.

Lin, Justin Yifu, Fang Cai, and Zhou Li, 1996. *The China Miracle: Development Strategy and Economic Reform*. The Hong Kong Centre for Economic Research.

Ravallion, Martin, Gaurav Datt, and Dominique van de Walle, 1991. "Quantifying Absolute Poverty in the Development World." *Review of Income and Wealth* 37: 345–361.

Sen, Amartya, 2001. "Economic Development and Capability Expansion," *Pacific Economic Review*, 6 (2): 179–191.

State Statistical Bureau (SSB), various years. *China Development Report*. Beijing: China Statistical Publishing House.

World Bank, 1992. *China: Strategies for Reducing Poverty in the 1990s*. Washington, DC.

World Bank, 2000. *China: Overcoming Rural Poverty*. Report No. 21105-CHA. Joint Report for the Leading Group for Poverty Reduction, UNDP, and The World Bank.

Yang, Danis Tao, and Cai Fang, 2000. "The Political Economy of China's Rural–Urban Divide," Center for Research on Economic Development and Policy Reform Working Paper No. 62, Stanford University.

6 Spatial inequality in education and health care in China

Xiaobo Zhang and Ravi Kanbur

Abstract

While increasing income inequality in China has been commented on and studied extensively, relatively little analysis is available on inequality in other dimensions of human development. Using data from different sources, this paper presents some basic facts on the evolution of spatial inequalities in education and health care in China over the long run. In the era of economic reforms, as the foundations of education and health care provision have changed, so has the distribution of illiteracy and infant mortality. Across provinces and within provinces, between rural and urban areas and within rural and urban areas, social inequalities have increased substantially since the reforms began.

6.1 Introduction

Since the start of the reforms in 1978, China has experienced unprecedented economic growth, which has led to spectacular reductions in income poverty (World Bank, 2000; Fan, Zhang, and Zhang, 2002). However, this growth has been accompanied by dramatic increases in inequality, especially in the 1990s. In recent years, the policy debate in China has begun to reflect strong concern with this increasing inequality (UNDP, 1999; CASS, 2005). Growing disparities along different dimensions (rural–urban, inland–coastal etc.) are cited as reasons for growing social unrest, not to mention the fact the poverty reduction would have been even more spectacular had the growth not been accompanied by a sharp increase in inequality. Most of the literature on inequality in China is about income inequality (Lyons, 1991; Tsui, 1991; Khan, Riskin, and Zhao, 1993; Hussain, Lanjouw, and Stern, 1994; Chen and Ravallion, 1996; Aaberge and Li, 1997; Kanbur and Zhang, 1999, 2005; Yang, 1999; Démurger et al., 2002). Relatively little analysis is available on inequality in other dimensions of human development. For example, West and Wong (1995) discuss fiscal decentralization and increasing regional disparities in education and health status. However, their study focuses on only rural areas in two provinces, Shandong and Guangdong. The China Human Development Report (UNDP, 1999) highlights the negative impact of fiscal decentralization on education and health. Although it presents a human development index at the province level in 1997, it does not quantify the change in social inequality over time. This paper is a contribution to the attempts at filling this gap in our knowledge. Using data from different sources, it presents a picture of the long term evolution of spatial inequalities in education and health care in China.

There are several reasons to worry about high social inequality. First, people live in a social setting and do care about their relative positions in a society. High social inequality is often in relation to low happiness. Second, large social inequality often leads to more crimes and social instability, which in turn contribute negatively to investment environment and economic growth. Third, the increasing gap of social development will reduce the trickle-down effect of economic growth on poverty reduction. For example, it is hard for an illiterate person to share the boat of rapid economic development. All in all, social inequality is equally important as income inequality.

The paper is arranged as follows. Section 6.2 provides an institutional and historical review of social welfare provision in rural areas and cities. Section 6.3 describes the spatial distribution of education and health development, respectively, using national level data that go back to the pre-reform period. Section 6.4 concludes, and an Appendix provides a description of the data used in the analysis.

6.2 Institutional changes in education and health care provision

Until the 1980s, China's distributional policies manifested a strong urban bias (Lin, Cai, and Li, 1996).[1] The rationing system introduced in the 1950s enabled urban residents to have access to food, housing, education, and health care at much lower prices. Almost all urban residents in the working age group had guaranteed jobs in the state or collectively owned firms. Because these jobs were permanent, the so called "iron rice bowl", urban unemployment was virtually nonexistent. These jobs also provided urban residents with many benefits such as free or subsidized education and health care. Basically, enterprises and government agencies were responsible for providing social welfare to urban residents.

Compared to the level of social expenditure in cities, rural areas received far less. Nevertheless, the government adopted an alternative strategy in rural areas to promote basic education and health care. For health care, the focus was on preventive rather than curative health care measures. The communes, production brigades, and production teams had authority to mobilize the masses to engage in public health and infrastructure works. With large manpower input, the government could implement various public health campaigns, such as fighting against the four pests (rats, flies, mosquitoes, and bed bugs), expanding nationwide immunization, and training indigenous rural health workers (so called "bare-foot doctors"). By the late 1970s, "bare-foot doctors" and clinics were set up in almost all the villages. As shown in Table 6.1, the numbers of hospital beds and health care personnel per thousand in rural areas rose dramatically from 0.08 and 0.95 to 1.48 and 1.81 from 1952 to 1980, respectively. In general, these public health measures were rather successful in controlling infectious and parasitic diseases. Mortality rates specific to infectious diseases declined noticeably in the pre-reform period (Yu, 1992).

Basic education relied largely on the communes. Agricultural collectivization created a large number of "commune schools," making access to basic education much easier. As shown in Table 6.1, the student–teacher ratio in primary school declined from 35.6 in 1952 to 25.7 in 1980 while the ratio in secondary school decreased from 27.4 to 17.6. By 1980 the enrollment rate among rural children reached was almost 90 percent (Fan, Zhang, and Zhang, 2002).

Overall, in the planned era, although health care and school conditions for rural residents were much worse than their urban cohorts due to an urban-biased policy, basic education and preventive health care were widely available. By the late 1970s, China's life expectancy and infant mortality rate were much higher than most developing countries, even many middle-income countries (World Bank, 2003). Despite the remarkable achievement in social equity, the collective system had well known economic drawbacks. Since the late 1970s, China has implemented a series of rural and urban reforms to introduce market incentives in order to enhance economic efficiency and dynamism. In addition, the center granted local governments more fiscal responsibility to improve their incentives to develop the local economy. Consequently, the redistributive power of central government has declined. With limited help from the center and tight budget constraints, many local governments in poor regions cut spending on social development and let individuals share more health care and education expenses (West and Wong, 1995). As shown in Table 6.2, the shares of both government and social spending in total health expenditure have declined dramatically.

In addition to the general fiscal reforms, rural and urban areas have undergone their own reforms. Following the rural economic reform, the communes were dissolved and households became the unit of decision-making, reducing the power of villages and directly affecting the provisions of education and health care. Not surprisingly, many rural health clinics have disappeared since the rural reform in the 1970s. The number of hospital beds per thousand has declined from 1.50 to 1.11 from 1985 to 1998 (Table 6.1). To fill the vacuum, in 1984, the government authorized private medical practices in rural areas. Because private medical practitioners provide their services according to patients' ability to pay, an increasing number of people have had to bear the full cost of medical care. The share of out-of-pocket expense in medical care for China as a whole increased from 16 percent in 1980 to 38 percent in 1988 to 61 percent in 2001 (Table 6.2). Table 6.3 shows that in 1998 the self-paid share in total health expenses was much greater for rural than for urban areas. After the reforms, most rural residents have been left out of health care

Table 6.1 Education and health care in China, 1952–1998

Year	Primary school enrollment rate (%)	Primary school graduates entering secondary schools (%)	Student/teacher ratio in primary school	Student/teacher ratio in secondary school	Hospital beds per 1000 people (city)	Hospital beds per 1000 people (rural)	Health care personnel per 1000 people (city)	Health care personnel per 1000 people (rural)
1952	49.2	96.0	35.6	27.4	1.46	0.08	2.71	0.95
1957	61.7	44.2	34.1	27	2.08	0.14	3.60	1.22
1962	56.1	45.3	27.6	24.8	3.88	0.45	5.07	1.50
1965	84.7	82.5	30.1	21.2	3.78	0.51	5.38	1.46
1970	n.a.	71.2	29.1	22.4	4.03	0.85	4.71	1.22
1975	96.8	90.6	29.0	21.1	4.46	1.23	6.70	1.41
1978	95.5	87.7	28.0	20.5	4.70	1.41	7.50	1.63
1979	93.0	82.8	27.2	19.1	n.a.	n.a.	n.a.	n.a.
1980	93.9	75.9	26.6	18.5	4.57	1.48	7.82	1.81
1981	93.0	68.3	25.7	17.6	n.a.	n.a.	n.a.	n.a.
1982	93.2	66.2	25.4	17.6	n.a.	n.a.	n.a.	n.a.
1983	94.0	67.3	25.0	17.6	4.62	1.47	8.37	1.99
1984	95.3	66.2	25.2	18.4	n.a.	n.a.	n.a.	n.a.
1985	96.0	68.4	24.9	18.4	4.48	1.50	7.81	2.06
1986	96.4	69.5	24.3	18.4	4.87	1.46	8.36	2.01
1987	97.2	69.1	23.6	17.9	5.22	1.46	8.72	1.97
1988	97.2	70.4	22.8	16.7	5.56	1.41	8.98	1.92
1989	97.4	71.5	22.3	15.8	5.71	1.38	9.08	1.89
1990	97.8	74.6	21.9	15.7	5.81	1.37	9.15	1.89
1991	97.8	75.7	22.0	15.7	5.86	1.36	9.17	1.89
1992	97.2	79.7	22.1	15.9	6.02	1.33	9.34	1.86
1993	97.7	81.8	22.4	15.7	6.06	1.30	9.24	1.83
1994	98.4	86.6	22.9	16.1	6.18	1.22	9.37	1.75
1995	98.5	90.8	23.3	16.7	6.09	1.19	9.31	1.73
1996	98.8	92.6	23.7	17.2	6.08	1.16	9.24	1.71
1997	98.9	93.7	24.2	17.3	6.10	1.14	9.25	1.72
1998	98.9	94.3	24.0	17.6	6.08	1.11	9.16	1.71

Source: Comprehensive Statistical Data and Materials on 50 Years of New China (China State Statistical Bureau, 2000).

Table 6.2 Recurrent health expenditures by source of finance

Year	Per capita expenditure (1980 yuan)	Government budget (%)	Social expenditure (%)	Personal expenditure (%)
1965	4.7	28	56	16
1970	5.1	27	57	15
1975	8.6	28	55	16
1980	10.9	28	56	16
1981	12.1	27	55	18
1982	13.9	26	53	20
1983	15.8	25	51	23
1984	17.3	25	50	25
1985	19.4	23	47	29
1986	22.0	22	45	32
1987	23.4	19	46	35
1988	26.3	18	44	38
1991	37.7	23	38	39
1995	51.7	17	33	50
2000	95.5	15	24	61
2001	101.7	16	23	61

Source: The data from 1965 to 1988 are from *China: Long-Term Issues and Options in the Health Transition* (World Bank, 1992), Annex Table 9.1. Information for later years are from the website of the Ministry of Health, http://www.moh.gov.cn/statistics/digest03/t28.htm. The health expenditure data from 1991 to 2001 are converted to 1980 yuan using the national consumer price index.

Table 6.3 China's health care coverage in 1998 (yuan per capita)

	Cities	Countryside	Total
Totally public paid	16.0	1.2	5.0
Labor related	22.9	0.5	6.2
Semi-labor related	5.8	0.2	1.6
Insurance	3.3	1.4	1.9
Cooperative	4.2	6.6	5.9
Self-paid	44.1	87.4	76.4
Other	3.7	2.7	2.9

Source: China Health Yearbook 1999 (Ministry of Health, 1999), p. 410.

coverage of any kind and paying for a health visit has become the norm. A special report in the *Economist* (2004) points out that even immunization is not free in many parts of China.

Table 6.4 compares some key indicators among several Asian countries. China's performance on literacy and infant mortality rate is more like a middle income country than many developing countries, and better than India. However, there are huge disparities in the distribution of access to health care. In rich areas, such as Shanghai, health indicators are on a par with many western countries. In western China, such as Guizhou, they are similar

Table 6.4 International comparisons on key indicators

Country	GDP per capita (current PPP dollars)	Infant mortality rate (deaths per 1000)	Illiteracy rate (%)	Ranking based on health expenditure per capita in international dollars	Ranking of overall health systems performance
China	3,740	32	15	139	144
India	2,730	68	43	133	112
Indonesia	2,970	35	13	154	92
Korea, Rep.	14,720	5	2	31	58
Malaysia	9,100	8	13	93	49
Philippines	3,790	30	5	124	60
Singapore	23,700	3	8	38	6
Thailand	6,230	25	5	64	47

Note: Data in the second to fourth columns are for 2000 and from the World Development Indicators (2003). The last two columns are from Annex Table 1 of the *World Health Report* (WHO, 2000).

to those of African countries. According to the World Health Organization (WHO), health expenditure per capita in international dollars ranks only at 139th, compared to 133rd in India although China has a higher GDP per capita measured in PPP. The ranking of overall health system performance, which takes into account the fairness of access to health care and individual contribution cost, puts China at 144th place, behind India's 112th place and far behind other Asian countries listed in Table 6.4. In other words, although China's health indicators are comparable to countries at the similar development level, the trend and distribution are more worrisome.

Although contested elections have been introduced over the past two decades partly in an attempt to improve the efficiency of public goods provision, the gains are not significant for at least two reasons (Zhang et al., 2004). First, privatization has made taxation or levies on rural enterprises more difficult. Second, in many villages, the power is not shared between the party secretary and the elected village head, limiting the impact of elections. It is likely that the increasing rural income inequality would translate into increasing health inequality, as villages do not have much fiscal power to provide public goods and service in poor areas under the current fiscal arrangement.

In cities, many people's livelihood is wrapped up with the fate of state-sector jobs. Unlike the simple objective of profit maximization in private enterprises, state owned enterprises (SOEs) have to bear multiple responsibilities of efficient production and social welfare provision (Bai et al., 2001). With greater integration of China into the world market, it becomes increasingly difficult for SOEs to compete with multinationals and private enterprises because of their full range of social obligations. In the initial stage, the government could afford to subsidize the SOEs through low-interest loans. But with the increasing burden of loss, the government's support to SOEs has declined. Therefore, since the mid-1990s, the government has carried out ambitious reforms to reduce the noneconomic burden of SOEs by allowing bankruptcy and more open unemployment. Since then, many SOEs have laid off workers and cut health and other benefits. To provide new impetus to the SOEs, the government has launched a series of urban reforms since the late 1980s. The central theme is to transfer welfare-provision obligations such as health care and housing from enterprises to social insurance agencies and individuals (China Development Report, 1997). Although China has made progress in reforming the health care and pension system, a well-functioning social safety net is still far from being in place (Liu et al., 2001). Therefore, the liberalization of the urban welfare system may have made some disadvantaged groups more vulnerable to sudden shocks such as catastrophic illness.

Similar to health care, both rural and urban residents are increasingly relying on themselves to pay for education. Table 6.5 lists the sources for education expenditure, showing that the out-of-pocket education expenses have increased significantly. The government's share in total education expenditure declined from 64.6 percent in 1990, when the data were first

Table 6.5 Sources of education expenditure

Year	Total education expenditure (100 million yuan)	Government budget (%)	Social expenditure (%)	Tuitions and incidentals (%)
1990	659.4	64.6	33.1	2.3
1991	731.5	62.8	34.6	2.5
1992	867.1	62.1	35.0	2.9
1993	1059.9	60.8	36.2	3.0
1994	1488.8	59.4	36.7	4.0
1995	1878.0	54.8	40.9	4.4
1996	2262.3	53.6	41.3	5.1
1997	2531.7	53.6	40.8	5.6
1998	2949.1	53.1	34.4	12.5

Source: Calculated by authors based on Table A-14 in *Comprehensive Statistical Data and Materials on 50 Years of New China* (China State Statistical Bureau, 2000), p. 14.

available, to 53.1 percent in 1998, while the share of tuitions and incidental fees rose from 2.3 percent to 12.5 percent in the nine-year period. With the increasing out-of-pocket expenses on education, children in the poor families may have difficulties in finishing the basic nine-year schooling, likely leading to more uneven access to education.

This completes our discussion of the institutional changes in education and health care provision in China since the start of the reform process. Sen (1992, 2000) expresses concerns about the social inequality consequences of these policy changes for two reasons. First, social development is the end of economic development and therefore a highly uneven distributional outcome of social development is not desirable in itself. Second, considering that the rather equal distribution of human capital was regarded as a key to China's success in economic reform, the uneven social development may have a long term negative impact on economic growth. We now turn to the evolution of inequality in health and education indicators, viewing them through the lens of spatial inequality.

6.3 Spatial inequality in education and health over the long run

We are interested in the evolution of social inequality in China over the long run, comparing the planned era with the more recent era of market reforms. As noted in Kanbur and Zhang (2005), although the ideal requirement for this exercise is household level survey data stretching back over fifty years, such data is simply not available for China. Analysts focusing on interpersonal inequality as revealed by household survey data have had to analyze much shorter periods or with severely restricted regional coverage – a few years for a few provinces, and mainly in the recent period. An alternative approach, as in Kanbur and Zhang (2005), is to view inequality through the lens of spatial inequality, meaning by this variations across provinces, sub-divided by rural and urban areas. Apart from the fact that such regional inequality is interesting in its own right, the advantage of taking this perspective is that data is more readily available at the national level for much longer periods. As shown in Kanbur and Zhang (2005) and in Table 6.6, regional income inequality calculated at the provincial level with a rural–urban divide has increased. The Gini coefficient rose from 29.3 percent in 1978 to 25.6 percent in 1984 and then to 37.2 percent in 2000. The question for this paper, however, is: what has happened to social inequality? We look at the spatial inequality of education and health outcomes in turn.

6.3.1 Education inequality

Focusing on the years for which census data is publicly available at the national level, we initially arrive at illiteracy rates for rural and urban areas

Table 6.6 Regional inequality

Year	Gini
1978	29.3
1979	28.6
1980	28.2
1981	27.0
1982	25.6
1983	25.9
1984	25.6
1985	25.8
1986	26.8
1987	27.0
1988	28.2
1989	29.7
1990	30.1
1991	30.3
1992	31.4
1993	32.2
1994	32.6
1995	33.0
1996	33.4
1997	33.9
1998	34.4
1999	36.3
2000	37.2

Note: The figures for Gini coefficients are calculated based on population weighted per capita expenditure at the provincial level with a rural–urban divide. The data sources for 1978–1998 and 1999–2000 are *Comprehensive Statistical Data and Materials on 50 Years of New China* (China State Statistical Bureau, 2000) and *China Statistical Yearbook* (China State Statistical Bureau, 2000 and 2001), respectively. See Kanbur and Zhang (2005) for details of the calculation.

and for females and males for the years 1981, 1990 and 2000. The illiteracy rate for 1981 is defined as the number of illiterate per hundred people who are 12 years old and above. The definition changes to 15 years old and above in the censuses of 1990 and 2000. Because the censuses do not report the aggregate illiteracy rate in coastal and inland areas, we compute it using data at the provincial level with population as weights. The upper panel of Table 6.7 presents the levels of illiteracy for overall, rural, urban, inland, coastal, females, and males in China. Several striking features stand out from the table. First, the illiteracy rate has declined steadily over the years, reflecting the success of nine-year compulsory education and the high primary-school enrollment rate. Second, there exist large rural–urban and gender-gaps. In 2000, the rural illiteracy rate was more than double the urban illiteracy rate. The illiteracy rate among females is more than twice as high as the male illiteracy rate, suggesting a strong gender bias against girls. The illiteracy rate in inland areas is about 15 percent higher than that in coastal areas.

Table 6.8 further displays the spread in the illiteracy rate across rural and urban areas, with the Gini and Generalized Entropy (GE) as inequality measures. The GE family of measures is discussed further in Zhang and Kanbur (2001) – the specific member of the family used in this paper is the famous Theil measure of inequality. Inequality is calculated using the population weighted values of illiteracy for spatial units. In the top panel of Table 6.8, the first two columns show that the Gini and the GE at the national level increased from 1981 to 2000. The same pattern holds true for inequalities across rural, urban, inland, coastal, female, and male population. It seems that the regional variation in health outcome has enlarged over the reform period in all dimensions.

As is well known, the GE family of inequality measures can be decomposed into the sum of a within- and a between-group component, for any given partitioning of the population into mutually exclusive and exhaustive groups. Table 6.8 also presents the evolution of the between-group components of inequality. The female–male component is larger than the rural–urban and inland–coastal components. Using the overall-inequality and between-inequality, we can calculate the polarization index following the method outlined by Zhang and Kanbur (2001).[2] As shown in the last column in Table 6.8, illiteracy rate is mostly polarized along the gender line although it has decreased from 59.0 in 1981 to 44.6 in 2000. The rural and urban areas became increasingly polarized from 17.8 in 1981 to 25.7 in 2000.

The above inequality analysis offers a snapshot for each of three years. To check whether the findings are robust over a long continuous period, we calculate regional inequality in rural illiteracy rate from 1978 to 1998, when the data at provincial level are available in various issues of *China Rural Statistical Yearbook*. Figure 6.1 plots the regional Gini coefficients of per capita income and illiteracy rate. As clearly shown in Figure 6.1, the regional inequality in illiteracy across rural areas has increased, consistent with the analysis based on data at the county and district level as shown in Table 6.7.

Table 6.7 The levels of illiteracy rate and infant mortality rate (IMR)

Year	National	Rural			Urban			Rural–Urban	Inland	Coastal	Inland–Coastal	Female	Male	Female–Male
		Total	Female	Male	Total	Female	Male							
Illiteracy rate														
1981	31.9	34.8	49.1	21.1	16.4	24.6	8.9	2.1	33.7	29.1	1.2	45.3	19.2	2.4
1990	22.2	26.2	37.1	15.7	12.0	18.4	6.1	2.2	23.8	19.6	1.2	31.9	13.0	2.5
2000	15.1	19.9	27.9	12.1	8.7	13.2	4.1	2.3	16.0	13.9	1.2	21.6	8.8	2.5
IMR														
1981	36.6	39.1	38.1	40.0	23.6	22.4	24.8	1.7	44.5	24.4	1.8	35.7	37.6	1.0
1990	30.5	32.4	34.9	30.0	19.1	19.5	18.8	1.7	35.8	17.2	2.1	30.6	26.8	1.1
2000	24.1	30.8	36.7	25.8	11.0	13.5	10.3	2.8	26.8	13.6	2.0	28.4	20.5	1.4

Note: For data sources, see Data Appendix. The 1981 census defines the illiteracy rate using age 12 as a benchmark, while the other two censuses refer to those people 15 years old and above. Therefore, they may not be totally comparable.

Table 6.8 Regional inequality in illiteracy rate and infant mortality rate (IMR)

Year	National Gini	National Theil	Rural	Urban	Rural–Urban	Rural–Urban/Total	Inland	Coastal	Inland–Coastal	Inland–Coastal/Total	Female	Male	Female–Male	Female–Male/Total
Illiteracy rate														
1981	30.3	14.5	11.5	17.3	2.6	17.8	13.0	16.5	0.2	1.7	4.8	8.6	8.6	59.0
1990	33.7	18.1	12.7	17.5	4.7	26.0	17.5	18.0	0.4	2.4	7.0	12.8	9.3	51.4
2000	36.5	21.3	13.8	23.9	5.5	25.7	19.8	23.6	0.2	1.1	9.8	16.7	9.5	44.6
IMR														
1981	27.0	11.9	10.9	7.3	1.3	11.1	9.6	3.7	3.8	31.6	11.3	12.3	0.0	0.3
1990	29.6	14.1	12.6	8.0	2.4	16.7	9.9	4.8	5.4	38.1	14.5	13.6	0.2	1.6
2000	36.7	22.5	17.8	13.7	8.1	35.9	19.5	11.5	4.6	20.6	23.2	18.8	1.2	5.1

Note: For data sources, see Data Appendix. The GE measure is parameterized so as to make it the Theil measure of inequality. National inequality in illiteracy and infant mortality rate (IMR) are calculated using population at the provincial level a rural–urban and gender divide. Rural–urban, female–male, inland–coastal polarization indexes are defined as the ratio of between-group GE to within-group GE. For a discussion of polarization measures, see Zhang and Kanbur (2001).

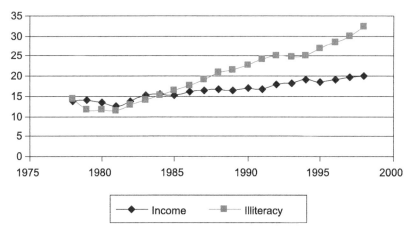

Figure 6.1 Twenty years of rural inequality in income and illiteracy rate.

Note: The income inequality measure is the Gini coefficient, calculated by authors based on population weighted per capita expenditure at the provincial level in rural areas. The data are from *Comprehensive Statistical Data and Materials on 50 Years of New China* (China State Statistical Bureau, 2000). The illiteracy inequality measure is also the Gini coefficient, calculated from population weighted province level data on rural illiteracy rates. The data source is *China Rural Statistical Yearbook* (China State Statistical Bureau, various issues).

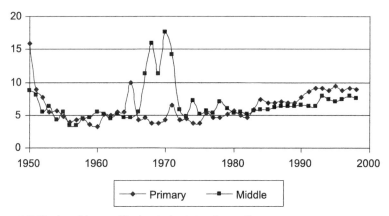

Figure 6.2 Regional inequality in student–teacher ratio.

Note: The figure reports regional Gini coefficients of student–teacher ratios in primary and secondary schools calculated by authors based on population weighted provincial data from *Comprehensive Statistical Data and Materials on 50 Years of New China* (China State Statistical Bureau, 2000).

The rural regional income inequality, measured by the Gini coefficient, increased from 13.7 percent to 24.1 percent in the period of 1978–1998, but the Gini coefficient of rural illiteracy worsened even more rapidly, from 14.5 percent to 32.4 percent.

Figure 6.2 plots the evolution of regional inequality in the provision of primary and secondary education. We calculate the Gini coefficients of student–teacher ratios in the two sectors using provincial data. The inequalities in the two ratios show a similar pattern, except for the Cultural Revolution period (1966–1976) when the middle school education system was disrupted. The regional inequality in the provision of public education has increased since the late 1970s, reflecting the fiscal decentralization policy in the reform period.

6.3.2 Health inequality

Similar to education inequality, we first look at the health outcomes using more disaggregated population census or survey data. The lower panel in Table 6.6 reports the levels of infant mortality rate (IMR), defined as the number of infant deaths per thousand births. For China as a whole, IMR declined dramatically from the 1960s to the 1980s and then leveled off. With careful adjustment, Banister and Hill (2004) even found that the mortality risks of girls at the national level in infancy increased during 1990 to 2000. IMR in rural areas was significantly higher than in cities and the gap widened from 1.5 in 1981 to 2.1 in 2000. The ratio of female to male IMR increased dramatically from 0.9 to 1.3 over the same period. More seriously, female IMR in rural areas rose from 34.9 to 36.7 in the period of 1990–2000. These figures probably reflect an outcome of family planning policy, as rural residents in general prefer to have boys.

Using the data set, we can further examine the regional distribution of IMR. As shown in the lower panel of Table 6.7, overall regional inequality increased from 1981 to 2000, so did the within-rural, within-urban, and between rural–urban inequalities. It seems that the regional variation in health outcomes has enlarged over the reform period in both rural and urban areas.

To understand the driving forces behind the observed changes in health outcome, we further investigate the distribution of health care provision. Based on the last four columns of Table 6.1, we plot the rural–urban ratios of health care personnel and hospital beds per thousand people in Figure 6.3. Figure 6.3 shows that the density of health care personnel and facilities in cities has been much higher than that in rural areas. For example, in 1980, hospital beds and health care personnel per 1000 people in cities were 4.57 and 7.82, respectively, compared to 1.48 and 1.81 in rural areas. Moreover, as shown in Figure 6.3, the gap between rural and urban areas has grown. The enlarging difference in access to health care appears to be a contributing factor to the widening gap in IMR between rural and urban residents.

While Figure 6.3 provides a rural–urban comparison at the national level, Figure 6.4 plots the regional distribution of the above two variables using data at the provincial level. Regional inequality declined steadily in the planned era but has leveled off since the late 1970s. The picture in Figure 6.4 is in contrast to the increasing trend of rural–urban disparity shown in Figure 6.3. This is probably due to the fact that the provincial level data used in

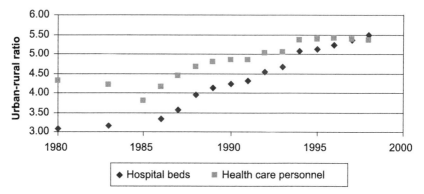

Figure 6.3 Rural–urban ratios in hospital beds per thousand people and health care personnel per thousand people.

Note: The vertical axis measures the rural–urban ratios of hospital beds per thousand people and health care personnel per thousand people, based on data at the national level reported in the last four columns of Table 6.1.

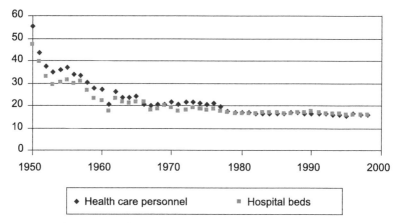

Figure 6.4 Regional inequality in health care.

Note: The vertical axis represents regional Gini coefficients of health care personnel and hospital beds per thousand people calculated by authors based on provincial data from *Comprehensive Statistical Data and Materials on 50 Years of New China* (China State Statistical Bureau, 2000).

Figure 6.4 does not have a rural–urban divide, masking the large variation in this dimension within a province.

6.4 Conclusion

In this paper, we have described the institutional and historical background on the public provision of education and health care and examined the patterns and evolution of social inequality. In the era of market reforms, the old foundations of education and health care provision have eroded. First, the increasing fiscal decentralization has reduced the central government's redistributive power. Many local governments, in particular those in poor regions with insufficient revenues, have largely withdrawn from their role in investing in human development. Second, increasing competition has doomed SOEs, as it is difficult to serve well the dual task of profit maximizing and welfare provision. As a result, a large number of SOEs have laid off employees and reduced welfare benefits. Third, weak governance at the village level makes it difficult to finance public infrastructure in rural areas. Fourth, governments cannot mobilize vast manpower in public works as they did in the planned era, because labor must be adequately compensated in the market economy.

With this background, we examine the spatial patterns of social development indicators. Not surprisingly, the changing distribution in outcome of education and public health has reflected the evolution of underlying institutions in the process of economic transformation. Social inequalities in rural, urban, inland, and coastal areas all have increased since the economic reforms. In particular, the rural–urban gap in IMR is increasing and the gender gap in literacy is still large.

It has been argued by many observers that to ensure a long-term sustainable development, China should adopt a broad-based development strategy. A healthy and well-educated labor force is a key asset to ensuring China's success in incorporating the challenges of WTO accession. However, the increasing economic integration will greatly intensify market competition, which will likely further weaken the central government's ability to redistribute wealth among provinces, and it will reduce the role of SOEs as social welfare providers. In addition, the increasing shocks associated with global integration may further worsen social inequality. Moreover, increasing social inequality may increase social instability, which in turn affects economic growth. The facts of social inequality presented in this paper call for more attention to improving the mechanisms of education and health care provision and reforming the fiscal arrangement between local and central governments so as to ensure more equitable education and health outcomes. In other words (UNDP, 1999), the state should play a more "substantial and vigorous role" in providing education and health care.

Data appendix

Per capita expenditure, population, hospital beds, health care personnel, school enrollment, teacher–student ratios, and education expenditures prior to 1999 are from *Comprehensive Statistical Data and Materials on 50 Years of New China* (China State Statistical Bureau, 2000). The information on per capita expenditure and population for 1999 and 2000 are from *China Statistical Yearbook* (China State Statistical Bureau, 2000 and 2001). The health care coverage data in 1998 is from *China Health Yearbook 1999* (Ministry of Health, 1999) and the sources of health expenditures are *China:*

Long-Term Issues and Options in the Health Transition (World Bank, 1992) and the website of Ministry of Health, http://www.moh.gov.cn/statistics/digest03/t28.htm.

The illiteracy and IMR are compiled from published provincial and national statistical volumes of the population censuses of 1981, 1990, and 2000. The official data report illiteracy and IMR rate at the provincial level with a rural–urban and gender disaggregation for each province. When calculating regional inequality in illiteracy and IMR, we use the corresponding population as weights. The rural illiteracy data at the provincial level annually from 1978–1998 is from *China Rural Statistical Yearbook* (China State Statistical Bureau, various issues).

Banister and Zhang (2005) find that the infant mortality rates reported from the census are lower than those from a large annual survey conducted by China's Ministry of Health, which is specially designed to get unusually-complete death reporting. This survey estimated that China's infant mortality rate was 50.2 infant deaths per thousand live births in 1991 and 32.2 in 2000 (China National Working Committee on Children and Women, 2001, p. 28). The World Development Indicator (2003) reports the higher figure from the second source, as shown in Table 6.4. Comparing the survey results in 1991 and 2000 with census results in 1990 and 2000, if assuming that the survey infant mortality data are accurate, we can conclude that infant deaths may have been only about 61 percent reported for 1990 in the 1990 census and over 70 percent reported in the 2000 census. However, without access to the survey data at the disaggregate level, we cannot make use of them for inequality measures. Considering that the two data series share similar trends, therefore the impact on the accuracy of inequality measures may not be that serious.

Notes

1 This bias still exists today, but in different forms (for example, government invests more in urban than in rural areas; universities post higher admission scores for rural students; and there are still visible and invisible restrictions on migration from rural to urban areas).
2 The polarization index is defined as the ratio of between-inequality to within-inequality.

References

Aaberge, R., & X. Li, 1997, The trend in urban income inequality in two Chinese provinces, 1986–90. *Review of Income and Wealth* 43(3): 335–355.
Bai, C., D. D. Li, Z. Tao, & Y. Wang, 2001, A multi-task theory of state enterprise reform, The William Davidson Institute Working Paper 367, University of Michigan.
Banister, Judith, & Kenneth Hill, 2004, Mortality in China, *Population Studies* 58(1): 55–75.
Banister, J., & X. Zhang, 2005, China, economic development and mortality decline, *World Development* 33(1): 21–41.

China National Working Committee on Children and Women, 2001 *Report of the People's Republic of China on the Development of Children in the 1990s.* Beijing: China State Council.

Chen, S. & M. Ravallion, 1996, Data in transition: assessing rural living standards in southern China, *China Economic Review* 7(1): 23–56.

China State Statistical Bureau (SSB), various issues. *China Rural Statistical Yearbook* (China Statistical Press: Beijing).

China State Statistical Bureau (SSB), 1997, *China Development Report* (China Statistical Press: Beijing).

China State Statistical Bureau (SSB), 2000, *Comprehensive Statistical Data and Materials on 50 Years of New China* (China Statistical Press: Beijing).

China State Statistical Bureau (SSB), 2000 and 2001, *China Statistical Yearbook* (China Statistical Press: Beijing).

Chinese Academy of Social Sciences (CASS), 2005, *Blue Report on Social Development in China* (China Social Science Literature Publishing House: Beijing).

The *Economist*, 2004, "Special report: China's health care," August 21st.

Fan, S., L. Zhang, & X. Zhang, 2002, *Growth, Inequality, and Poverty in Rural China: The Role of Public Investments.* International Food Policy Research Institute (IFPRI) Research Report 125. Washington, DC.

Hussain, A., P. Lanjouw, & N. Stern, 1994, Income inequalities in China: Evidence from household survey data, *World Development* 22(12): 1947–1957.

Kanbur, R., & X. Zhang, 1999, Which regional inequality: The evolution of rural–urban and inland–coastal inequality in China, *Journal of Comparative Economics* 27: 686–701.

Kanbur, R., & X. Zhang, 2005, Fifty years of regional inequality in China: a journey through revolution, reform and openness, *Review of Development Economics* 9(1): 87–106.

Khan, A. R., K. G., C. Riskin, & R. Zhao, 1993, Sources of income inequality in post-reform China, *China Economics Review* 4(1): 19–35.

Lin, J. Y., F. Cai, & Z. Li, 1996, *The China Miracle: Development Strategy and Economic Reform* (The Chinese University Press: Hong Kong).

Liu, G., X. Wu, C. Peng, & A. Wu, 2001, Urbanization and access to health care in China, paper presented at the International Conference on Urbanization in China: Challenges and Strategies of Growth and Development, June 26–28, Xiamen, China.

Lyons, T. P., 1991, Interprovincial disparities in China: Output and consumption, 1952–1987, *Economic Development and Cultural Change* 39(3): 471–506.

Ministry of Health, 1999, *China Health Yearbook 1999* (People's Health Publishing Press: Beijing).

Sen, A., 1992, Life and death in China: A Reply, *World Development* 20(9): 1305–1312.

Sen, A., 2000, *Development as freedom* (Random House, Inc.: New York).

Sylvie, D., J. D. Sachs, W. T. Woo, Shuming Bao, Gene Chang, & Andrew Mellinger, 2002, Geography, economic policy and regional development, *Asian Economic Papers* 1(1): 146–197.

Tsui, K., 1991, China's regional inequality, 1952–1985. *Journal of Comparative Economics* 15(1): 1–21.

United Nations Development Programme (UNDP), 1999, *China Human Development Report 1999: Transition and the State* (Oxford University Press).

West, L. A., & C. P. W. Wong, 1995, Fiscal decentralization and growing regional disparities in rural China: Some evidence in the provision of social services, *Oxford Review of Economic Policy* 11(4): 70–84.

World Bank, 1984, *China: The Health Sector* (World Bank: Washington, DC.).

World Bank, 1992, *China: Long-Term Issues and Options in the Health Transition* (World Bank: Washington, DC.).

World Bank, 2000, *China: Overcoming Rural Poverty* (World Bank: Washington, DC.).

World Bank, 2003, *World Bank Development Indicators* (World Bank: Washington, DC.).

World Health Organization (WHO), 2000, *World Health Report* (World Health Organization, Geneva).

Yang, D. T., 1999, Urban-biased policies and rising income inequality in China, *American Economic Review* (Paper and Proceedings) 89(2): 306–310.

Yu, D., 1992, Changes in health care financing and health status: The Case of China in the 1980s, Economic Policy Series, No. 34. International Child Development Centre, UNICEF.

Zhang, X., & R. Kanbur, 2001, What difference do polarization measures make? An application to China, *Journal of Development Studies* 37(3): 85–98.

Zhang, X., S. Fan, L. Zhang, & J. Huang, 2004, Local governance and public goods provision in rural China, *Journal of Public Economics* 88(12): 2857–2871.

Part II

Explanations and policy responses

7 Resource abundance and regional development in China[1]

Xiaobo Zhang, Li Xing, Shenggen Fan, and Xiaopeng Luo

Abstract

Over the past several decades, China has made tremendous progress in market integration and infrastructure development. Demand for natural resources has increased from the booming coastal economies, causing the terms of trade to favor the resource sector, which is predominantly based in the interior regions of the country. However, the gap in economic development level between the coastal and inland regions has widened significantly. In this paper, using a panel data set at the provincial level, we show that Chinese provinces with abundant resources perform worse than their resource-poor counterparts in terms of per capita consumption growth. This trend that resource-poor areas are better off than resource-rich areas is particularly prominent in rural areas. Because of the institutional arrangements regarding property rights of natural resources, most gains from the resource boom have been captured either by the government or state owned enterprises. Thus, the windfall of natural resources has more to do with government consumption than household consumption. Moreover, in resource-rich areas, greater revenues accrued from natural resources bid up the price of non-tradable goods and hurt the competitiveness of the local economy.

7.1 Introduction

Over the past several decades, China has made tremendous progress in market integration and infrastructure development (Bai et al., 2004; Fan and Chang-Kan, 2005; Zhang and Tan, 2007). Market reforms have eased restrictions on the flows of products, labor, and capital. The newly built interprovincial highway system provides better transport links between regions and promotes trade flow. Rapid productivity growth has lowered the price of manufactured goods and led to soaring demand for raw materials, which are supplied by the natural resource-abundant interior regions. As shown in Figure 7.1, the terms of trade have shifted in favor of the resource sector. Given this situation – increasing market integration, better transport systems, and more favorable terms of trade – growth theory predicts regional convergence. However, the gap in living standards between the coastal and inland

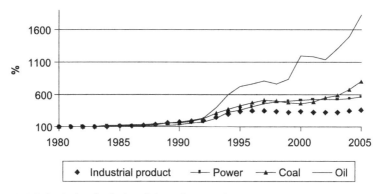

Figure 7.1 Price index for industrial products and energy.

regions has widened (Kanbur and Zhang, 1999, 2005), as shown in Table 7.1. Various explanations to this puzzle have been put forward, including agglomeration, biased development policy, decentralization, and globalization (Démurger et al., 2002; Hu, 2002; Zhang and Zhang, 2003; Zhang, 2006). However, few studies have examined the link between natural resource endowment and the imbalance in regional development patterns in China.[2]

Natural resources serve as important capital in economic development. In principle, revenues generated from the natural resource sector should be good for the economy. However, many resource-rich countries have worse economic performance than their resource-poor counterparts, a phenomenon known as the "resource curse." In the present study, we seek to link the two strands of the literature on regional inequality and resource curse to explain the rapidly increasing inequality between resource-rich and resource-poor regions in China from the viewpoint of the resource curse.

In this study, we make use of a provincial-level panel data set from China. The unique characteristics of China make it particularly suitable for testing whether natural resource abundance has a statistically significant negative impact on economic development. First, the institutional and governance structures are rather homogeneous across provinces. Second, in terms of population and geographic size, many Chinese provinces are as large as countries and there are large regional variations in terms of resource endowment and development. The homogeneous institutional structure and large temporal and spatial variations enable us to better identify the effect of natural resources on growth and distribution.[3]

The results show that provinces with abundant resource wealth grow slower than their resource-poor counterparts in terms of per capita consumption, particularly in rural areas. We explain this phenomenon primarily from the perspective of property rights. Due to the arrangement of property rights on natural resources, local residents, in particular farmers, do not enjoy a fair share of the rise in rents associated with the booming natural resource sector. Most rents go to the government and state-owned enterprises

Table 7.1 Summary statistics by region and year

Region	Year	Per capita GDP	Per capita consumption	Per capita rural consumption	Resource share	Population share	GDP share	Per capita resource (kg CE)	Resource/GDP (TNCE/10000 yuan)
Inland	1985	625	310	248	72.2	59.1	45.8	979	15.7
	2005	3,497	1,046	696	77.7	56.4	36.5	1,926	5.5
	Annual growth rate (%)	9.0	6.3	5.3	0.4	-0.2	-1.1	3.6	-5.4
Coastal	1985	1,069	396	318	27.8	40.9	54.2	546	5.1
	2005	7,857	1,766	1,063	22.3	43.6	63.5	715	0.9
	Annual growth rate (%)	10.5	7.8	6.2	-1.2	0.3	0.8	1.4	-8.7

Note: Calculated by authors. The units of per capita GDP and consumption are in 1985 yuan.

(SOEs). Moreover, greater revenues accrued from natural resources lead to increased prices for non-tradable goods and hurt the competitiveness of local economies.

The next section offers empirical evidence of the negative impact of resource abundance on consumption growth. Section 7.3 analyzes the transmission channels of natural resources. Finally, in Section 7.4 we present our conclusions and explore policy implications. The data used in the analysis are described in the Appendix.

7.2 Is there a resource curse in China?

The cross-country empirical growth literature has shown mixed evidence to support the curse of natural resources. By looking at the period of 1970–1989 when oil prices plummeted, Sachs and Warner (2001) show strong empirical support for the hypothesis. However, if the period is extended to a later time, the findings do not hold (Auty, 2001). In addition, it is hard to control for institutional factors and rigorously test the hypothesis in a strictly controlled environment for cross-country data sets. When institutional factors are accounted for, the direct negative impact of resource abundance vanishes (Bulte, Damania, and Deacon, 2005; Mehlum, Moene, and Torvik, 2006).

Due to the large size of Chinese provinces and homogeneous governance structures, China provides a good test ground for examining whether the resource curse is a real phenomenon. Following the spirit of Sachs and Warner (2001), Figure 7.2 plots per capita GDP growth from 1985 to 2005 against a resource intensity variable, namely the ratio of resource production to total GDP in 1985.[4] Resource production is defined as the total standard energy units of coal, oil, natural gas, and hydraulic power. See the Appendix for details on the data sources. The figure shows a negative link between natural resource abundance in 1985 and the growth rate of per capita GDP in the following two decades. Most provinces with rapid growth started as resource poor, such as Zhejiang Province, while resource rich provinces, such as Guizhou, Shanxi, and Heilongjiang, grow slower than average. Figures 7.3 and 7.4 reveal the same negative associations of resource abundance with change in per capita consumption and poverty.[5] These findings thus suggest that resource abundance is more closely related to per capita consumption growth than to GDP growth.

The bivariate plots in Figures 7.2–7.4 show a negative relationship between the resource intensity variable and several outcome variables. However this finding should be viewed with caution, as confounding variables may have given rise to the observed negative association. For example, the negative correlation may be due to geographic factors, because most natural resources are produced in remote areas. That is, the remoteness of the production site rather than the resource abundance may be the causal factor. Therefore, multivariate analysis must be used to control for key variables.

Before undertaking more rigorous quantitative analyses, we first briefly

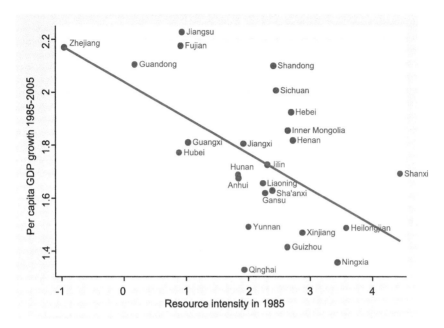

Figure 7.2 GDP growth and resource abundance.

Note: The resource intensity variable is in logarithmic form.

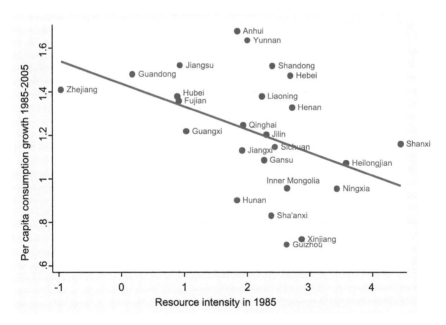

Figure 7.3 Consumption growth and resource abundance.

Note: The resource intensity variable is in logarithmic form.

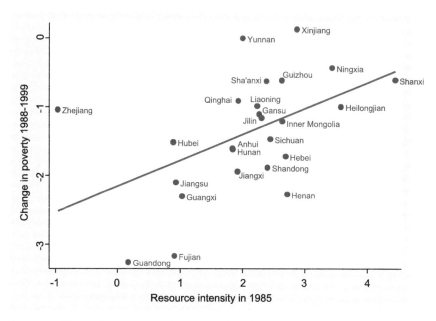

Figure 7.4 Change in poverty and resource abundance.

Note: The resource intensity variable is in logarithmic form.

review the history of price reform in China's natural resource sector.[6] In the planned economic era (1949–1978), the state artificially set low prices for minerals and other natural resources to support the manufacturing sector, which largely consisted of SOEs and was concentrated in resource-poor provinces. Since 1978, China has implemented a series of price reforms. From 1979 to 1984, the general price reform focused on lifting controls on consumer prices. The state, on realizing that low energy prices hindered supply, increased the price on three separate occasions, during the period of 1979–1983. In 1984, the state permitted collectively-owned and local government-owned coal mines to sell coal at the market price.

A milestone in price reform occurred in 1985, when a dual-track system was put in place. Prior to this reform, SOEs under the control of the central, provincial, or municipal governments, enjoyed privileged access to a variety of scarce materials through quotas. There were few quotas, however, for other lower-level SOEs and even fewer for collectively-owned enterprises. The dual pricing system allowed SOEs to sell unused input quota at market price to township and village enterprises, which were outside the command economy. This dual-track system presented a price-discovery mechanism. The planned and market prices gradually converged. By 1993, the coal price was largely liberalized, except for the portion earmarked for electricity generation, which was still subject to state price control and accounted for about 30 percent of total output. In October 1993, the state introduced a dual-track system for crude oil production. Under this system, crude oil produced outside the state quota could be sold at the market price. On May 1 1994, the state raised the planned price for crude oil to bring it into line with the international market price.

In summary, there has been a continuous process of price liberalization from the late 1970s to the mid-1990s in China. Under the price control regimes in place during this period, the resource curse may have resulted from China's heavy industrial-oriented development strategies and may have had little to do with the traditional resource curse. Only after reforms, when the energy price reflected market supply and demand, did the original interpretation of the resource curse discussed in the literature become relevant to China. Therefore, in our analyses presented below, we not only cover the whole sample period of 1985–2005, but also the sub-period of 1995–2005, during which energy and raw material prices were liberalized.[7]

As a first step, we examine the link between resource abundance and several outcome variables for the whole period and the post-price liberalization period using cross-provincial data (Table 7.2). The upper panel reports the regression results for the whole period of 1985–2005, while the lower panel lists the results obtained when the same regressions were repeated for the post-price liberalization period of 1995–2005. The regressions estimate the relationship between historical resource abundance and the growth in outcome variables conditional on the initial value of the dependent variable. The outcome variables include the change in the logarithmic values of per capita GDP, per capita consumption, per capita rural consumption, and the change in rural poverty incidence. The regressors include the logarithm of the initial value of the dependent and resource intensity variables. The initial value of

Table 7.2 The impact of resource intensity on change in several outcome variables from 1985 to 2005 and from 1995 to 2005

	Per capita GDP	Per capita consumption	Per capita rural consumption	Rural poverty
1985–2005				
Initial value	0.099	−0.079	−0.201	−0.033
	(0.67)	(0.31)	(0.66)	(3.02)***
Resource intensity	−0.130	−0.109	−0.106	0.446
	(3.98)***	(3.54)***	(3.19)***	(2.65)**
Adjusted R-squared	0.289	0.120	0.080	0.331
1995–2005				
Initial value	−0.04	0.091	0.035	
	(0.42)	(0.83)	(0.30)	
Resource intensity	−0.023	−0.028	−0.036	
	(0.99)	(1.49)	(2.48)**	
Adjusted R-squared	−0.058	0.066	0.078	

Note: Robust *t* statistics in parentheses; * significant at 10%; ** significant at 5%; *** significant at 1%. Due to a lack of data, the rural poverty regression is from 1988 to 1999.

the dependent variable can help capture the mean reversion property of most economic variables. A negative coefficient for the variable suggests growth convergence across provinces. The resource intensity is defined as the ratio of resource production to total GDP in the first year of the sample period.

For the whole period of 1985–2005 (upper panel, Table 7.2), the coefficient for the resource variable is negative and statistically significant in all four regressions, providing tentative evidence in support of the presence of a resource curse. For the post-price liberalization period (lower panel, Table 7.2), by contrast, the coefficient for the resource variable is only significant in the regression on rural consumption growth. However, given the potential problem of omitted variables in cross-sectional regressions, this finding is only suggestive. It seems that the results are not robust to the sample period covered.

With only 25 observations, it is difficult to add more control variables to test the robustness of the results more rigorously.[8] To overcome this constraint, we divide the two-decade period into four five-year sub-periods and create a panel data set with 100 observations. The resulting larger data set enables us to control for more factors by taking advantage of the panel structure.

Table 7.3 presents the estimated results on the link between resource abundance and per capita GDP growth obtained using the above panel data set for six distinct specifications. Once again, we run the regressions for the whole period (1985–2005) and the post-price liberalization period (1995–2005). In all the specifications, we include year dummy variables to control for time-specific effects. The resource intensity variable is defined as the ratio of resource production to comparable GDP in the initial year of each panel period.[9] The terms of trade variable is defined as the ratio of the fuel price index to the overall retail price index used in 1985 as a base.[10] Due to the location-specific nature of resource variables, we cannot add provincial dummy variables, which are highly correlated with the resource intensity variable, in the regressions.

The independent variables in the first regression include the initial value of per capita GDP, the resource intensity, and the change in the terms of trade for the resource sector. For the whole period (upper panel, Table 7.3), the resource intensity variable has a significant negative coefficient, indicating the possible existence of the resource curse. The coefficient for the terms of trade variable is also statistically significant. For the post-price liberalization period (lower panel, Table 7.3), however, neither the coefficient for the resource intensity variable, nor that for the terms of trade variable, is significant.

In the second regression, the coastal dummy variable is added to capture potentially omitted variables, such as the geographic advantage of the coast along with globalization and coast-biased development policies. In the third regression, we replace the coastal dummy variable with explicit geographic (the share of population living within 100 kilometers from the coast) and policy variables taken from Démurger et al. (2002). When these variables are

Table 7.3 Per capita GDP growth and resource abundance

	R1	R2	R3	R4	R5	R6
1985–2005						
Initial per capita GDP	0.037	0.028	0.028	0.039	0.034	0.033
	(2.99)***	(2.09)**	(1.89)*	(3.21)***	(2.24)**	(2.38)**
Resource intensity	−0.019	−0.012	−0.012	0.003	0.002	
	(1.81)*	(1.22)	(0.96)	(0.25)	(0.20)	
Change in terms of trade	0.149	0.136	0.136	0.100	0.094	
	(2.04)**	(1.91)*	(1.84)*	(1.77)*	(1.58)	
Coastal dummy		0.043				
		(1.79)*				
Pop ≤ 100 km from coast			0.026			
			(0.67)			
Policy			0.013			
			(0.86)			
Distance to nearest seaport					−0.013	−0.017
					(0.59)	(0.80)
Observations	100	100	100	68	68	68
Adjusted R-squared	0.537	0.544	0.532	0.532	0.528	0.527
1995–2005						
Initial per capita GDP	0.031	0.035	0.035	0.037	0.030	0.028
	(2.67)**	(2.45)**	(1.86)*	(2.10)**	(1.24)	(1.30)
Resource intensity	0.003	−0.001	0.001	−0.001	−0.002	
	(0.31)	(0.07)	(0.09)	(0.08)	(0.13)	
Change in terms of trade	0.210	0.236	0.208	0.286	0.280	
	(1.34)	(1.36)	(1.16)	(1.38)	(1.28)	
Coastal dummy		−0.019				
		−0.64				
Pop ≤ 100 km from coast			0.008			
			−0.13			
Policy			−0.019			
			−0.77			
Distance to nearest seaport					−0.02	−0.022
					−0.53	−0.64
Observations	50	50	50	34	34	34
Adjusted R-squared	0.275	0.264	0.253	0.198	0.183	0.200

Note: Robust *t* statistics in parentheses; * significant at 10%; ** significant at 5%; *** significant at 1%. The year dummies, which are not reported here, are jointly significant in all the specifications.

included, the coefficient for the resource intensity variable is nonsignificant for both the whole period and the post-price liberalization period. In China, most natural resources are concentrated in the inland regions. As a result, the resource variable is highly associated with the coastal dummy, geographic, and policy variables mentioned above.[11] The resultant multicollinearity problem poses a challenge to empirically disentangle the impact of resource abundance.

Considering that the geographic and policy variables vary to only a small degree in the inland region, in the next three regressions we use only the inland sample to take advantage of the fact that variations in the geographic and policy variables will not obscure regional variations of the resource variable within the inland region. In so doing, we can separate the geographic and policy effects from the resource effect to a large degree. As indicated in the results obtained using only the inland region sample for the whole period (specification R4, upper panel, Table 7.3), the terms of trade variable appears to have a significant positive impact on GDP growth. When the distance to the nearest seaport is included (specification R5), the significance of this association between the terms of trade variable and GDP growth drops slightly. For the period of 1995–2005 (lower panel, Table 7.3), however, the coefficients for the terms of trade variable in R4 and R5 are not significant.

To control for the possibility that the high correlation between the resource intensity and distance variables may mask the inference precisions in the last regression, we replace the resource variable with the distance variable. When this is done, the coefficient for the distance to the nearest seaport variable is insignificant in both specifications. Overall, the initial per capita GDP has a positive coefficient in all the specifications when the resource variable is included, indicating a divergence in regional growth in both 1985–2005 and 1995–2005. However, the results showing a negative impact of resource intensity on GDP growth are not robust to variations in the specifications and the sample period considered.

It has been argued that GDP growth is an imperfect welfare indicator (Bulte, Damania, and Deacon, 2005). In Tables 7.4 and 7.5, we examine the impact of resource abundance on per capita consumption growth and per capita rural consumption growth following a parallel specification, as in Table 7.3. For the whole period, the resource abundance variable is significant in specifications R1, R2, and R4, and marginally significant in R5. For the sub-period of 1995–2005, this variable is significantly negative in R1 and R4.

For the whole sample, when both the geography and policy variables are included, the coefficient for the resource variable becomes insignificant due to the inherent multicollinearity among the three variables. When the regression is run on only the inland sample, the magnitude of the negative coefficient is larger than when the whole sample is used. To check if the negative impact of resource abundance on consumption growth is due to the inclusion of the geographic variable in the last equation, we repeat the calculation without the resource intensity variable. The sign and significance level of the coefficient for the geography variable remain largely the same (specifications R5 and R6).

Because most natural resources are produced in remote rural areas, it is interesting to investigate the impact of natural resources on growth in consumption by rural residents. Table 7.5 lists the results obtained when the same calculations were applied to the growth of per capita rural consumption. The negative coefficient for the resource abundance variable is statistically

Table 7.4 Per capita consumption growth and resource abundance

	R1	R2	R3	R4	R5	R6
1985–2005						
Initial per capita	−0.013	−0.04	−0.043	−0.064	−0.059	−0.037
consumption	(0.28)	(0.78)	(0.79)	(0.81)	(0.76)	(0.48)
Resource intensity	−0.028	−0.019	−0.01	−0.031	−0.029	
	(3.11)***	(1.79)*	(0.60)	(1.82)*	(1.65)	
Change in terms of	0.183	0.164	0.149	0.21	0.197	
trade	(2.07)**	(1.78)*	(1.67)*	(1.73)*	(1.62)	
Coastal dummy		0.05				
		(1.55)				
Pop ≤ 100 km from			0.075			
coast			(1.50)			
Policy			0.015			
			(0.68)			
Distance to nearest					−0.023	−0.034
seaport					(0.79)	(1.24)
Observations	100	100	100	68	68	68
Adjusted R-squared	0.385	0.392	0.396	0.276	0.272	0.235
1995–2005						
Initial per capita	0.027	0.005	−0.036	0.045	0.041	0.053
consumption	(0.55)	(0.09)	(0.57)	(0.65)	(0.61)	(0.72)
Resource intensity	−0.022	−0.017	0.001	−0.032	−0.027	
	(2.27)**	(1.36)	(0.07)	(1.81)*	(1.45)	
Change in terms of	0.663	0.619	0.574	0.816	0.784	
trade	(2.73)***	(2.52)**	(2.60)**	(3.01)***	(2.83)***	
Coastal dummy		0.034				
		(0.93)				
Pop ≤ 100 km from			0.117			
coast			(2.41)**			
Policy			0.024			
			−0.79			
Distance to nearest					−0.045	−0.051
seaport					(2.07)**	(2.51)**
Observations	50	50	50	34	34	34
Adjusted R-squared	0.347	0.344	0.411	0.360	0.400	0.253

Note: Robust *t* statistics in parentheses; * significant at 10%; ** significant at 5%; *** significant at 1%. The year dummies, which are not reported here, are jointly significant in all the specifications.

significant in all the specifications in which it is present, except for R3. A resource boom in rural areas does not necessarily trickle down to the local population and lead to consumption growth. In fact, having abundant resources may be more of a curse than a blessing for rural residents. Comparison of the coefficient for the resource intensity variable in specification R4 in Tables 7.4 and 7.5 shows that the negative impact of resource abundance on consumption growth is greater for rural areas than for China as a whole. This finding suggests that rural residents benefit less from positive

Table 7.5 Per capita rural consumption growth and resource abundance

	R1	R2	R3	R4	R5	R6
1985–2005						
Initial per capita rural consumption	−0.09	−0.131	−0.154	−0.19	−0.186	−0.127
	(1.54)	(2.23)**	(2.87)***	(2.03)**	(2.02)**	(1.53)
Resource intensity	−0.036	−0.027	−0.02	−0.038	−0.038	
	(3.25)***	(2.09)**	(1.15)	(1.88)*	(1.84)*	
Change in terms of trade	0.143	0.119	0.104	0.126	0.13	
	(1.63)	(1.30)	(1.17)	(1.02)	(1.03)	
Coastal dummy		0.064				
		(1.88)*				
Pop ≤ 100 km from coast			0.081			
			(1.43)			
Policy			0.022			
			(1.00)			
Distance to nearest seaport					0.008	0.001
					(0.25)	(0.03)
Observations	100	100	100	68	68	68
Adjusted R-squared	0.249	0.264	0.26	0.151	0.138	0.114
1995–2005						
Initial per capita rural consumption	−0.066	−0.121	−0.238	−0.109	−0.112	−0.037
	(1.24)	(2.10)**	(3.61)***	(1.20)	(1.22)	(0.37)
Resource intensity	−0.039	−0.030	−0.020	−0.047	−0.046	
	(3.33)***	(2.39)**	(1.44)	(2.29)**	(2.25)**	
Change in terms of trade	0.769	0.683	0.728	0.761	0.758	
	(2.88)***	(2.72)***	(3.36)***	(2.54)**	(2.50)**	
Coastal dummy		0.080				
		(2.07)**				
Pop ≤ 100 km from coast			0.159			
			(2.85)***			
Policy			0.065			
			(2.00)*			
Distance to nearest seaport					−0.006	−0.01
					(0.21)	(0.39)
Observations	50	50	50	34	34	34
Adjusted R-squared	0.228	0.274	0.360	0.228	0.201	0.080

Note: Robust *t* statistics in parentheses; * significant at 10%; ** significant at 5%; *** significant at 1%. The year dummies, which are not reported here, are jointly significant in all the specifications.

resource shocks than their urban counterparts, even though they are physic-ally closer to the point of production.

The estimation results in Tables 7.3–7.5 indicate that the negative impact of resource abundance is more closely related to per capita consumption growth, in particular rural per capita consumption growth, than to per capita GDP growth. The standard of living of rural residents in resource-rich regions does not grow in tandem with the level of natural resource wealth.

7.3 The channels of the resource curse

At least six transmission channels contributing to the resource curse have been put forward (Ross, 1999; Stevens, 2003), namely a long-term decline in terms of trade, revenue volatility, the Dutch disease, weak linkage with other sectors of the economy, rent-seeking behavior, and institutional quality. For a country relying on natural resources as a primary revenue source, a prolonged drop in real prices directly affects economic development. In the period of 1985–2005, the terms of trade in China favored the resource sector, as shown in Figure 7.1. Thus, worsening terms of trade can be excluded as a contributing factor. Because natural resource prices were fairly stable during this period, we also exclude revenue volatility as an explanation for the observed curse of natural resources on consumption growth.

The last two of the six channels relate to institutions. The institution school (Bulte, Damania, and Deacon, 2005; Mehlum, Moene, and Torvik, 2006) posits that institutional arrangements regarding the distribution of resource rents have the greatest effect on welfare outcomes. The above studies use indicators of the rule of law and government competitiveness as measures of institutional quality. In China, the *de jure* institutional and governance structures are highly homogeneous and there are no systematic indicators on government competitiveness (Zhang, 2006). As a consequence, we cannot directly use the method in the literature to directly test whether institutional arrangements in China contribute significantly to the resource curse. Instead, we look in-depth at the institutional arrangements in regard to the distribution of resource rents and examine how such arrangements may affect the outcome variable.

According to the Chinese constitution, all natural resources beneath the ground belong to the state.[12] In the decades between the establishment of the People's Republic of China in 1949 and the enactment of the Natural Resource Law in 1986, SOEs did not provide any compensation to local people for mining natural resources because both the enterprises and resources were owned by the state. The state sector enjoyed exclusive property rights on mining. Following the market reforms since the 1970s, the demand for natural resources went up dramatically. The monopoly mining rights granted to SOEs inhibited the development of this sector. It became imperative to reform the property rights arrangement, allow more private and foreign investment, and increase the supply of natural resources. Although the Mineral Resource Law was passed in 1986, it was not put into full practice until 1994 when the Implementation Regulations on the Mineral Resource Law were introduced.[13] Overall, from 1949 to 1994, SOEs were the dominant players in the mining sector and the accrued rents did not necessarily improve local welfare.

Under the new regulations, local governments were allowed to auction the development rights of mineral resources to the private sector, including multinational companies. Local governments were also permitted to explore and develop mineral resources. However, under the new regulations, SOEs still enjoyed preferential treatment in developing large mineral reserves. Collective enterprises and private investors were able to explore and develop small-scale reserves left over by the state sector. The Ministry of Land and Natural Resources grants permits for the exploration and mining of large-scale reserves, while provincial and county-level governments are responsible for issuing permits for medium- and small-scale reserves falling within their jurisdictions.

During the late 1980s and early 1990s, China began a fiscal decentralization process (Zhang, 2006). Under the new fiscal arrangements that emerged from this process, local governments have a strong incentive to generate more revenue. Faced with limited and mobile capital, local governments compete vigorously to attract new investment (Cai and Tresman, 2005). In areas with natural resources, selling exploration and mining rights is a quick way to create revenues. As a result, many small-scale mines have been privatized since 1994. However, the process of privatizing natural resources lacks transparency. In the absence of elections and the associated checks and balances, the interests of government officials may not be aligned with the interests of local residents.

When conflicts arise between developers and local residents, the Natural Resource Law stipulates that mediation and resolution are the responsibility of local courts. However, local courts are not independent of local governments, leaving open the possibility of collusion between local courts, local governments and investors. Such collusion allows local governments to meet their objective of generating quick revenues, but may result in the unfair allocation of resource rents. When the price of a natural resource increases, the ambiguous property rights on natural resources may encourage rent-seeking behavior, to the detriment of rural residents, who usually do not have direct voices in the process. Although it is impossible to directly test the impact of institutional quality, useful indirect information on the importance of institutional arrangements governing resource rents can be gleaned by examining the investment and consumption patterns of governments and individuals associated with resource abundance. Given the framework within which resources are governed in China, we test the following two hypotheses:

- *Hypothesis I: The share of investment by the state sector in total investment is positively related to the abundance of natural resources.*
- *Hypothesis II: The ratio of government consumption to private consumption is larger in resource-rich regions.*

To test the first hypothesis, the first regression presented in Table 7.6 examines the change in the ratio of private capital to SOE capital. As shown by the negative coefficient, the ratio of private capital to SOE capital grows more slowly in resource-abundant regions than in resource-poor regions. This result supports the first hypothesis that, in resource-rich regions, most investment is made by the state sector. Because investment data with a

Table 7.6 Channels of the resource curse

	Non-SOE/SOE fixed investment	Industrial GDP/GDP	Government/household consumption	Schooling	Price level
Initial value	-0.74	-0.383	0.587	-0.104	-0.029
	(7.65)***	(4.06)***	(7.43)***	(2.99)***	(0.31)
Resource intensity	-0.236	0.019	0.057	-0.001	0.028
	(3.37)***	(1.54)	(2.54)**	(0.36)	(2.06)**
Change in terms of trade	-0.384	-0.025	-0.194	-0.003	0.042
	(1.26)	(0.34)	(1.79)*	(0.10)	(0.71)
Observations	45	68	68	68	68
Adjusted R-squared	0.740	0.598	0.631	0.768	0.859

Note: Robust t statistics in parentheses; * significant at 10%; ** significant at 5%; *** significant at 1%. Because the breakdown of fixed investment by ownership was not published after 1995, the first regression is limited up to 1995. To obtain one more panel from 1980 to 1985 for the first regression, we assume the total resource output by province in 1985 is the same as that in 1980.

breakdown by ownership is only available up to 1994/1995, we cannot further examine the change in the composition of private and public capital since the passing of the Implementation Regulations on Natural Resource Law in 1994.

Hirschman (1958) argued that the root cause of slower growth in resource-rich economies is a weak linkage between resource enclaves and the rest of the economy. To test this hypothesis, ideally we should examine the connection between resource abundance and growth of the manufacturing sector. However, no systematic data is available for the manufacturing sector in China. Here we use the ratio of industrial GDP to overall GDP as a proxy measure of manufacturing development. However, this approach has the problem that the industrial GDP includes not only the manufacturing sector, but also the construction and transportation sectors. A resource boom may hurt the manufacturing sector, yet benefit the local construction and transportation sectors. As shown in Table 7.6, the linkage between resource abundance and industrial sector growth is not significant. Because of the problem inherent in this proxy variable, our results on the linkage between resource abundance and negative manufacturing growth are only suggestive. Future studies with better manufacturing data are called for.

Based on comparative advantage, it is natural for lagging regions to focus on the resource sector. Provided rents are fairly distributed among local residents, governments, and business, the favorable terms of trade in the resource sector should have a trickle-down effect on household consumption. However, the estimation results in Tables 7.3 and 7.4 suggest otherwise. The question then arises: to where have the rents from the booming resource sector flowed?

Under the current rule of resource rent allocation, the state sector should distribute rents fairly among local residents. However, if there is rent seeking behavior or if the distribution channels are blocked, local residents may receive a smaller share of the rising resource rents they are entitled to.

In testing the above proposition, we examine the change in the ratio of government to household consumption in the GDP account by expenditure. The positive coefficient for the resource variable suggests that the government benefits more from the natural resource windfall than do local residents. The results thus offer support to hypothesis II.

In the literature, the most commonly discussed channel of the resource curse is the Dutch disease. The Dutch disease model postulates that a resource boom will cause a country's exchange rate to appreciate, which will make exports more expensive in the international market. The increase in the price of exports will, in turn, inhibit the country's growth. In essence, the Dutch disease hypothesis refers to the crowding-out effect on the tradable sector in terms of higher prices. Since there is only one form of currency in China, the transmission channel of price impact of natural resources is not through the standard exchange rate, as occurs in cross-country cases. However, there is still a potential price effect. As argued by Sachs and Warner (1999), positive shocks from natural resources tend to increase demand for non-traded goods, leading to higher overall local prices. This will in turn increase the cost of living and hurt the competitiveness of local businesses that produce tradable goods.

Empirical evidence on the Dutch disease hypothesis based on cross-country data is inconclusive (Auty, 2001). An interesting feature of using provincial data within a country to test the hypothesis is that we do not need to deal with the complications arising from foreign exchange rate regimes. Because China does not publish the non-traded price index at the provincial level, we cannot directly test the impact of resource abundance on the price level of non-tradable goods. However, if we assume that the price level for tradable goods is similar across regions, then a higher non-traded price will be reflected in the general price index. In support of this assumption, transportation improvements and market reform have caused China's domestic market to become increasingly integrated and prices to converge (Bai et al., 2004; Wei and Fan, 2004; Zhang and Tan, 2007). Therefore, the above assumption on the law of one price in the tradable sector appears to be reasonable.

One potential link between resource abundance and negative economic performance is education, as shown in Papyrakis and Gerlagh (2007). Unlike the manufacturing sector, expansion of the resource sector usually does not require a highly skilled labor force, likely leading to underinvestment in human capital. In the next regression, we use the average years of schooling as an outcome variable.[14] The coefficient for the resource intensity variable is negative but nonsignificant. This may reflect the fact that the Chinese government has played a strong role in promoting basic education, in particular in the planned economic era. In addition, there is a long lag time in investment in human capital. Thus, any effects of underinvestment in human capital due to resource abundance may take decades to manifest.

In the last column of Table 7.6, we regress the change in general retail price level on the historical resource endowment conditional upon the initial price level, akin to specification R4 in Tables 7.3–7.5.[15] To remove regional effects, the sample includes only the inland provinces. The results show that areas with more intensive resource exploitation tend to exhibit a more rapid price hike, suggesting the non-traded price in resource intensive regions must have risen faster to offset the decline in the real price of tradable goods incurred through lower transportation costs and a more integrated market.[16] The above-normal price levels in resource-abundant regions may cause businesses in these regions to become less competitive in both the domestic and international markets. In other words, the natural resource sector may crowd out other tradable sectors through the price effect. This finding is consistent with those of Sachs and Warner (2001), and provides evidence that the Dutch disease may occur even within a country.

7.4 Conclusions

Despite increasing market integration and better transport infrastructure, regional inequality has risen significantly in China since economic reforms were initiated. This paper offers an explanation for the observed increase in regional inequality from the perspective of natural resource endowments and the mechanism governing rent allocations. China's booming economy bids up demand for natural resources. In China, natural resources nominally belong to the state, and farmers have no right to a share of the rent. Consequently their welfare has little to do with the booming resource sector. In resource-rich regions, most resource rents go to the government and SOEs, crowding out private capital accumulation. Greater revenues from a positive resource stock tend to boost government consumption more than household consumption. In short, the root of the problem lies in the rules governing resource rent allocations.

Another contribution of this paper is that it performs empirical testing of the resource curse hypothesis within a country. In contrast to the present work, the majority of the large body of empirical literature on the resource curse hypothesis uses cross-country data. The identification problem inherent in a cross-sectional data set makes it a daunting task to empirically test the resource curse hypothesis. Using panel data at the provincial level in China and estimating the sample only for inland regions, this paper distinguishes geographic effects from resource effects, thereby revealing the existence of a resource curse in terms of per capita consumption growth. The present results provide only weak support for a direct link between resources and GDP growth. Our findings indicate that, to a large extent, growth dividends do not trickle down to rural residents in resource-abundant regions. Since many of the poor live in regions rich in natural resources, the existence of a resource curse may help explain the recent widening regional inequality and stagnant poverty prevalent in resource-rich regions, in particular western China.

The negative linkage between natural resource abundance and consumption growth suggests that the institutional roots of rural poverty may be deeper than previously thought. To eliminate poverty and reduce inequality in rural areas, it is critical to reform the property rights arrangements regarding natural resources. In the absence of such reform, it will be difficult to increase the income of the poor and to reduce the income gap by relying primarily on fiscal transfers.

Even in the absence of the foreign exchange rate effect that forms the basis of the traditional Dutch disease hypothesis, a resource curse can still occur through the channel of non-traded price. Resource booms tend to boost non-traded prices and raise the cost of living in resource-rich regions. This hurts the competitiveness of manufacturing sectors.

With globalization, both factor and product markets become more integrated worldwide. The rise of emerging economies such as China and India means that demand for natural resources will likely continue to increase in the near future. Given that resource exports are the major revenue source of many severely indebted poor countries, it is important to understand the sources of the resource curse and turn resources into a blessing for all. Insights from

Chinese provinces may assist in resolving similar problems affecting other poor but resource-rich countries.

Appendix

Consumption   The per capita consumption data (at the provincial level) from 1952 to 1998 come from *Comprehensive Statistical Data and Materials on 50 Years of New China* (CNBS 1999), while consumption data for later years are from various issues of the *China Statistical Yearbook*. The consumption expenditures are comparable across years. For details on the construction of the data series, see Kanbur and Zhang (2005, Data Appendix).

GDP   The real GDP growth rates, nominal GDP, household consumption, and government consumption prior to 1996 come from *Data of Gross Domestic Product of China: 1952–1995* (CNBS) while the data for the period 1996–2002 are from *Data of Gross Domestic Product of China: 1996–2002* (CNBS). Data for the later years are from *China Statistical Yearbook*. Using the GDP in 1985 as a base, we calculate the real GDP for the whole period using the comparable GDP growth rates.

Geography and policy variables   The share of population within 100 kilometers of coastline and the policy variables are obtained from Démurger et al. (2001). The distance to the nearest seaport variable is from Bao et al. (2002).

Population   Population data were used as weights in the calculation of the inequality measures. Data on total and rural population for 1985–1998 come from *Comprehensive Agricultural Statistical Data and Materials on 50 Years of New China* (CNBS 1999), and those for 1999 onwards come from *China Statistical Yearbook* and *China Agricultural Statistical Yearbook* (CNBS 1999–2005).

Rural poverty   The rural poverty data are from Ravallion and Chen (2007).

Resources   The data for coal, hydroelectric power, oil, and natural gas are from various issues of the *China Energy Statistical Yearbook* (CNBS, various). They are converted into standard coal using the technical conversion coefficient provided at the end of the yearbook.

Terms of trade   The terms of trade for the resource sector are defined as the ratio of fuel price index to the overall consumer price index. The general consumer price index for 1985–1998 is from *Comprehensive Statistical Data and Materials on 50 Years of New China* (CNBS 1999) and for 1999 onwards is from the *China Statistical Yearbook*. The fuel price index is from various issues of the *China Statistical Yearbook*. Because the fuel price index is not available at the provincial level prior to 1985, we use the national fuel price index as a proxy for each province. Considering that the fuel prices were largely under control of the planned economy in the early 1980s, the use of a national-level price index should have minimal impact on the results.

Rural education   We use the percentage of rural population with different education levels to calculate the average years of schooling, assuming 0 years for a person who is illiterate or semi-illiterate, 5 years for primary-school education, 8 years for a junior high-school education, 12 years for a high-school education, 13 years for a professional school education, and 16 years for a college education. The data are from population censuses and *China Rural Statistical Yearbook*.

Notes

1 The authors acknowledge funding support provided by the Natural Science Foundation of China (Approval number 70525003). The authors also thank staff and students from the International Center for Agricultural and Rural Development (ICARD) for their help in inputting data. The authors are grateful for the comments from Regina Birner, Erwin Bulte, Xinshen Diao, Nico Heerink, Samuel Morley, Li-An Zhou, and participants of the Chinese Economists Society annual meetings at Changsha and of seminars held at the International Food Policy Research Institute, Wageningen University, and Zhejiang University.
2 Xu and Wang (2006) is one of the few Chinese papers we have found on this topic.
3 In spirit, the paper echoes the work of Papyrakis and Gerlagh (2007), who examine resource abundance and regional economic growth by making use of state level data in the United States.
4 Ideally, we should use resource stocks as a measure of resource abundance. However, systematic stock data at the provincial level are not available for the resource variables used in this paper.
5 The vertical axis label in Fig.7.4 is only for 1988–1999 as opposed to the other 1985–2005 data in Figs. 7.2 and 7.3.
6 This review is largely drawn from Chen and Zeng (1997) and Zhang (2000).
7 China did not publish energy production data by province until 1985. The rural poverty data at the provincial level provided by Ravallion and Chen (2007) are only available from 1988 to 1999.
8 Due to a lack of data, Tibet, Hainan, and Chongqing are not included. In addition, the three principal cities, Beijing, Shanghai, and Tianjing, are excluded from our analysis on account of their special status and negligible natural resource base. The main results remain the same if these areas are included.
9 Sachs and Warner (2001) argue that the share of resource production in GDP is a better measure than per capita resource production as it captures the importance of natural resources in the economy. Nonetheless, to test the robustness of our results, we also perform all the regressions in Tables 7.2–7.5 using alternative measures of resource intensity, including per capita resource production in 1985, per capita resource production in the initial year of each panel period, and the ratio of resource production to GDP in 1985. The basic findings are the same. The detailed regressions are available upon request.
10 We also use the ratio of the fuel price index to the GDP deflator at the provincial level as an alterative measure. The results are similar.

11 Its correlation coefficients with the coastal dummy, share of population within 100 km from coast, and policy variables are –0.46, –0.50, and –0.63, respectively.
12 A good reference on the evolution of natural resource property rights is Zhang (2000).
13 The regulations are available at www.mlr.gov.cn/pub/mlr/documents/ t20041125_74922.htm.
14 We also use illiteracy rate as an outcome variable. The results are similar.
15 The finding still holds even after controlling for per capita consumption.
16 There are numerous news reports in Chinese on rocketing real estate prices in coal mining towns (e.g., www.people.com.cn/GB/news/37454/37461/2992927.html).

References

Auty, R. (2001) *Resource Abundance and Economic Development*. Oxford: Oxford University Press.
Bai, C., Y. Duan, Z. Tao, and S. Tong (2004) Local Protectionism and Regional Specialization: Evidence from China's Industries. *Journal of International Economics*, 63(2): 397–417.
Bao, S., G. Chang, J. Sachs, and W. Thye Woo (2002) Geographic Factors and China's Regional Development under Market Reforms, 1978–98. *China Economic Review*, 13: 89–111.
Bulte, E., R. Damania, and R. Deacon (2005) Resource Intensity, Institutions, and Development. *World Development*, 33 (7): 102–91044.
Cai, H., and D. Tresman (2005) Does Competition for Capital Discipline Governments? Decentralization, Globalization, and Public Policy. *American Economic Review*, 95 (3): 817–830.
Chen, Y., and X. Zeng (1997) An Overview and Output on China's Energy Price Reform (Zhongguo Nengyuan Jiage Gange Huigu yu Zhanwang). *Coal Research (Meitan Jingji Yanjiu)*, 6: 5–9. [in Chinese]
China National Bureau of Statistics (CNBS), various years. *China Energy Statistical Yearbook*. Beijing: China Statistics Press.
China National Bureau of Statistics (CNBS), various years. *China Rural Statistical Yearbook*. Beijing: China Statistics Press.
China National Bureau of Statistics (CNBS), various years. *China Statistical Yearbook*. Beijing: China Statistics Press.
China National Bureau of Statistics (CNBS 1997), The *Gross Domestic Product of China: 1952–1995*. Dalian: Dongbei University of Finance and Economics Press.
China National Bureau of Statistics (CNBS 1999), *Comprehensive Statistical Data and Materials on 50 Years of New China*. Beijing: China Statistics Press.
China National Bureau of Statistics (CNBS 2004), *Data of Gross Domestic Product of China: 1996–2002*. Beijing: China Statistics Press.
Démurger, S., J. Sachs, W. Thye Woo, and S. Bao (2002) Geography, Economic Policy, and Regional Development in China. *Asian Economic Papers*, 1 (1): 146–197.
Fan, S., and C. Chan-Kang (2005) *Road Development, Economic Growth, and Poverty Reduction in China*. International Food Policy Research (IFPRI) Report No. 138. Washington: IFPRI.
Fan, S., L. Zhang, and X. Zhang (2004) Reform, Investment and Poverty in Rural China. *Economic Development and Cultural Change*, 52 (2): 395–422.
Hirschman, A. (1958) *The Strategy of Economic Development*, New Heaven CT: Yale University Press.

Hu, D. (2002) Trade, Rural-Urban Migration, and Regional Income Disparity in Developing Countries: A Spatial General Equilibrium Model Inspired by the Case of China. *Regional Science and Urban Economics*, 32: 311–338.

Kanbur, R., and X. Zhang (1999) Which Regional Inequality: Rural–Urban or Coast–Inland? An Application to China. *Journal of Comparative Economics*, 27: 686–701.

Kanbur, R., and X. Zhang (2005) Fifty Years of Regional Inequality in China: A Journey Through Central Planning, Reform and Openness. *Review of Development Economics*, 9(1): 87–106.

Mehlum, H., K. Moene, and R. Torvik (2006) Institutions and Resource Curse. *Economic Journal*, 116: 1–20.

Papyrakis, E., and R. Gerlagh (2007) Resource Abundance and Economic Growth in the United States. *European Economic Review*, 51 (4): 1011–1039.

Ravallion, M., and S. Chen (2007) China's (Uneven) Progress against Poverty. *Journal of Development Economics*, 82 (1): 1–42.

Ross, M. (1999) The Political Economy of the Resource Curse. *World Politics*, 51 (2): 297–322.

Sachs, J., and A. Warner (1999) The Big Push, Natural Resource Booms and Growth. *Journal of Development Economics*, 59: 43–76.

Sachs, J., and A. Warner (2001) Natural Resources and Economic Development: The Curse of Natural Resources. *European Economics Review*, 45: 827–838.

Stevens, P. (2003) Resource Impact: Curse or Blessing: A Literature Survey. *Journal of Energy Literature*, 9 (1): 1–42.

Wei, X., and C. Simon Fan (2004) *Converge to the Law of One Price in China*, paper presented the Allied Social Sciences annual meetings at San Diego, January 3–5.

Xu, K., and J. Wang (2006) An Empirical Study of a Linkage Between Natural Resource Abundance and Economic Development. (Ziran Ziyuan Fengyu Chengdu yu Jingji Fazhang Shuiping de Guanxi), *Economic Research (Jingji Yanjiu)*, 1: 78–89. (in Chinese).

Zhang, W. (2000) Evolution and Development Orientation of Property Rights System of Mineral Resources in China (Woguo Kuangchan Ziyuan Caichan Quanli Zhidu de Yanhua he Fazhang Fangxiang). *China Geology and Mining Economics (Zhongguo Dizhi Kuangchan Jingji)*, 1: 1–10.

Zhang, X. (2006) Fiscal Decentralization and Political Centralization in China: Implications for Growth and Regional Inequality. *Journal of Comparative Economics*, 34 (4): 713–726.

Zhang, X., and K. Yam Tan (2007) Incremental Reform and Distortions in China's Product and Factor Markets. *World Bank Economic Review*, 21(2): 279–299.

Zhang, X. and Zhang, K. (2003). How does FDI affect regional inequality within a developing country? Evidence from China, *Journal of Development Studies*, 39(4): 47–67.

8 How does globalization affect regional inequality within a developing country?

Evidence from China

Xiaobo Zhang and Kevin H. Zhang

Abstract

Developing countries are increasingly concerned about effects of globalization on regional inequality. This paper develops an empirical method for decomposing the contributions of two major driving forces of globalization, foreign trade, and foreign direct investment (FDI), on regional inequality and applies it to China. Even after controlling for many other factors, globalization is still found to be an important factor contributing to the widening regional inequality. The paper ends by investigating the role of factor market segmentations in aggravating the distributional effect of changing regional comparative advantages in the process of globalization.

8.1 Introduction

Globalisation has integrated the product and financial markets of economies around the world through the driving forces of trade and capital flows cross borders. One of the main debates on globalization is the effect of growing economic integration on income distribution. The antiglobalization movement argues that globalization is widening the gap between the haves and the have-nots (Mazur, 2000). The pro-globalization position claims that the current wave of globalization since the 1980s has actually promoted economic equality and reduced poverty (Dollar and Kraay, 2002).

In view of the importance of the subject and the wide divergence in positions, many studies have been conducted to assess the role of globalization in income inequality (Cline, 1997; Lawrence, 1996). However, much of the literature on the relationship between globalization and inequality has focused on developed countries, especially the case of the United States (for example, Feenstra and Hanson 1996; Richardson, 1995; Rodrik, 1997). The number of studies on this issue for developing countries has been relatively small, and existing studies have been limited to the effects of trade liberalization on wage inequality (Wood, 1997; Robbins, 1996; Hanson and Harrison, 1999) and world income inequality (Kaplinsky, 2000). Few studies have shed light on the effect of globalization on regional inequality within a developing country.

Increased trade and capital movements have led to greater specialization in production and the dispersion of specialized production processes to geographically distant locations. Theoretically globalization thus would make a developing country more egalitarian through raising wages of its abundant low-income unskilled labor, because the country has comparative advantage in producing unskilled-labor intensive goods and services (Deardorff and Stern, 1994). However, evidence tells us an opposite story. The average Gini coefficients in the transitional and developing countries rose from about 0.25 to 0.30 in the period from the late 1980s to the mid-1990s, an era of rapid globalization (IMF, 1998). This appears to be a significant increase in such a short period of time, since the Gini coefficients tend to be stable in the short term. Has globalization merely coincided with widening income inequality, or has it contributed to the phenomena?

In this study we attempt to tackle this issue by providing evidence from China. Being the largest trading nation and the largest recipient of FDI in the developing world, China has obviously been a major participant in the process of globalization for the past two decades. It is virtually certain for China to become even more important in the world economy in the future because of its huge size, dynamic economic growth, continuing policy reforms, and especially its recent entry of the World Trade Organization. Perhaps like other developing countries, China's economic integration with the world has been accompanied with growing regional inequality. Especially the income gap between coastal and inland areas, which has risen dramatically since the mid-1980s (Kanbur and Zhang, 1999; Zhang and Kanbur, 2001). Commentators in China have expressed concern about regional inequality and some even warned that further increases in regional disparities might lead to China's dissolution, like the former Yugoslavia (Hu, 1996).

Regional inequality might be a result of many factors such as geographic and institutional barriers in product and factor markets, and possibly globalization. Many studies have examined the factors behind China's widening regional gap, such as factor productivity, institutional bias, and development strategies (for example, Tsui, 1991; Jian, Sachs, and Warner, 1996; Fleisher and Chen, 1997; and Kanbur and Zhang, 1999). Yet there have been few studies investigating the effect of globalization on regional inequality. This study thus aims to close the gap by assessing to what extent globalization may affect regional inequality in China and to suggest appropriate policies to help the lagging inland provinces catch up with more prosperous coastal areas. In particular, special attention will be paid to the role of foreign trade and inward FDI in China's widening regional inequality. We extend Shorrocks' decomposition method (Shorrocks, 1982) to evaluate the effects of globalization and other factors on the rising regional inequality. The empirical results suggest that foreign trade and inward FDI indeed have contributed significantly to China's regional inequality.

The rest of the paper is organized as follows. Section 8.2 describes recent trends of foreign trade, FDI, income growth, and regional inequality over the past two decades. A conceptual framework and empirical specifications are developed in Section 8.3. Section 8.4 presents our estimates of the production functions needed to decompose the sources of regional inequality. Section 8.5 highlights our conclusions and policy implications.

8.2 Foreign trade, FDI, and regional inequality in China

In recent years, few developments in economic globalization have been more important than the sudden emergence of China as a trading nation and a leading FDI recipient (Lardy, 2002). For the two decades since China began to integrate with the world economy in 1978, the role of the globalization in the Chinese economy has burgeoned in ways that no-one anticipated.

China's economic reforms and open-door policy have resulted in a phenomenal growth of trade and FDI inflows. Between 1984 and 1998, the value of exports grew 19 percent annually while manufactured exports grew 24 percent per year. By 1994 China exported manufactured goods worth over $100 billion and was the eighth largest exporter in the world. While China accounted for only 0.75 percent of world exports in 1978, its share rose to nearly four percent in 1998 (IMF, 1999). Changes in FDI flows into China are even more astonishing. From the economy virtually without any foreign investment in the late 1970s, China has become the largest recipient of FDI among the developing countries and globally the second (next only to the US) since 1993. FDI flows into China in 1993–2000 constitute over 30 percent of total FDI in the developing world. By 2000, the total FDI received in China reached as much as $347 billion (UNCTAD, 2001).

Table 8.1 indicates the pattern of globalization, economic growth, and regional inequality in China over the period of 1978–98. The degree of China's integration with the world economy may be captured by the rapid increase in foreign trade and FDI flows. The ratio of trade (the sum of exports and imports) to GDP (usually defined as openness) has increased five-fold, from 0.05 to 0.30, during the period of twenty years. This ratio of 0.30 is quite large for a huge country like China, contrasting the same ratio of 0.12 for the United States.[1] The importance of FDI in Chinese economy may be seen from the rising share of FDI flows in GDP, which was almost zero in 1978 and reached 6.56 percent in 1994, and then fell slightly to 4.43 percent in 1998. China's boom in trade and inward FDI has been accompanied by rapid economic growth. Chinese economy grew at a rate of about ten percent in the two decades, resulting in a more than six-fold increase in real GDP. The role of foreign trade and FDI in Chinese economy has become increasingly important. Many studies have shown that trade and inward FDI have contributed significantly to the outstanding performance of the Chinese economy (for example, Lardy, 1995; Zhang, 1999 and 2001). The trade boom not only directly raises Chinese output through production for exports, but also increases productivity through efficient allocation of resources and technological upgrading. The contributions of inward FDI to Chinese economy

Table 8.1 Trade, FDI, GDP, and regional inequality

Year	Trade/GDP (exchange rate)	Trade/GDP (PPP)	FDI/GDP (%)	Real GDP (1978=100)	Gini (regional)
1978	9.80	5.19	0.00	100.0	0.22
1979	11.26	5.98	0.01	107.6	0.20
1980	12.62	7.08	0.04	116.0	0.20
1981	15.13	8.24	0.07	122.0	0.19
1982	14.55	8.64	0.07	133.3	0.19
1983	14.44	7.26	0.09	148.2	0.19
1984	16.67	6.36	0.22	170.9	0.19
1985	22.99	6.49	0.31	193.5	0.19
1986	25.29	7.23	0.41	209.9	0.19
1987	25.80	6.30	0.45	234.1	0.20
1988	25.61	5.98	0.70	260.5	0.20
1989	24.57	7.11	0.72	271.5	0.20
1990	29.90	7.33	0.85	283.0	0.20
1991	33.36	6.77	1.10	308.8	0.21
1992	34.22	6.67	2.55	352.2	0.22
1993	32.61	7.04	4.54	398.4	0.24
1994	43.67	7.21	6.56	448.7	0.24
1995	40.87	7.82	5.49	489.1	0.23
1996	36.10	8.36	5.08	536.8	0.24
1997	36.87	8.05	5.00	582.9	0.24
1998	34.42	8.59	4.43	628.4	0.26
Growth (%)					
1978–84	3.57	1.47		9.34	−1.04
1985–98	3.86	−0.09	11.80	9.48	0.63
1978–98	3.77	1.09		9.63	0.34

Note: Trade ratio is defined as the ratio of total trade to total GDP. FDI/GDP are in percentages. Real GDP is an index with 1978 as a benchmark. Because total trade volume is usually only reported in US dollars, we use both the official exchange rate and the PPP index to derive the trade ratio. The Gini coefficient is calculated by the authors using labor productivity (GDP/Labor) with total labor force as weights at the provincial level.

Source: Author's computation based on *Comprehensive Statistical Data and Materials on 50 Years of New China* (SSB, 1999) and various issues of *China Statistical Yearbook*.

include increasing capital formation, transferring technology and management know-how, generating employment, and promoting exports. Both trade and FDI have brought extra gains to Chinese economy in facilitating China's transition toward a market-oriented system, which in turn enhanced the income growth. Higher levels of trade and inward FDI in China have stimulated domestic market expansion, contributed to reforms of state-owned enterprises and privatization, and promoted competition (Zhang, 1999).

However, the grains of economic growth have not been evenly distributed across regions. As shown in Table 8.1, the regional Gini coefficient rose significantly from 0.19 in 1985 to 0.26 in 1998. While the rise in the regional inequality may be caused by many factors, foreign trade and inward FDI seem to play a certain role, as suggested by the strong correlation between the three indices in the table. To see more details about the link between globalization and regional inequality, we present the patterns of trade, FDI, and per capita income by province for 1986–98 in Table 8.2. A striking feature from the table is that coastal provinces have generated more trade volume (over 86 percent of total) and attracted far more FDI (over 87 percent) than inland provinces.[2] In 1998, the three coastal provinces, Guangdong, Jiangsu, and Shanghai, rank top three, while the three inland provinces, Guizhou, Inner Mongolia, and Jilin, are bottom three in terms of attracting FDI. The above

Table 8.2 Trade, FDI, and GDP per capita in China by regions: 1986–98

Provinces	Share of value of trade in nation (%)		Share of FDI inflows in nation (%)		GDP per capita (in Chinese yuan)	
	1986–91	1992–98	1986–91	1992–98	1986–91	1992–98
Coastal areas	**85.96**	**88.08**	**91.93**	**87.42**	**1449**	**3055**
Beijing	2.76	2.16	9.04	3.76	3575	5786
Tianjin	2.85	2.70	2.39	4.13	2828	4311
Shanghai	9.61	8.05	9.11	8.95	4595	7865
Liaoning	7.02	4.58	5.40	4.42	1978	3046
Hebei	2.12	1.30	1.09	2.13	968	1746
Shandong	4.64	5.40	3.42	6.37	1165	2248
Jiangsu	5.07	7.08	4.03	12.54	1504	3096
Zhejiang	3.04	4.65	1.66	3.30	1474	3081
Fujian	3.30	6.03	9.47	10.04	1329	2861
Guangdong	44.45	45.00	44.87	29.75	1337	2863
Guangxi	1.11	1.13	1.47	2.04	638	1152
Inland areas	**14.04**	**11.92**	**8.04**	**12.58**	**853**	**1489**
Jilin	1.30	0.94	0.28	0.94	1326	2007
Heilongjiang	1.83	1.44	0.85	1.21	1450	2091
Shanxi	0.65	0.57	0.14	0.36	1046	1568
Inner Mongolia	0.56	0.51	0.06	0.15	1141	1697
Anhui	0.95	0.96	0.26	0.97	831	1330
Jiangxi	0.78	0.65	0.29	0.86	814	1366
Henan	1.22	0.74	1.04	1.30	790	1283
Hubei	1.64	1.29	0.84	1.83	1038	1672
Hunan	1.24	1.21	0.37	1.58	824	1278
Sichuan	1.09	1.02	0.70	1.70	743	1192
Guizhou	0.23	0.24	0.16	0.13	614	843
Yunnan	0.87	0.74	0.16	0.38	718	1177
Shaanxi	0.69	0.71	2.47	0.86	908	1319
Gansu	0.26	0.22	0.10	0.15	926	1346
Qinghai	0.08	0.06	0.00	0.01	1591	1889
Ningxia	0.12	0.10	0.02	0.05	1487	1757
Xinjiang	0.54	0.53	0.30	0.12	1258	1940
Nation	**100.00**	**100.00**	**100.00**	**100.00**	**1098**	**2136**

Note: GDP per capita is expressed in 1986 constant prices.

Source: Calculated from *Comprehensive Statistical Data and Materials on 50 Years of New China* (SSB, 1999) and *China Statistical Yearbooks* (SSB, various years from 1990 to 2000).

three coastal provinces alone contribute to more than 60 percent of the total foreign trade in 1998. The last two columns of the table show GDP per capita by province and region, indicating a widening gap between the two regions (the ratio rises from 1.70 in the 1980s to 2.05 in the 1990s). In fact the coastal provinces enjoyed higher growth rate than inland regions by three percentage points per year in 1978–98.

To further investigate this issue, we calculate the mean ratios of GDP, domestic capital, education levels, FDI, and foreign trade along the coastal and inland areas in Table 8.3. Two features are discernible from these mean ratios. First, there indeed exist significant disparities between the coastal and inland areas. GDP in the coastal region is more than 40 percent higher than that in the inland region in 1998. Both the levels of domestic capital and FDI per unit of labor in the coastal region are much higher than those in the inland region. The average year of schooling in inland areas has been over 25 percent less than that in coastal provinces. The share of trade in total GDP in the coastal region has been at least two times higher than in the inland region. It seems that the higher labor productivity in coastal areas is associated closely with more capital input, better education, and higher degree of integration with the world economy.

Second, the inland–coastal gap has increased significantly throughout the period. The GDP gap between the two regions rose by 29 percent between 1985 and 1998. Domestic capital investment has become increasingly

Table 8.3 Inland–coastal ratios

Year	GDP	Capital	Education	FDI	Trade
1985	1.12	1.20	1.27	13.23	4.68
1986	1.13	1.24	1.26	7.35	3.37
1987	1.15	1.26	1.26	8.69	4.92
1988	1.18	1.30	1.25	7.42	5.19
1989	1.20	1.34	1.26	11.83	5.26
1990	1.16	1.27	1.28	16.04	5.93
1991	1.22	1.35	1.29	16.38	5.50
1992	1.28	1.48	1.33	9.35	4.90
1993	1.36	1.61	1.32	6.81	4.70
1994	1.41	1.64	1.27	7.15	4.91
1995	1.39	1.67	1.24	7.03	4.86
1996	1.38	1.69	1.29	7.36	5.45
1997	1.38	1.56	1.32	6.21	6.14
1998	1.45	1.52	1.35	6.82	5.90
Increase (%)	29	26	6	−48	26

Note: (1) Authors' calculation. GDP, capital formulation (K), and foreign direct investment (FDI) are from various issues of *China Statistical Yearbooks*. The education variable is the literacy rate among population above 15-years old. Trade is defined as the ratio of trade (the sum of import and export) to GDP. (2) The coastal zone includes the following provinces: Beijing, Liaoning, Tianjin, Hebei, Shandong, Jiangsu, Shanghai, Zhejiang, Fujian, Guangdong, and Guangxi. The remaining provinces are classified as the inland zone. Tibet is excluded due to the lack of data. Hainan is included in Guangdong Province.

concentrated in the coastal region with a rise of 26 percent during the period. The difference in economic openness also has increased by 26 percent. The average year of schooling between the two regions has widened by six percent. Most FDI has been concentrated in the coastal areas although the ratio does not indicate a clear trend due to the severe year-to-year fluctuation. It appears that the increased disparity in output levels among regions might have been caused in large part by differences in input levels. The question is: which factors have contributed more to the overall increase in inequality?

It is reasonable to speculate that regional comparative advantages in the context of the globalization might be an important factor behind the changes in regional inequality. Figure 8.1 plots the relationship between regional inequality and trade while Figure 8.2 plots the correlation between FDI and regional inequality. The two figures suggest a positive relationship between openness and FDI and inequality. However, we cannot simply infer causation from these two figures. There are possibly many other factors affecting regional inequality as well during this period. A more systematic framework is needed to quantify the contributions of various components to the overall regional disparity.

8.3 Model specifications

While there is considerable literature on the causes of China's regional inequality (Lyons, 1991; Tsui, 1991; Jian et al., 1996; Fleisher and Chen, 1997; Kanbur and Zhang, 1999; Yang, 1999), few studies have systematically examined the role of globalization in China's growing regional inequality. One constraint to assessing the distributional impact of FDI and other production factors is the lack of a suitable analytical framework to decompose the contributions of production factors, such as FDI, toward regional inequality. In the literature, inequality is decomposed based on either exogenous population groups or income sources (Shorrocks, 1982 and 1984). The distributional effect of production factors cannot be directly analyzed

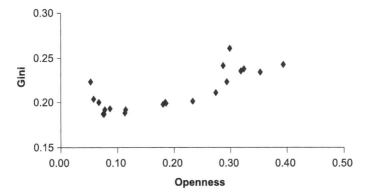

Figure 8.1 Openness and regional inequality.

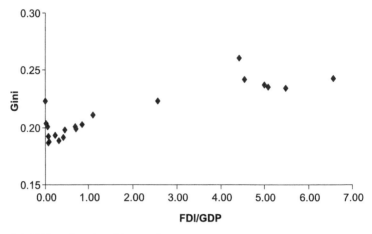

Figure 8.2 FDI and regional inequality.

with these existing frameworks. Moreover, because the returns to FDI have not been documented in the official GDP statistics, it is hard to directly evaluate the impact of FDI on inequality. In this paper, we develop an indirect approach based on Shorrocks' method to quantify the impact of FDI and economic openness on both growth and regional inequality using a panel data set at the provincial level.

We assume that each region has the same production function at a given time but the regions lie at different points on the production surface. That is to assume that the coefficients are the same across provinces. Following standard procedures in the literature, we assume that the aggregate production functions are of Cobb-Douglas form as follows:

$$Y = AL^{\beta_1} K_D^{\beta_2} K_F^{\beta_3} E^{\beta_4} V^{\beta_5} \tag{1}$$

where $Y =$ total GDP,
         $A =$ intercept,
         $L =$ labor input,
         $K_D =$ domestic capital stocks,
         $K_F =$ foreign capital stocks,
         $E =$ education,
         $V =$ trade-to-GDP ratio,
         $\beta_1 =$ parameters to be estimated.

In equation (1), labor (L) and capital (both K_D and K_F) are traditional inputs in production, and education (E) as an input is suggested by the new growth theory to capture the growth impact of human capital (Barro and Sala-i-Martin, 1995). Domestic and foreign capital is treated separately not only to capture their individual effects but also because of the view that growth effects of foreign capital (K_F) may not be identical to those of domestic capital. Inward FDI may foster economic growth in a host country through transferring technology and expanding exports, in addition to contribution to capital formation and employment (Borenstein, De Gregorio, and Lee, 1998; Caves, 1996; Ram and Zhang, 2002). There are several ways in which one can rationalize the notion that the openness, defined as the trade-to-GDP ratio (V), may be treated as a production input in the sense that the level of openness affects aggregate output for given levels of other inputs. It has been widely recognized that a high level of openness leads to a better allocation of resources in terms of concepts of comparative advantages and specialization (Krueger, 1980; Ram, 1987 and 1990; World Bank, 1993). Trade liberalization in a developing country may also facilitate exploitation of scale economies due to an enlargement of effective market size; afford greater capacity utilization; and induce more rapid technological changes (Bliss, 1988; Edwards, 1993; Feder, 1983; Pack, 1988).[3]

Since each region varies by size, it does not make sense to calculate regional inequality using total GDP. Therefore, we use labor productivity to compare the regional difference. Both output and conventional inputs (excluding education and trade) in (1) are divided by the number of laborers L, to yield:

$$\frac{Y}{L} = AL^{\delta-1}\left(\frac{L}{L}\right)^{\beta_1}\left(\frac{K_D}{L}\right)^{\beta_2}\left(\frac{K_F}{L}\right)^{\beta_3} E^{\beta_4} V^{\beta_5}, \tag{2}$$

where $\delta = \sum_{i=1}^{3}\beta_i$. Notably, labor still appears on the right-hand side of equation (2) unless constant returns to scale is imposed on the production function so that $\delta = 1$. As the standard practice in the literature, we assume constant returns to scale.[4] The logarithmic form of equation (2) thus is given by:

$$y = a + \beta_2 k_D + \beta_3 k_F + \beta_4 e + \beta_5 v + \varepsilon, \tag{3}$$

where lower cases indicate logarithms. An error term ε is added to represent the stochastic shocks to output and is assumed to be unrelated to the other variables.

Following Shorrocks (1982), the variance of y in equation (3) can be decomposed as:

$$\sigma^2(y) = \text{cov}(y, \beta_2 k_D) + \text{cov}(y, \beta_3 k_F) + \text{cov}(y, \beta_4 e) + \text{cov}(y, \beta_5 v)$$
$$+ \text{cov}(y, \varepsilon) = \beta_2 \text{cov}(y, k_D) + \beta_3 \text{cov}(y, k_F) + \beta_4 \text{cov}(y, e)$$
$$+ \beta_5 \text{cov}(y, v) + \sigma^2(\varepsilon), \tag{4}$$

where $\sigma^2(y)$ is the variance of y and $\text{cov}(y, \cdot)$ represents the covariance of y with other variables. Since the right-hand side variables in equation (3) are not correlated with the error term, the covariance of y and ε is equal to the variance of ε. Considering that y is already in the logarithmic form, $\sigma^2(y)$ is a standard inequality measure known as the logarithmic variance (Cowell, 1995). It has the property of invariance to scale. According to Shorrocks (1982), the covariance terms on the right hand side of (4) can be regarded as the contributions of the factor components to total inequality.

The equations (3) and (4) constitute the basis for our panel analysis of the impact of globalization on regional inequality. In particular, we first estimate the labor productivity function specified in (3), and then decompose the inequality into the components of production factors following (4).

8.4 Data and empirical results

A panel data set including 28 provinces over the period 1986–98 was constructed from various issues of *China Statistical Yearbook*. Tibet is excluded from the analysis, due to the lack of consistent GDP data. Hainan Province is included in Guangdong Province because data for Hainan are not available before 1988 when it became a separate province. Both nominal GDP and annual growth rates of GDP for each province are published in the *China Statistical Yearbook*. We assume that prices were the same for all provinces in the initial year of 1978 and that the nominal GDP was equal to the real GDP. Under this assumption, real GDP estimates for the whole period can be derived from nominal GDP data for 1978 and the published annual growth rates in real GDP.

Although capital investment data is readily available, information on China's capital stocks is rather scarce. There are several studies reporting domestic capital stocks. Chow (1993) derived capital stocks at the national level from 1952 to 1985 using newly increased fixed assets. Fan, Zhang, and Robinson (2002) constructed capital stocks series from 1978 to 1995 at the provincial level using gross capital formation data with depreciation adjustment. But so far, we have not seen any figures on foreign capital stocks in China. In this paper, we make efforts to calculate both domestic and foreign capital stocks based on available information.

For domestic capital stocks, we use published information of gross capital formation and fixed asset depreciation. For the period of 1978–95, the data by province are taken from *The Gross Domestic Product of China: 1952–1995*, while for other years, the data are from the *China Statistical Yearbooks*. The gross capital formation is defined as the value of fixed assets and inventory acquired minus the value of fixed assets and inventory disposed. To construct a domestic capital stock series, we use the following procedure. Define the capital stock in time t as the stock in time $t-1$ plus investment minus depreciation with price adjusted.

$$K_t = \frac{I_t - D_t}{P_t} + K_{t-1} \tag{5}$$

where K_t is the capital stock in year t, I_t is the gross capital formation in year t, and D_t is depreciation in year t. P_t is an accumulative price index with year 1978 as 1, which is derived from the annual price index for fixed assets as published in the *China Statistical Yearbooks*. The price index is available by province from 1988 to 1998 but only available at the national level from 1978 to 1987.

To obtain initial values for the capital stock, we used a procedure similar to that of Kohli (1982). That is, we assume that prior to 1978, real investment in each province has grown at a steady rate (r) which is supposed to be the same as the rate of growth of real GDP from 1952 to 1977 in the corresponding province. Thus,

$$K_{1978} = \frac{I_{1978}}{\delta + r} \tag{6}$$

where δ is the depreciation rate. This approach ensures that the 1978 value of the capital stock is independent of the 1986–98 data used in our analysis. Moreover, given the relatively small capital stock in 1978 and high levels of investment in the following years, the estimates for capital stocks are not sensitive to the 1978 benchmark value of the capital stock.

For foreign capital stocks in China, we do not need to worry about the initial stocks because virtually no foreign capital flows went to China until 1979. The foreign capital stocks are constructed as follows:

$$K_t = I_t / P_t + (1 - \delta_t) K_{t-1}. \tag{7}$$

China Statistical Yearbooks (SSB, 1995) reports the depreciation rate of fixed assets for years from 1952 to 1992. Since 1992, SSB has ceased to publish official depreciation rates. For the years after 1992, we used the 1992 depreciate rate.

FDI data are adjusted using a three-year moving average to overcome the year-to-year fluctuations at the province level. Similar to the domestic capital, FDI is converted to constant values at 1978 using a constant deflator for US dollars. The total trade volume data are from *Comprehensive Statistical Data and Materials on 50 Years of New China*. We use literacy rate among population above 15-years old as proxy for education level. The data are from various issues of *China Population Statistics*.

The labor productivity function outlined in equation (3) is estimated under different specifications. Table 8.4 reports the estimation results. To check the sensitivity of including foreign capital as a separate variable, we also present estimates with an aggregate capital stock. As noted earlier, the values of trade-to-GDP ratio may be subject to the changes in official exchange rate. Considering that exchange rate is year-specific and common to all provinces, including year dummies in estimations can eliminate this particular and other

Table 8.4 The estimation results for labor productivity

Variables	R1	R2	R3	R4	R5	R6
Intercept	−3.160**	−3.103**	−3.102**	−3.445**	−3.592**	−3.690**
	(0.347)	(0.358)	(0.357)	(0.339)	(0.348)	(0.348)
Domestic	0.627**	0.635**	0.634**			
capital	(0.010)	(0.019)	(0.019)			
Foreign capital	0.027*	0.041**	0.043**			
	(0.011)	(0.010)	(0.009)			
Total capital				0.645**	0.666**	0.670**
				(0.018)	(0.018)	(0.018)
Education	0.908**	0.863**	0.863**	0.960**	0.957**	0.986**
	(0.079)	(0.081)	(0.081)	(0.077)	(0.079)	(0.079)
Trade ratio	0.093*	0.056**	0.057**	0.109**	0.088**	0.105**
	(0.019)	(0.017)	(0.017)	(0.015)	(0.015)	(0.013)
Regime dummy		0.009			0.053**	
(1992–98)		(0.024)			(0.022)	
Year dummies	Yes**			Yes**		
Coastal region	0.052**	0.063**	0.058**	0.076**	0.093**	0.067**
	(0.025)	(0.024)	(0.020)	(0.023)	(0.023)	(0.021)
Hausman Test	0.958	0.366	0.229	0.780	0.010	0.001
(p-value)						
Adjusted R^2	0.939	0.933	0.933	0.939	0.931	0.930

Note: All variables are in logarithms. GDP, domestic capital, and foreign capital are in constant price of 1978. The dependent variable is GDP per unit of labor. The Hausman Test is used to test the endogeneity of domestic and foreign capital. Standard errors are in parentheses. * and ** denote statistical significance at the five percent and ten percent level, respectively.

year-specific effects. As all the variables are in logarithmic form, the difference in conversion factor for total trade only affects the year-specific intercepts. In another specification, a regime dummy instead of year dummies is included to capture the policy shift toward a more open system beginning from 1992 when the late supreme leader Deng Xiaoping traveled to the south and promoted opening up. Finally, we drop both year dummies and the regime dummy to check the robustness of the estimations.

There might be issues of endogeneity in the regressions. For example, both domestic and foreign capital might be affected by the output level. To check the possible endogeneity issue for capital stocks and openness, we conduct a Hausman Test and present the p-values in the second to last row in the table. Following Greene (2000), we use the lagged dependent variable, lagged capital stocks and trade ratio, current values of other regressors, and exogenous population variable as instruments in the test. For most specifications except for the last two columns, p-values are larger than five percent, implying that the null hypothesis of no endogeneity cannot be rejected.

The adjusted R^2s for the labor productivity functions range from 0.930 to 0.939, implying good fit. The two regressions with year dummies have the highest adjusted R^2s and p-values for the endogeneity test. Coefficients for all the variables except for regime dummy in regression R2 are statistically significant and have expected signs. In general, the results are rather robust to different specifications. However, there are still some slight differences. When the total capital stock is included, the coefficients for the total capital are higher than for the domestic capital stock in regressions with separate capital stocks. The coefficients for the trade ratio also become higher when the aggregate capital stock is used.

Because we assume constant returns to scale, the labor elasticities can be calculated by subtracting the elasticities for domestic capital and foreign capital or total capital from one. The labor elasticities range from 0.323 to 0.355 across the six specifications. Among the production factors and shift variables considered in the estimation, the elasticity of education has the largest value, implying the importance of human capital. The elasticities with respect to domestic capital or total capital also show high values between 0.6 and 0.7. Both regions have greater capital elasticities than labor elasticities. The coefficients for two variables of globalization, foreign capital, and trade ratio, are statistically significant and positive despite with smaller values compared to those for domestic capital and education. The significant coefficients for the regional dummy suggest the existence of systematic difference in labor productivity between inland and coastal regions.

Given the estimated coefficients for labor productivity functions, we can now apply the inequality decomposition method outlined in equation (4) to quantify the contributions of the production factors, human capital, and openness to total regional inequality in labor productivity. Table 8.5 presents the overall inequality and the contributions from these factors to total inequality.

The inequality index, measured as the log variance, in the second column in Table 8.5 has increased from 0.198 in 1986 to 0.301 in 1998, indicating a widening gap in labor productivity over the period. The contributions of domestic capital, foreign capital, education, and the trade-to-GDP ratio are 75.1 percent, 8.1 percent, −8.0 percent, and 11.1 percent, respectively, of the total increase in regional inequality.

The uneven distribution of domestic capital has been a dominant factor behind the increase in regional inequality. China has adopted a preferential policy for the coastal regions since the 1980s. Almost all the inland provinces have set up offices or investing companies in the special zones in the coastal areas. Because of the favorable investment policy, even domestic capital has flown to south and east (China Development Report, 1995). With the trend of fiscal decentralization, provinces are allowed to keep a larger share of revenues locally, which further reduces the central government's redistribution power and enlarges the existing regional disparity.

Education has been the only equalizing factor. The education disparity between inland and coastal regions has been much smaller and increased rather slower than most other factors as shown in Table 8.3. Despite a slight increase in inequality in education, the covariance between education and

Table 8.5 Inequality decomposition by factors

Year	Inequality	Domestic capital	Foreign capital	Education	Foreign trade	Inland– Coastal	Other factors
1986	0.198	0.102	0.011	0.036	0.023	0.006	0.020
		(51.6)	(5.6)	(18.1)	(11.6)	(2.8)	(10.3)
1987	0.206	0.110	0.014	0.036	0.022	0.006	0.018
		(53.6)	(6.6)	(17.6)	(10.8)	(2.8)	(8.6)
1988	0.213	0.119	0.015	0.036	0.024	0.006	0.012
		(55.9)	(7.1)	(17.2)	(11.2)	(2.9)	(5.8)
1989	0.213	0.125	0.015	0.035	0.025	0.006	0.007
		(58.8)	(7.3)	(16.3)	(11.6)	(2.9)	(3.2)
1990	0.220	0.136	0.016	0.030	0.025	0.006	0.007
		(61.6)	(7.4)	(13.5)	(11.6)	(2.7)	(3.2)
1991	0.226	0.138	0.017	0.028	0.025	0.007	0.011
		(61.1)	(7.5)	(12.4)	(11.1)	(2.9)	(5.0)
1992	0.238	0.143	0.017	0.030	0.025	0.007	0.016
		(60.0)	(7.0)	(12.4)	(10.7)	(3.0)	(6.8)
1993	0.254	0.151	0.016	0.029	0.028	0.008	0.022
		(59.5)	(6.3)	(11.5)	(10.9)	(3.1)	(8.6)
1994	0.259	0.152	0.016	0.030	0.027	0.008	0.025
		(58.9)	(6.3)	(11.4)	(10.4)	(3.3)	(9.8)
1995	0.274	0.161	0.017	0.030	0.029	0.009	0.028
		(59.0)	(6.2)	(10.9)	(10.5)	(3.3)	(10.1)
1996	0.284	0.169	0.018	0.027	0.032	0.009	0.029
		(59.5)	(6.4)	(9.4)	(11.2)	(3.2)	(10.3)
1997	0.293	0.175	0.019	0.027	0.034	0.009	0.030
		(59.6)	(6.4)	(9.2)	(11.5)	(3.2)	(10.1)
1998	0.301	0.180	0.019	0.027	0.034	0.010	0.030
		(59.7)	(6.5)	(9.1)	(11.4)	(3.2)	(10.1)
Growth (%)	52.5	39.4	4.3	−4.2	5.8	2.0	5.2
Contribution	100.0	75.1	8.1	−8.0	11.1	3.8	9.9

Notes

(1) The decomposition method is based on formula outlined in equation (4).

(2) The second column refers to the measure of inequality (log variance). Columns (3)–(8) are contributions to the overall inequality by domestic capital, foreign capital, education, trade ratio, inland–coastal difference, and unexplained factors. In mathematical formula, the overall inequality in year t, y_t, is decomposed to the sum of factor components $y_t = \sum_i x_{it}$ where x_i represents the factor components from column 3 to column 8.

(3) The total increase in inequality can be expressed as follows:
$$\frac{\Delta y_t}{y_{t-1}} = \sum_i \frac{x_{it-1}}{y_{t-1}} \frac{\Delta x_{it}}{x_{it-1}} \equiv \sum_i s_{it-1} \frac{\Delta x_{it}}{x_{it-1}},$$ where s_{it-1} is the share of the ith factor's contribution to overall inequality in year $t-1$ and $\frac{\Delta x_{it}}{x_{it-1}}$ is the growth rate of the ith factor's contribution from $t-1$ to t.

labor productivity has declined from 0.036 to 0.027 as shown in the fifth column in Table 8.5. China has been well known for expansion of basic education to its vast population over the past five decades. The widespread access to basic education has been argued to be an asset for the widely shared and participatory economic growth after the economic reforms in China (Sen, 1995). Improvement in education not only enhances one's productivity but also increases one's ability to move, therefore reducing regional inequality.

The variation in the degree of globalization across provinces, indicated by foreign trade and foreign capital, explained 19.2 percent of increase in total regional inequality. In short, after controlling for other factors, globalization through foreign trade and foreign capital is still a rather important force behind the widening regional disparity.

In this paper we argue that the implicit assumption of integrated factor markets underlying the standard analysis does not hold in China. Segregated factor markets can aggravate the distributional impact of changes in regional comparative advantages associated with globalization. In a closed economy with agriculture as the predominant mode of production, the comparative advantage is mainly determined by the difference in land/labor ratios across regions within a country. When the economy opens its door to the rest of the world, a region's comparative advantage is evaluated in a broader global context. In that context, regions adjacent to more developed economies may enjoy a far better location advantage for trade and development than land-locked regions, and therefore may have a faster growth.

For instance, Guangdong province did not enjoy any obvious comparative advantage for trade or location advantage for FDI than inland provinces before the open-door policy was adopted in 1978. Labor productivity in Guangdong ranked 14th in that year among 30 provinces, which was almost the same as the inland Sichuan province. Since 1978 Guangdong has become the most favored place for foreign investors as well as the largest trading province largely due to its proximity to Hong Kong. Meanwhile, the rank of labor productivity for Sichuan has declined from 15th in 1978 to 23rd in 1998. Clearly, the relative comparative advantages between the two provinces have changed significantly with global economic integration.

In the ideal case with fully integrated factor markets, changes in comparative advantages will not affect regional disparity. With labor and capital's free movement, regional differences in returns to labor and capital can in large part be mitigated. However, because of geographical and institutional barriers, there exist strong segmentations and distortions in China's factor markets, as shown in Kanbur and Zhang (1999) and Yang (1999). Restrictions on rural–urban and regional migrations have been argued to be a major factor contributing to labor market inefficiency.

In addition to segmentations in the labor market, there exist large distortions in China's capital market as well. Over the past two decades, China has implemented a coast-biased development policy in utilizing the locational advantages of coastal regions since the early 1980s. For instance, up to the early 1990s, almost all special economic zones had been established in the coastal provinces, which enjoyed far more favorable polices regarding attracting FDI and foreign trade than the inland regions. As a result, the capital/labor ratio between the coastal and inland regions has increased significantly. Fan, Zhang, and Robinson (2002) show an increasing variation in marginal returns to capital since 1985, implying the existence of distortions in the capital market.

In summary, globalization has led to changes in regional comparative advantages, which, in turn, has aggravated regional inequality due to segmentations in labor and capital markets.

8.5 Conclusions

The world economy has become increasingly integrated through cross-border trade and capital movements. The correlation between globalization and widening income inequality has led to a growing concern about the distributional impact of globalization, in particular its detrimental effect on the more vulnerable populations and regions. While there has been a large body of literature on the issue, studies about effects of globalization on regional inequality within a developing country have been limited. The purpose of this study is to close this gap through providing a method for investigating the impact of globalization on regional inequality in developing countries and applying the method to China. Using a provincial level data set for the period of 1986–98, we estimate a model that quantitatively decomposes the effects of foreign trade and inward FDI on Chinese regional inequality. The estimates suggest that globalization through foreign trade and FDI indeed played an important role in worsening Chinese regional inequality.

The increasing trend of regional disparity can be largely explained by the uneven distribution of production factors and variations in openness among regions. Both domestic and foreign capital investments have been concentrated in the more developed coastal region, leading to a faster growth in these areas. Even after controlling for many other factors, we find FDI and trade have played important roles in contributing to changes in overall regional inequality. This finding is in contrast to theoretical predictions of the standard trade model that implicitly assumes integrated factor markets. Our empirical finding can be explained by the fact that China's factor markets have been rather segmented. Because of the segmentation, most gains from globalization have just gone to part of the country, leading to widening regional disparity.

With its entry of WTO, China is expected to become more integrated with the rest of the world, probably resulting in large changes in regional comparative advantages. If the government continues to favor the coastal region in its investment strategy, then regional disparity will widen. Further liberalizing the economy in the inland region is an important development strategy for the government both to promote economic growth and reduce regional inequality. In general, removing distortions in factor markets will help mitigate the negative distributional effect of the globalization process. To further promote the nine-year compulsory basic education as widely as possible is also likely to be an effective strategy to ensure that people from all regions participate in and share the benefits of globalization.

Notes

1 Although the official statistics report trade volume both in US dollars and Chinese currency, the trade volume in local currency is converted based on the conventional exchange rate. As exchange rates have changed dramatically, the trade-to-GDP ratio is largely subject to the changes in exchange rate. When using the purchasing power parity (PPP) as a conversion factor, the trade-to-GDP ratio becomes much lower as shown in Table 8.1. Therefore, one should be cautious of the trend of trade dependency. However, one should be also aware that the accuracy of the PPP is also a subject of controversy because the sample used for PPP calculation was extremely small and limited to only one city in China (personal correspondence with Michael Ward, the Development Data Group, the World Bank).
2 In order to better analyze these issues, we divide China into two zones: the coastal zone including Beijing, Liaoning, Tianjin, Hebei, Shandong, Jiangsu, Shanghai, Zhejiang, Fujian, Guangdong, and Guangxi; the inland zone comprising all the remaining provinces. Haninan is included in Guangdong province.
3 The Marxist or the neo-Marxist argument would, however, view international trade and FDI as one mechanism for exploitation of the developing countries by the industrialized West.
4 The assumption of constant returns to scale might be restrictive. But without imposing this assumption, labor would appear in the right-hand side of equation (3), making it harder to explain the results.

References

Barro, Robert and Sala-i-Martin, Xavier, 1995, *Economic Growth*, London: McGraw-Hill, Inc.

Bliss, Christopher, 1988, "Trade and Development", in Henry Chenery and T. N. Srinivasan eds. *Handbook of Development Economic*, II, Amsterdam; New York: North-Holland.

Borenstein, E., De Gregorio, J., and Lee, J.-W., 1998, "How Does Foreign Direct Investment Affect Economic Growth?", *Journal of International Economics*, Vol.45, pp.115–35.

Caves, Richard, 1996, *Multinational Enterprise and Economic Analysis*, 2nd Edition, Cambridge; New York: Cambridge University Press.

China State Statistics Bureau (SSB), 1995, *China Development Report*, Beijing: China Statistical Press.

China State Statistics Bureau (SSB), 1997, *The Gross Domestic Product of China*. Dalian: Dongbei University of Finance and Economics Press.

China State Statistics Bureau (SSB), *China Statistical Yearbook*, various issues, Beijing: China Statistical Press.

China State Statistics Bureau (SSB), *China Population Statistics*, various issues, Beijing: China Statistical Press.

China State Statistics Bureau (SSB), 1999, *Comprehensive Statistical Data and Materials on 50 Years of New China*, Beijing: China Statistical Press.

Chow, G.C. (1993) "Capital Formation and Economic Growth in China", *Quarterly Journal of Economics*, Vol.108, No.3, pp.809–42.

Cline, William, 1997, *Trade and Income Distribution*, Washington, DC: Institute for International Economics.

Cowell, Frank, 1995, *Measuring Inequality*, 2nd ed., London, New York: Prentice Hall/Harvester Wheatsheaf.

Deardorff, A. and Stern, R., 1994, *The Stolper-Samuelson Theorem: A Golden Jubilee*, Ann Arbor: University of Michigan Press.

Dollar, David and Kraay, Aart, 2002, "Spreading the Wealth", *Foreign Affairs*, Vol.81 No.1, pp.120–33.

Edwards, W., 1993, "Openness, Trade Liberalization, and growth in Developing Countries", *Journal of Economic Literature*, Vol.31, No.3, pp.1358–93.

Fan, Shenggen, Zhang, Xiaobo, and Robinson, Sherman, 2002, "Structural Change and Economic Growth in China", *Review of Development Economics*, forthcoming.

Feder, Gershon, 1983, "On Exports and Economic Growth", *Journal of Development Economics*, Vol.12, pp.59–73.

Feenstra, R. and Hanson, G. 1996, "Foreign Investment, Outsourcing and Relative Wages", in R. Feenstra and D. Irwin, eds. *The Political Economy of Trade: Papers in Honor of Jagdish Bhagwati*, Cambridge: MIT Press.

Fleisher, Belton M., and Chen, Jian, 1997, "The Coast-Noncoast Income Gap, Productivity, and Regional Economic Policy in China", *Journal of Comparative Economics*, Vol.25, No.2, pp.220–36.

Greene, H. William, 2000, *Econometric Analysis*, New Jersey: Prentice Hall International Inc.

Hanson, G. and A. Harrison, 1999, "Trade Liberalization and Wage Inequality in Mexico", *Industrial and Labor Relations Review*, Vol.52, pp.271–88.

Hu, Angang, 1996, "Excessively Large Regional Gaps are Too Risky", *Chinese Economic Studies*, Vol.29, No.6, pp.72–5.

International Monetary Fund (IMF) (1999), *International Financial Statistics Yearbook* 1999, Washington, DC.

IMF Fiscal Affairs Department, 1998, "Should Equity Be a Goal of Economy Policy?" *The Economic Issues Series*, No.16.

Jian, Tianlun, Sachs, Jefferey, and Warner, Andrew, 1996, "Trends in Regional Inequality in China", *China Economic Review*, Vol.7, No.1, pp.1–21.

Kanbur, Ravi and Zhang, Xiaobo, 1999, "Which Regional Inequality? The Evolution Of Rural–Urban And Inland–Coastal Inequality in China, 1983–1995", *Journal of Comparative Economics*, Vol.27, pp.686–701.

Kaplinsky, Raphael, 2000, "Globalization and Unequalization: What Can Be Learned from Value Chain Analysis?" *Journal of Development Studies*, Vol.37, No.2, pp.117–46.

Kohli, U., 1982, "A Gross National Product Function and the Derived Demand for Imports and Exports", *Canadian Journal of Economics*, Vol.18, pp.369–86.

Krueger, Ann, 1980, "Trade Policy as an Input to Development", *American Economic Review*, Vol.70, May, pp.288–92.

Lardy, Nicholas R., 1995, *China in the World Economy*, Washington, DC: Institute for International Economics.

Lardy, Nicholas R., 2002, *Integrating China into the Global Economy*, Washington, DC: Brookings Institution Press.

Lawrence, Robert, 1996, *Single World, Divided Nations?* Washington, DC: Brookings Institution Press and OECD Development Center.

Lyons, Thomas P., 1991, "Interprovincial Disparities in China: Output and Consumption, 1952–1987", *Economic Development and Cultural Change*, Vol.39, No.3, pp.471–506.

Mazur, Jay, 2000, "Labor's New Internationalism", *Foreign Affairs*, Vol.81, No.1, pp.79–93.

Pack, Howard, 1988, "Industrialization and Trade", in H. Chenery and T. N. Srinivasan eds. *Handbook of Development Economics*, I, Elsevier Science B. V.

Ram, Rati, 1987, "Exports and Economic Growth in Developing Countries: Evidence from Time-Series and Cross-Section Data", *Economic Development and Cultural Change*, Vol.36, No.1, pp.51–72.

Ram, Rati, 1990, "Imports and Economic Growth: A Cross-Country Study", *Economia Internazionale /International Economics*, Vol.43, No.1, pp.45–66.

Ram, Rati and Zhang, Kevin, 2002, "Foreign Direct Investment and Economic Growth: Evidence from Cross-Country Data for the 1990s", *Economic Development and Cultural Change*, Vol.51, pp.205–15.

Richardson, J., 1995, "Income Inequality and Trade: How to Think, What to Conclude", *Journal of Economic Perspectives*, Vol.9, pp.33–55.

Robbins, D., 1996, "HOS Hits Facts: Facts Win; Evidence on Trade and Wages in the Developing World", Developing Discussion Paper # 557, Harvard Institute for International Development.

Rodrik, Dani, 1997, *Has Globalization Gone Too Far?* Washington DC: Institute for International Economics.

Sen, Amartya Kumar, 1995, "Economic Development and Social Change: India and China in Comparative Perspectives", Development Economics Research Programme Discussion Paper No. 67. Suntory and Toyota International Centres, London School of Economics and Political Science, London.

Shorrocks, Anthony F., 1982, "Inequality Decomposition by Factor Components", *Econometrica*, Vol.50, No.1, pp.193–211.

Shorrocks, Anthony F., 1984, "Inequality Decomposition by Population Subgroups", *Econometrica*, Vol.52, No.6, pp.1369–85.

Tsui, Kai-yuen, 1991, "China's Regional Inequality, 1952–1985", *Journal of Comparative Economics*, Vol.15, No.1, pp.1–21.

United Nations Conference on Trade and Development (UNCTAD), 2001, *World Investment Report 1998 and 2001*, New York: United Nations.

Wood, A., 1997, "Openness and Wage Inequality in Developing Countries: The Latin American Challenge to East Asian Conventional Wisdom", *World Bank Economic Review*, Vol.11, pp.33–57.

World Bank, 1993, *The East Asian Miracle: Economic Growth and Public Policy*, London: Oxford University Press.

Yang, Danis, 1999, "Urban-Biased Policies and Rising Income Inequality in China", *American Economic Review* (Paper and Proceedings), Vol.89, No.2, pp.306–10.

Zhang, Kevin H., 1999, "How Does FDI Interact with Economic Growth in a Large Developing Country? The Case of China", *Economic Systems*, Vol.23, No.4, pp.291–303.

Zhang, Kevin H., 2001, "Roads to Prosperity: Assessing the Impact of FDI on Economic Growth in China", *Economia Internazionale / International Economics*, Vol.54, No.1, pp. 113–25.

Zhang, Xiaobo and Kanbur, Ravi, 2001, "What Difference Do Polarization Measures Make?" *Journal of Development Studies*, Vol.37, No.3, February, pp.85–98.

9 China's WTO accession

Impacts on regional agricultural income – a multi-region, general equilibrium analysis

Xinshen Diao, Shenggen Fan, and Xiaobo Zhang[1]

Abstract

This study constructs a regional Computable General Equilibrium (CGE) model of China to analyze the impact of China's WTO accession on rural income. The results show that total welfare will improve but regional income gaps will widen. The agricultural sector will suffer if only agricultural trade is liberalized. Lifting both agricultural and nonagricultural trade barriers will benefit farmers at the national level. However, rural income will increase less than urban income, implying that the rural–urban income gap will widen further. Among the regions, farmers in China's least-developed rural areas will benefit little or even suffer because agriculture, especially traditional agriculture, is still an important source of their livelihood.

9.1 Introduction

China was finally admitted to the World Trade Organization (WTO) in December 2001 after 15 years of preparation. During this period, China made considerable progress in economic liberalization and reforms, even without being a member of the WTO. The ongoing process of reform is in harmony with the general trend of globalization, in which flows of trade, financial capital, technology, and information across national boundaries have led to, and will continue to lead, to a restructuring of the world economy.

China has achieved remarkable economic growth as a result of its economic reform and opening since 1979. The nation's GDP has grown at nine to ten percent per annum, outperforming most countries throughout the world. Reform initiated in the agricultural sector has led to rapid transformation in rural China. Grain output increased from 305 million tons in 1978 to 508 million tons in 1999, with an annual growth rate of 2.5 percent. Such growth is much faster than the population growth rate of one percent per annum. The value added in agriculture rose at an even higher annual rate of 4.8 percent due to increased diversification of agricultural production. Rapid growth in agriculture has led to an even more impressive reduction in rural poverty. At the beginning of the reforms, about 260 million people, or one-third of the rural population, lived under the poverty line without access to adequate food supplies or income to maintain a healthy and productive life. By 1999, the number of rural poor had declined to less than 34 million, accounting for less than four percent of rural population (Ministry of Agriculture, 2000). Many development indicators, including agricultural products possessed per capita and both average calorie and nutrition intake, have reached or even surpass the world average. Various studies show a strong positive relationship between openness and economic growth based on data from the past several decades; this relationship is particularly strong for low-income countries. Thus, WTO accession will accelerate China's economic growth by spurring closer integration into the world economy and by enabling it to take advantage of globalization's benefits.

However, the gains from past reforms are not distributed equally among regions. Less-developed areas, such as the Northwest and Southwest, have gained very little. Moreover, regional inequality has increased over the past two decades (Kanbur and Zhang, 1999). With China's entry into the WTO, the less-developed regions may suffer even more because their economies are still predominantly agricultural. Agricultural prices are expected to drop, leading to a decline in farmers' income. With poor infrastructure and a shortage of human capital in the less-developed regions, it will be hard for farmers to switch from grain production to other high value-added crops or to non-farm activities. Without the implementation of proper government policies, these factors may contribute to an increase in the concentration of rural poor in these regions.

The objective of this study is to quantify the effect of WTO accession on China's economy at the regional level, particularly on the rural economy of the less-developed regions. The analytical framework is a multi-sector, multi-region Computable General Equilibrium (CGE) model. Previous CGE studies on China's WTO accession focus on the possible impacts at the national level (Development Research Center, 1998; U.S. International Trade Commission, 1999; Wang, 1999; Martin, Dimaranan, and Hertel, 1999; Hertel and Walmsley, 2000; Lejour, 2000; Fan and Zheng, 2000).[2] Although the aggregate effect at the national level is positive, all regions in China may not benefit equally. Some regions may be hurt due to the existing differences in economic development and openness. Thus, a national-level assessment is not sufficient to understand the full impact of WTO accession on China's economy. For policymakers, it is imperative to identify region-specific adverse effects and implement appropriate policies to cope with them.

In this paper, we first sketch the differences in economic development and openness among regions within China. Then we employ a CGE model with disaggregated regional production to simulate the effects of WTO accession on the agricultural and rural economy at the regional level, particularly in the less-developed regions. We conclude by presenting policy implications and future research directions.

9.2 Regional disparities in the rural economy

We divide China into seven regions according to geographic location, agricultural production structure, and the level of economic development at the provincial level. Table 9.1 lists the regional classification. Differences in economic development among the seven regions can be gauged by per capita GDP and agriculture's share in regional GDP, as well as by per capita income in the rural areas in Table 9.2. Measured by both per capita GDP and rural income, the Northwest and Southwest are China's two least-developed regions. In 2000, per capita GDP in the Southwest and Northwest was around 5,000 yuan, about half the income level in the East and South. Per

Table 9.1 Regions in China

Region (number of provinces included)	Province
Northeast (3)	1. Liaoning 2. Jilin 3. Heilongjiang
North (7)	4. Beijing 5. Tianjin 6. Hebei 7. Shanxi 8. Shandong 9. Shaanxi 10. Henan
Northwest (6)	11. Inner Mongolia 12. Gansu 13. Qinghai 14. Ningxia 15. Xinjiang 16. Tibet
Central (4)	17. Anhui 18. Jiangxi 19. Hubei 20. Hunan
East (3)	21. Shanghai 22. Jiangsu 23. Zhejiang
Southwest (4)	24. Sichuan 25. Chongqing 26. Guizhou 27. Yunnan
South (4)	28. Guangdong 29. Guangxi 30. Hainan 31. Fujian

Table 9.2 Major economic indicators in the seven regions, 2000

Region	Population (millions)	Per capita GDP (yuan)	Agriculture's share of GDP (%)	Rural per capita income (yuan)
Northeast	104.5	9,328	13	2,175
North	355.6	7,747	15	2,592
Northwest	54.1	5,317	20	1,518
Central	163.6	6,092	19	2,200
East	189.4	11,716	11	3,845
Southwest	190.3	4,496	23	1,662
South	155.5	10,280	15	2,733

Source: Fan *et al.* 2001.

capita rural income in the Northwest and Southwest is 1,518 and 1,662 yuan, respectively, only 40 percent of the income level in the East. Shares of agriculture in GDP are higher for these two regions at 20 percent and 23 percent than those in the other regions at between 11 percent and 19 percent, which indicates that farming is still a major source of rural income in the two poorest regions.

The different shares of the rural labor force employed in the rural non-farm sector contribute significantly to the regional gap in rural income (Rozelle, 1994). Many factors, including economic, social, cultural, and geographical, restrict labor mobility in the less-developed regions. Such restrictions are a major factor contributing to the widening regional disparity (Kanbur and Zhang, 1999). For the nation as a whole in 1997, about 29 percent of the rural labor force was engaged in nonagricultural activities, such as rural industry, construction, and services, and this non-farm sector provided more than one-third of rural income. However, in the Northwest and Southwest, the two least-developed regions, less than 20 percent of the rural labor force was employed in non-farm activities compared to 40 percent in the more developed areas, such as the East.

With an overwhelmingly large share of the rural labor force employed in agricultural activities, labor productivity is low in the less-developed regions. For example, labor productivity in the Southwest was half the national average in 1997. Poor natural resource endowments and infrastructure limit the potential yield of agricultural land, while high illiteracy and the lack of both investment and personnel in science and technology restrain the adoption of new technologies and the potential to increase agricultural productivity. Moreover, difficulty in accessing both national and international markets constrains the choice of crop mix and the development of high-value agricultural products in the less-developed regions. A study by Fan, Zhang, and Zhang (2002) shows that the growth rates of agricultural land and labor productivities in the Northwest and Southwest are far below the national average over the past two decades. With the growing agricultural productivity and rural income gap between the less-developed regions and the rest of the nation, the incidence of poverty is increasingly concentrated in the less-developed regions. More than 60 percent of China's rural poor lives in the two least-developed regions (Fan et al., 2001), even though these regions account for only 20 percent of national population.

Difference in the degree of openness among regions also contributes to the regional income gap (Kanbur and Zhang, 2001). After China adopted its opening-to-the-outside-world policy in 1978, the degree of openness, measured both by trade and foreign capital flows, increased dramatically. For example, the trade to GDP ratio quadrupled, from 8.5 percent in 1978 to 36.5 percent in 1999 (Wei and Wu, 2001). However, due to differences in geographical and social economic conditions, the degree of openness varies significantly across the provinces and regions. In Table 9.3, we use data on the trade-GDP ratio and per capita foreign direct investment to measure openness in the provinces and regions in China. As the table shows, from 1997 to 1999, the three-year average of the trade-GDP ratio was as high as 97 and 40 percent for the South and East, respectively, but as low as 7 to 9 percent for the Southwest, Central, and Northwest regions. Similarly, per capita foreign investment in 1999 in the South and East was 1,860 and 1,452 U.S. dollars, respectively, but only 92 and 121 US dollars for the Northwest and Southwest, respectively.

9.3   The data and the model

9.3.1   The data

Our regional CGE model is based on various sources of data. A national level social accounting matrix (SAM) for China in 1997 is used as the base. However, the original 1997 SAM includes only two aggregate primary agricultural sectors, namely, crops and livestock. Since we focus on agriculture, we need a much more disaggregate agricultural sector. Such disaggregation is done according to the GTAP (Global Trade Analysis Project, 2001) version 5 database. Using the production data taken from China's Statistical Yearbook and the input-output relationship provided by the GTAP database, the aggregated crop sector is split into nine sectors, namely, wheat, rice, other cereals, vegetables, fruits, soybeans, other oilseeds, cotton, and other crops. Sector details are provided in appendix.

A standard multi-regional CGE model would have production and consumption activities disaggregated at the regional level, with details on inter-regional activities, such as commodity and factor flows across regions, included. To develop such a multi-region model requires data equivalent to social accounting matrices at the regional level. Unfortunately, such data, especially the regional input-output relationships and inter-regional commodity and factor flows, are unavailable for China. Regional input-output data have never been published and inter-regional economic relationships are

Table 9.3 Measures of openness by province and region

Province/region	Trade to GDP ratio 3-year (1997 to 1999) average (%)	Per capita foreign investment 1999 (US$)
Beijing	68.9	3,129
Tianjin	72.5	3,067
Hebei	8.3	220
Shanxi	12.4	147
Inner Mongolia	7.4	96
Liaoning	31.0	1,033
Jilin	12.8	273
Heilongjiang	10.4	239
Shanghai	74.6	6,156
Jiangsu	30.6	1,011
Zhejiang	29.5	614
Anhui	7.9	145
Fujian	46.8	1,490
Jiangxi	6.3	115
Shandong	23.2	429
Henan	4.4	127
Hubei	7.1	274
Hunan	5.5	110
Guangdong[a]	136.7	2,968
Guangxi	9.5	231
Sichuan[b]	6.9	149
Guizhou	6.6	54
Yunnan	7.7	104
Tibet	12.1	100
Shaanxi	11.7	213
Gansu	5.3	72
Qinghai	6.5	172
Ningxia	11.9	151
Xinjiang	12.3	72
North	22.3	430
Northwest	8.7	92
Northeast	20.5	559
East	40.1	1,452
Central	6.7	163
South	96.6	1,860
Southwest	7.1	121
Nation	33.8	615

a. Including Hainan.
b. Including Chongqing.

Source: Computed from *China Statistical Yearbook*.

very complex, not to mention difficult to measure correctly. To overcome this data shortcoming, we focus only on agriculture.

We first disaggregate the agricultural production data included in the national SAM into the seven regions according to *The China Statistical*

Yearbook and *China's Agricultural Statistical Materials*. While almost all crops, i.e., the nine aggregate crop groups included in the national SAM, are produced in each region, production systems, i.e., either the level of productivity or the combination of land, labor, and capital, are quite different. For example, land is abundant in the Northeast, while production is relatively labor-intensive in the East. Thus, it would be improper to use the national input-output coefficients provided by the national SAM for all seven regions. Without regional input-output data, we depend on the maximum entropy approach employed by Zhang and Fan (2001) to estimate reasonable region-specific input-output coefficients for agriculture. Specifically, their data set covers 25 provinces from 1979 to 1996. The three centrally administrated cities, namely, Beijing, Shanghai, and Tianjin, are not included because they represent relatively small shares of agricultural production and are not typical agricultural areas. Tibet is excluded due to data unavailability. The provincial data on two aggregate crops, namely, grains and cash crops, and five inputs, namely, land, labor, chemical fertilizer, machinery, and draft animals, are taken from *China's Agricultural Yearbook*, *China's Commodity Price Yearbook*, *China's Rural Statistical Yearbook*, and *Collections of Provincial Historical Statistical Materials*.

Due to data constraints for non-crop agriculture and rural nonagricultural activities, our estimation of regional production focuses only on crop production. To reduce the need for unknown parameters, all production functions are assumed to be Cobb-Douglas. However, the elasticity of each input changes over time through an interaction term between input variable and the time trend. The entropy estimation gives us both production elasticities for each input by crop and shares of each crop in total input use for regions. We use three-year average estimated shares for the inputs and data on output by region to disaggregate the inputs of land, labor, capital, and intermediates included in the national SAM to the regional level.

While the input-output data for crop production is disaggregated to the regional level, other agricultural production included in the six sectors, all nonagricultural production included in the 13 sectors, and other economic activities, such as trade and consumption, are measured by national level values due to the data constraint. This is a shortcoming of the model, because resource adjustments between crop and non-crop production within a region or across the seven regions cannot occur in the simulations. Moreover, the model includes only two aggregate household groups, namely, rural and urban, at the national level, so the feedback effect from consumers to production at the regional level is not captured properly. In order to account partially for these deficiencies, we modify the structure of the model.

9.3.2 The model

Most CGE models are neoclassical in spirit. Similarly, the regional CGE model for China assumes that the representative producer for each production sector, in the case of crop production for each sector within each region, maximizes profits by making production decisions, i.e., choosing levels of inputs and outputs. The consumers, who are aggregated into rural and urban at the national level, maximize their utility function by making consumption decisions subject to income constraints. While labor and capital are categorized as rural and urban, land is employed only in crop production and returns to land go only to the rural household.

To account for rapid growth in rural non-farm activities, rural labor and capital are assumed to be involved in both agricultural and nonagricultural activities, although urban labor and capital are employed in nonagricultural sectors only. Shares of nonagricultural labor and capital in the total supplies of rural labor and capital are calculated using the share of the gross value of rural industrial products in the gross value of national industrial products. Since rural industry is more labor-intensive at the sector level, we allow the share of the rural contribution to be high in the labor-intensive sectors, such as in textiles, apparel, transportation, sales, and construction. The share of the urban contribution is high in capital-intensive sectors, such as other industry, urban electricity supply and other utility services, financial services, and social services.

In order to account partially for the deficiencies caused by lack of data on both non-crop and nonagricultural production and factor allocation at the regional level, we allow factor mobility between crop production within regions and labor migration from regional crop production to non-crop and nonagricultural activities at the national level. Specifically, we allow labor forces to migrate from crop production into a pool of labor employed by all the other production activities at the national level, when the returns to labor in crop production at the regional level decline relative to the returns to non-crop and nonagricultural production at the national level in the simulations. Moreover, the degree of factor mobility is controlled by the different employment opportunities for rural labor across sectors and the elasticity of the substitution between rural and urban labor. Specifically, even though rural labor and capital can be employed by the nonagricultural sector, rural labor and urban labor are not perfectly substitutable. Moreover, migrated rural labor cannot be employed by some urban industries, such as other industry, excluding textiles and agriculture-related industries, urban electricity supply and other utility services, financial services, and social services, but it can move into textiles, construction, transportation, and sales, in which production is quite labor-intensive.

All agents, namely, producers and consumers, respond to prices. For example, when relative prices change due to the removal or reduction of import tariffs, producers adjust their production level and consumers adjust their demand for commodities. In the international market, the country is assumed to be small so that it takes world prices as given. Following a commonly used assumption in CGE models, there exists imperfect substitution between foreign goods and domestically produced goods; hence, the domestic price for a commodity, e.g., wheat, is not necessarily equal to, but may be highly affected by, the world price for that same commodity.

With regional disaggregation of crop production, we allow commodities produced by each region to be differentiated further. Specifically, the same commodity, such as rice, produced by different regions is not a perfect substitute. Since most commodity groups are quite aggregate, many different varieties exist within a commodity group. Moreover, considering China's market size, differences in distance between producers and consumers, and discrepancies in transportation and other transaction costs, we consider this to be a reasonable assumption.

The seven regions are distinguished further as import-substitutable and export-substitutable according to different crops. The specification of a region is based on its trade to GDP share, its income level, and its crop mix. Given this distinction, removing or reducing trade barriers will have different effects on relative prices for commodities within a region or across regions. As the imported commodities compete mainly with domestic production in the import-substitutable regions, the production effects due to trade liberalization are relatively large in these regions. On the other hand, trade liberalization may stimulate exports from some other sectors, such as vegetables and fruits, in which trade barriers are relatively low. However, such export opportunities cannot be equally realized across regions. The export opportunities will be captured mainly by the regions with advantages in information, transportation, and technology and, hence, relatively easy access to foreign markets. We define such regions as export-substitutable and distinguish them from the other regions.[3]

Like other static CGE models, our regional model has a medium-run focus. We report the results of comparative static experiments in which we first shock the model by changing or eliminating tariff and tariff-equivalent rates and then compute the new equilibrium solution. We do not consider explicitly how long it might take the economy to reach the new equilibrium or what other adjustments, such as an increase in total labor supply, more capital investment, technology transfer, and productivity shifts, might also occur. The model's time horizon must be viewed as long enough for a full adjustment of currently employed factors, including labor, land, and capital, to occur after the shock. While the approach is useful for an understanding of the change in the economy after the shock, it has obvious shortcomings. In particular, it fails to consider the costs of adjustment, such as transitional unemployment, that might be incurred while moving to the final equilibrium. Moreover, the model neglects many dynamic factors, e.g., the link between economic opening and growth, that have been shown statistically to be strong and important factors in explaining China's economic growth and rural development.

This regional CGE model is used to evaluate both the national and the regional effects of China's WTO accession. The detailed terms of China's commitments for 2002 were made available to the public only recently and its commitments for 2003 and 2004 are still unavailable. Thus, the U.S.-China agreement, which is the only publicly available one with information on 2003 and 2004, is used as the policy base for our study. Based on this information, China will reduce its average tariff rate on agricultural imports from 22 percent to 17.5 percent in the next three years, starting from 2002. It will also reduce many of its current non-tariff barriers to trade, including quotas, import licenses, and the use of state trading companies. Tables 9.A1 and 9.A2 in the appendix present the commitments on tariff and non-tariff barrier reductions for selected agricultural commodities.

We simulate China's WTO accession using two different scenarios. In the first scenario, the agricultural tariff rate and the tariff-equivalent rate, which is used to capture the non-tariff barriers to imports of grains, vegetable oil, and meat products, are reduced. In the second scenario, in addition to the reduction in the agricultural sector, tariff protections in the nonagricultural sectors are reduced. Although it is almost impossible for China to choose to liberalize only its agricultural sector, a comparison between the two scenarios helps us to evaluate the general equilibrium effect on agriculture from liberalizing nonagricultural sectors. Given the focus of our study on agriculture and the difficulty of obtaining data on non-tariff barriers for nonagricultural sectors, the model does not take into account the reduction and elimination of non-tariff barriers in the nonagricultural sectors, such as the automobile industry and services. Nonetheless, these are crucial components of China's commitments and will have a large effect on the Chinese economy. Furthermore, this study takes no account of potential conflicts between China's domestic policies and institutional arrangements and its WTO requirements. While harmonizing China's domestic policies and institutions with its commitments to the WTO is necessary for the calculated effects (Colby, Diao, and Francis, 2001), we ignore these important linkages due to the difficulties of identifying quantitatively these domestic policies and institutions.

9.4 The aggregate effect of China's WTO accession

At the national level, we focus on evaluating the effect of China's WTO accession on macroeconomic indicators as well as on agricultural trade, including imports and exports. As expected and similar to many other studies, China's WTO accession is shown to benefit the economy at the aggregate level by reducing or eliminating import tariffs. We use the change in real GDP at factor prices and total consumption in quantity, weighted by the expenditure share for each sector's commodity, to evaluate the welfare effect at the national level. Welfare gains come only from a more efficient allocation of current factor endowments.

While liberalizing agricultural trade in the first scenario raises GDP by 1.4 percent, liberalizing both agricultural and nonagricultural trade in the second scenario more than doubles the gain in GDP to 3.7 percent. This result is comparable to those found in other studies, e.g., China's GDP rises by one percent in USITC (1999) and by 1.4 to 2.0 percent in Lejour (2000). With more imports of foreign goods at lower prices, the domestic price declines. However, the decline happens mainly in agricultural prices when agricultural trade is liberalized. Once both agricultural and nonagricultural trade are fully liberalized, the decline in agricultural prices becomes much smaller and is comparable to the changes in nonagricultural prices and the consumer price index as Table 9.4 indicates. The result is due to the higher demand for agricultural products from higher income levels after full liberalization.

World prices, especially prices for wheat, soybeans, and some other agricultural products, would almost certainly rise if China increases its grain imports, because China is a large consumer of these commodities. To capture this effect of China's WTO accession, a worldwide CGE model in which world prices are determined endogenously is appropriate and used in many studies, e.g., Wang and Schuh (2002) use a world CGE model with 16 countries or regions to study the impact of economic integration of the Chinese Economic Area. However, we are focusing on regional impacts, especially the effects on the less-developed regions within China, and regional aggregation within China is difficult to handle in a worldwide CGE model. Moreover, if a comprehensive trade liberalization after China's joining the WTO affects world prices for a wide range of agricultural and nonagricultural

Table 9.4 Macroeconomic effects (% change from base year)

	EXP-1	*EXP-2*
Real GDP at factor cost	1.41	3.67
Total consumption	0.62	1.76
Consumer price index (CPI)	−1.64	−0.45
Real exchange rate[a]	0.79	5.65
Level of agricultural prices	−4.07	−0.26
Level of nonagricultural prices	0.41	−0.72
Value of total imports	6.13	34.69
Value of total exports	4.13	23.37
Rural income, nominal	−1.88	2.83
Rural income, real[b]	−0.24	3.29
Income from agriculture, nominal	−5.68	1.07
Income from agriculture, real[b]	−4.10	1.52
Urban income, nominal	1.32	3.58
Urban income, real[b]	3.02	4.05

a. Measured by the price ratio between tradable goods and home goods.
b. Normalized by CPI.
EXP-1: Eliminating agricultural tariffs.
EXP-2: Eliminating all tariffs.

Note: The difference between changes in GDP and in total consumption is due to the specification of closure in the model. By fixing government investment expenditure and foreign trade surplus to close the model, the increase in consumers' total consumption would be smaller than the increase in GDP at factor cost.

commodities, many effects would be canceled. Hence, the relative level of agricultural prices may not rise as much as predicted by a commodity or sector analysis. In fact, domestic prices fall by less than one percent in both scenarios (Table 9.4); hence, the magnitude of possible bias due to the small country assumption is minimal.

The welfare effect on rural and urban households is evaluated by the changes in rural and urban income. Because part of rural labor and capital is employed in the nonagricultural sector, changes in both agricultural and nonagricultural activities affect the income of rural households. If only agricultural trade is liberalized, the income of rural households from agriculture declines due to the fall in returns to labor employed in agriculture, to land, and to agricultural capital. Income from the nonagricultural sector increases, because more rural labor is employed in nonagricultural activities. However, because nonagricultural income accounts for one-third of the total income of rural households at the national level, rural income measured at the national level would decline in both nominal and real terms. In contrast, urban incomes rise in this scenario.

If both agricultural and nonagricultural trade are liberalized, agricultural and rural incomes increase in both real and nominal terms, but the increase in income from agriculture is much smaller than that from nonagricultural activities. Hence, rural households still gain less than urban households (Table 9.4). These results indicate that the income gap between rural and urban areas may widen further after China joins the WTO, although liberalizing the nonagricultural sectors would help raise rural income. Hence, analyzing the WTO effect partially by considering agricultural liberalization only may overestimate the negative effect on the rural sector.

As usual, trade liberalization stimulates trade, both in exports and imports. When the trade surplus is fixed at the base level, agricultural trade liberalization raises total trade modestly, as total imports and exports increase by six and four percent, respectively, at border prices. These increases are due mainly to more agricultural trade. However, full trade liberalization permits total imports and exports to increase by 35 and 23 percent, respectively.

Most of the increase in agricultural imports comes from grains, except for rice, and from cotton, vegetable oil, and meat products. The gains in agricultural exports are concentrated in rice, vegetables, fruits, and other crops, an aggregate category that represents a variety of cash crops. Total grain imports more than double after restrictions on imports are lifted in the simulation. The increase in grain imports is driven by a sharp increase in wheat and corn imports. However, while grain imports rise sharply, the ratio of imports to total domestic consumption is still below five percent, rising from two percent at its base. Among the four major grain crops, the ratio of imports to total domestic consumption increases to 6.6 and 7.4 percent for wheat, from less than one percent in the base, around 10 percent for corn, from a 4.6 percent base, 0.8 percent for rice, and 27 to 28 percent for soybeans, from a 15 percent base. Table 9.5 presents the important results.

Table 9.5 Effects on the imports and exports for selected agricultural products

	Base	Exp-1	Exp-2
Imports, % change from the base			
All grains		146.0	162.1
Wheat		1024.2	1157.3
Corn		123.0	134.6
Soybeans		61.1	72.1
Cotton		87.0	78.3
Meat		392.7	383.1
Other processed food		192.1	172.1
Imports/consumption, %			
All grains	1.79	4.38	4.60
Wheat	0.60	6.63	7.40
Corn	4.56	10.08	10.44
Soybeans	14.86	26.86	28.27
Cotton	13.57	24.12	22.41
Meat	4.58	22.00	20.63
Other processed food	1.04	3.02	2.78
Exports, % change from the base			
Rice		13.08	18.81
Vegetables		13.41	21.29
Fruits		31.56	23.34
Other crops		29.96	23.12
Exports/production, %			
Rice	1.60	1.79	1.85
Vegetables	4.23	4.81	5.14
Fruits	4.88	6.48	6.06
Other crops	13.34	16.68	15.83

We emphasize that the import-consumption ratios obtained from our simulations still do not reach the expected limits set by government. In our model, the mobility of land and capital among crops is restricted realistically at the regional level; in many other studies, agricultural resources are reallocated among different crops at the national level. In addition, by controlling labor mobility from agriculture to nonagricultural activities and restricting the change in cropping mix in the Northwest and Southwest, we also take into account reasonable constraints on labor migration, natural resources, and market conditions in these less-developed regions. Moreover, these ratios are the result of full trade liberalization as simulated in the second scenario, which is obviously a long-term goal and beyond the requirements of the WTO until the year 2004. If China reduces agricultural tariff and tariff-equivalent rates by only 50 percent, i.e., from an average rate of 29 percent to 16 percent, the ratio of imports to domestic consumption for total grains is 2.6 percent and wheat imports account for only 1.6 percent of domestic consumption.

With regional aggregation in agricultural production and reasonable constraints on the mobility of labor and other factors, agricultural production at the national level does not change much, except for soybeans, for which output declines 22 percent as imported foreign goods replace domestic production. Even though imports of wheat and corn increase dramatically due to trade liberalization, domestic production of wheat and corn falls by only 3 to 4 percent. On the other hand, the production of exportable commodities rises slightly due to increased exports. Table 9.6 reports these results.

9.5 Differential effects of China's WTO accession at the regional level

At the regional level, we focus on the possible effect of China's WTO accession on rural income. Currently, non-farm income is known to account for about one-third of rural income in China. However, due to the lack of data on rural non-farm sectors, the model cannot disaggregate rural non-farm activities from national nonagricultural sectors and, hence, from the distribution of rural non-farm income at the regional level. Thus, the effects of China joining the WTO on rural income at the regional level are captured by net labor migration from agricultural activities within the regions to nonagricultural activities at the national level. Specifically, we consider only the net increase in rural labor income for each region caused by the net increase in employment in non-crop or nonagricultural activities, while the increase or decrease in rural income due to labor mobility between or across the non-crop and nonagricultural activities is ignored.[4]

Moreover, given that non-farm income accounted for only 10 percent of rural income in the less-developed regions, which is far below the national average of one-third, we assume that agricultural labor in the Northwest and Southwest cannot move freely into nonagricultural activities in the simulations. Given this assumption, we actually segment the labor market and, hence, differentiate the rural wage rate. While a uniform wage rate exists for rural labor from the other five regions, the wage rate for the Northwest and

Table 9.6 Change in agricultural production

	EXP-1	EXP-2
Wheat	−3.18	−3.34
Rice	0.71	2.12
Corn	−4.00	−2.92
Soybeans	−22.23	−22.29
Other oilseeds	−5.30	−4.69
Cotton	−6.47	−2.19
Vegetables	0.88	2.63
Fruits	2.51	3.13
Other crops	4.86	4.43
Livestock products	−2.56	0.29

Southwest is determined endogenously by the labor market clear condition within each of these two regions. Furthermore, natural resource constraints, such as lack of water, and difficulties in market access lead to a lack of export opportunities that restrict the choice of cropping mix in these two regions. Specifically, we assume that exportable commodities are produced mainly in the other five regions, while agricultural production in the two less-developed regions is for the domestic market only. Moreover, the production of rice, vegetables, and fruits is fixed in the Northwest at the levels observed in the base year's data.

Regional analysis reveals large differential impacts on agricultural production as Table 9.7 indicates. For example, wheat production is expected to decline by around three percent in the second scenario at the national level. However, if only agricultural trade is liberalized, wheat production falls significantly more in the Central and Southwest regions than in the nation as a whole. If both agricultural and nonagricultural trade are fully liberalized, South and East become the regions in which wheat production declines substantially. In the North, a major wheat production region that accounts for almost 60 percent of national wheat output, wheat production falls by only 2.6 percent in the second scenario. About 10 percent of China's wheat is produced by the Northwest region; given the limited choice of cropping mix, wheat production actually rises slightly in this region in both scenarios.

Given regional differences in cropping mix, and especially differences in the share of non-farm income in total rural income, WTO accession has even larger regional differential effects on rural income. Four regions would benefit

Table 9.7 Change in crop production at the regional level (% change from base year)

EXP-1	North	Northwest	Northeast	Central	East	South	Southwest	Nation
Wheat	−2.04	0.42	−3.29	−9.91	−3.22	−4.44	−8.69	−3.18
Rice	1.27	0.00	0.00	3.54	−4.44	−4.60	5.76	0.71
Corn	−7.31	−0.32	2.21	−15.17	−11.66	−13.93	−25.63	−4.00
Vegetables	1.81	0.00	−2.82	−4.32	4.32	1.82	7.71	0.88
Fruits	4.72	0.00	2.81	−0.99	3.65	−0.58	−3.72	2.51
Soybeans	−23.50	−24.40	−17.06	−29.46	−34.39	−36.45	−38.70	−22.23
Other oilseeds	−0.70	1.32	−2.91	−8.65	−7.45	−9.38	−9.01	−5.30
Cotton	−7.55	−0.98	−7.94	−9.82	−7.80	−3.65	−4.06	−6.47
Other crops	4.60	14.08	9.23	0.90	5.82	7.18	4.98	4.86
EXP-2								
Wheat	−2.58	0.53	−0.52	−6.61	−6.77	−13.62	−8.20	−3.34
Rice	4.92	0.00	0.00	2.11	2.49	0.58	4.90	2.12
Corn	−5.26	−1.75	1.19	−9.97	−8.38	−12.80	−13.14	−2.92
Vegetables	5.31	0.00	−0.02	−1.97	5.62	1.55	3.39	2.63
Fruits	5.16	0.00	9.65	1.10	1.39	−1.62	−3.10	3.13
Soybeans	−25.86	−26.58	−16.70	−28.22	−27.48	−29.50	−37.82	−22.29
Other oilseeds	−2.09	7.03	3.22	−5.81	−7.75	−10.23	−7.06	−4.69
Cotton	−2.52	2.46	−1.15	−4.85	−4.73	−5.03	−2.13	−2.19
Other crops	8.52	22.79	19.01	4.60	5.15	2.69	6.18	4.43

from full liberalization as Table 9.8 indicates, while the less-developed regions, especially the Northwest, would suffer. The Northeast, which is the major soybean producing region in China, would gain little due to a rapid decline in soybean production caused by competition from imported soybeans and soybean oil. If only agricultural trade is liberalized, income falls in all of the regions because of the decline in agricultural income. In this scenario, the two less-developed regions suffer disproportionately, as rural income falls by 9.4 and 8.0 percent, respectively, compared to a 3.6 percent drop at the national level.

In the more advanced regions, such as the East and the South, non-farm income accounts for as much as 70 to 80 percent of total rural income (Fan et al., 2001). In the less-developed regions, the share is often less than 20 percent. As Table 9.4 shows, returns to nonagricultural activities rise more than do returns to agriculture; the result benefits the advanced regions because their non-farm income ratio is high. Moreover, as the wage rate of non-farm labor increases more rapidly than the agricultural wage rate after liberalization, more labor moves from agriculture to nonagricultural sectors, which benefits further the developed regions because these regions have more non-farm employment opportunities. However, since agriculture is still the main income source in the less-developed regions, rural households gain very little from engaging in non-farm activities. With the decline in agricultural prices and most of the rural labor force still in agriculture, rural income declines in these regions. Table 9.9 presents the changes in rural income by source and by region, while Table 9.10 displays the additional migration of rural labor from agriculture to nonagricultural activities due to trade liberalization.

If only agriculture is liberalized, about seven percent of the rural labor force in the five more developed regions would move from agriculture into nonagricultural activities. However, liberalizing fully both agriculture and nonagriculture reduces labor migration in these regions to between only two to four percent. Due to the decline in agricultural employment, rural income from agriculture falls by eight to nine percent in all regions if only agriculture

Table 9.8 Change in rural income by region[a] (% change from base year)

	EXP-1	EXP-2
North	−3.99	1.46
Northwest	−9.39	−1.98
Northeast	−5.90	0.03
Central	−4.32	1.43
East	−0.93	2.89
South	−1.17	2.94
Southwest	−8.07	−0.10
Nation	−3.55	1.64

a. Income from livestock production is not included.

Table 9.9 Change in rural income by source and by region (% change from base year)

	EXP-1	EXP-2
Agriculture		
North	−9.04	−0.58
Northwest	−9.39	−1.98
Northeast	−9.45	−1.81
Central	−8.17	−0.36
East	−8.99	0.00
South	−8.38	0.76
Southwest	−8.07	−0.10
Non-agriculture		
North	2.75	4.18
Northeast	3.16	4.73
Central	4.73	5.62
East	1.59	3.79
South	1.69	3.81

Note: The Northwest and the Southwest are assumed not to have rural–urban migration and additional non-agricultural income in the simulations.

Table 9.10 Decline in agricultural labor by region (% change from base year)

	EXP-1	EXP-2
North	−6.73	−2.06
Northeast	−7.35	−3.76
Central	−7.11	−3.72
East	−7.49	−1.90
South	−6.49	−1.59

is liberalized. However, both agriculture and nonagriculture are liberalized, rural income from agriculture declines only slightly or even rises in the South. Moreover, rural income from nonagricultural sources rises in both scenarios for all five regions, in which migration opportunities exist. Among these five regions, non-farm income rises most in the Central region, even though the East and South are the two most advanced regions in China. In the base data, non-farm employment accounts for 40 and 31 percent of the total rural labor force in the East and South, respectively, but only 27 percent in the Central region. With trade liberalization, the speed of labor migration and the resulting increase in non-farm income in the Central region is more rapid than in the East and South, but the final share of non-farm income in total rural income is still higher in the East and South.

To test the robustness of our results with respect to the assumptions about migration, we carry out an additional experiment in which the constraint on labor mobility between agriculture and nonagricultural activities in the less-developed regions is relaxed, while all other assumptions remain. The results show that, without the migration constraint, 3.8 and 4.8 percent of the labor force move out of agriculture in the Northwest and Southwest, respectively after full trade liberalization in both the agricultural and nonagricultural sectors. This migration leads to a rise in rural income in the Southwest of 0.5 percent, versus a decrease of 0.1 percent without migration, and a smaller decline in the Northwest of 1.4 percent versus 2.0 percent without migration. Comparing results from this experiment with those obtained from the previous scenarios, migration plays an important role in improving the income of rural households. Declines in rural income in the less-developed regions, where the poverty ratio is already high, affect poor people more significantly. Moreover, in these regions, the poverty ratio is strongly associated with the change in rural income (Fan et al., 2001). Therefore, government policies that diminish the adverse effects of WTO accession on the less-developed areas deserve close attention.

9.6 Conclusions: policy implications

Using a regional CGE model, we analyze the differential regional impacts of China's accession to the WTO on agricultural production, trade, and farmers' income. We divide China into seven regions for agricultural production, and 28 sectors, including 15 disaggregated agricultural sectors for grain, cash crops, livestock, and processing agricultural activities. We simulate the effects of China's WTO accession by reducing or removing tariff and tariff-equivalent protections. Our results indicate that WTO accession will improve total welfare by generating an additional 1.4 to 3.7 percent in GDP in China. However, existing gaps among regions and sectors will widen. The agricultural sector is expected to suffer most if only agricultural trade is liberalized, because cheap imports of agricultural products, particularly grains, will increase and domestic agricultural production and farmers' agricultural income will decline. Full trade liberalization, which consists of lifting trade barriers in both the agricultural and nonagricultural sectors, benefits farmers and agriculture at the national level but rural income increases less than urban income so that the rural–urban income gap widens. Furthermore, the least-developed rural areas benefit little or are even hurt because most of their income still comes from agriculture, especially from traditional agricultural activities such as grain production.

The difficulties in migrating to the non-farm sector, e.g., to rural township and village enterprises and to cities, and in switching from grain to high value-added cash crop production are the two key factors that cause the less-developed regions to lag behind. Our simulation results show that WTO accession may enable non-farm income to rise more rapidly than income from agriculture, especially from grain production. This would stimulate the advanced regions to increase further non-farm employment and to shift from low-return grain production to high-return cash crops. Since they face lower prices for grain crops due to increased competition from imports, farmers in the less-developed regions may have to return to traditional subsistence farming.

Policymakers must re-evaluate current policies and attempt to minimize or to avoid the potential adverse effects of WTO accession on the less-developed areas. The government is already implementing a strategy to develop the Western areas, but Chinese agriculture, farmers, and rural areas in the less-developed regions, which is called the *Shan Nong* problem, should receive a much higher priority in the development strategy. Since farmers in these regions still earn most of their income from agriculture, continued agricultural growth is the most effective way to increase their income and reduce rural poverty. Growth in agriculture in these regions is expected to have the largest impact on poverty reduction through a trickle-down process. In the near future, increasing non-farm employment should also receive high priority once the effects of agricultural growth on poverty reduction have been exhausted.

Apart from natural resource problems, such as the lack of water and poor soil fertility, the major reason that less-favored areas still have a high concentration of rural poor is the government's past neglect of public investment. As a result, the development of infrastructure, technology, and education lags behind that in other regions. For example, in many areas of the Northwest and Southwest, less than half of the rural population over 15-years old is literate, compared to an 80 percent literacy rate at the national level. In terms of agricultural research, the less-developed regions have large numbers of agricultural researchers per 10,000 farmers but spending per agricultural scientist is only half the national average, which indicates a lack of research funds. Given that government spending in rural areas is unlikely to increase after China joins the WTO, more government resources must be targeted to the less-developed regions in order to maximize overall poverty reduction. More investment in these regions might yield high economic returns, making it a win-win development strategy.

Appendix

Sector Aggregation
<u>Agricultural and processed food sectors</u>
Wheat
Rice
Corn and other cereals
Vegetables
Fruits
Soybeans
Other oilseeds
Cotton

Other crops
Livestock and products
Meat, processing eggs and dairy products
Grain mill products
Vegetable oil and forage
Other agricultural products
Other food products

Manufacturing sectors
Fertilizer and pesticides
Agricultural machinery
Cotton textile
Other textile
Wearing and apparel
Leather products
Other industry

Service sectors
Electricity and other utility
Construction
Transport services
Sales services
Financial services
Social services

Table 9.A1 Selected tariff cuts

Item	Base (%)	2004 (%)
Beef	45	12
Pork	20	12
Poultry	20	10
Citrus	40	12
Grapes	40	13
Apples	30	10
Almonds	30	10
Wine	65	20
Cheese	50	12
Ice cream	45	19

Source: U.S.–China bilateral agreement.

Table 9.A2 China's TRQ system quotas, tariff rates, and private trade share

	Quota amount		In-quota tariff rate (%)	Over-quota tariff rate		Private share	
	2000 (mil tons)	2004 (mil tons)		2000 (%)	2004[a] (%)	2000 (%)	2004[a] (%)
Wheat	7.30	9.64	1	77	65	10	10
Indica rice	1.33	2.66	1	77	65	10	10
Japonica rice	1.33	2.66	1	77	65	50	50
Corn	4.50	7.20	1	77	65	25	40
Cotton	0.74	0.89	4	69	40	67	67
Soy oil[b]	1.72	3.26	9	74	9	50	100

a. 2004 is the final year of implementation for every commodity *except* soy oil (see note 2 below).
b. The final year of implementation for soy oil is 2005 (the TRQ quota reaches 3.26 million tons), and the TRQ is eliminated in 2006, converting to 100% private trade with a tariff rate of nine%.

Source: U.S.–China bilateral agreement.

Notes

1 An early version of this paper was presented at the International Conference on Rural Investments, Growth and Poverty, November 5–6, 2001, Beijing, China. The authors acknowledge comments from participants at the conference. They also acknowledge gratefully Rebecca Harris for her editorial assistance and three anonymous referees of the journal for their comments and suggestions.
2 Gilbert and Wahl (2002) provide a comprehensive survey of CGE assessments of trade liberalization in China.
3 A detailed description about the model is available from the authors upon request.
4 While rural labor engaged in non-farm economic activities has increased steadily in China during the last three decades, most rural persons engaged in non-farm activities also work in agricultural sector. According to China's 1997 Agricultural Census, only 11.4 percent of rural labor was employed full time in the non-agricultural sector (Tuan, Somwaru, and Diao, 2000). Moreover, due to the current systems of land tenure and resident registration (*hu ko*), rural–urban and inter-provincial labor migration numbers are small. For this reason, China's SAM does not provide data on transfers or remittances, which constrains us from analyzing their impact on rural income.

References

Colby, Hunter, Diao, Xinshen, and Tuan, Francis, "China's WTO Accession: Conflicts with Domestic Agricultural Policies and Institutions." *The Estey Center Journal of International Law and Trade Policy* 2, 1:190–210, Apr. 2001.

Development Research Center (DRC), The State Council of People's Republic of China, *The Global and Domestic Impact of China Joining the World Trade Organization.* Beijing: DRC, The State Council of People's Republic of China, 1998.

Fan, Mingtai and Zheng, Yuxin, "The Impact of China's Trade Liberalization for WTO Accession – A Computable General Equilibrium Analysis." Paper presented for the Third GTAP Annual Conference, Melbourne, Australia, June 2000.

Fan, Shenggen, Zhang, Linxiu, and Zhang, Xiaobo, *Growth, Inequality, and Poverty in Rural China: The Role of Public Investment*. Washington, DC: International Food Policy Research Institute Research Report 125, 2002.

Fan, Shenggen, Zhang, Linxiu, Zhang, Xiaobo, and Ma, Xiaohe, "Regional Priorities of Public Investment in Rural China: A County-Level Analysis." Report No. 1 prepared for the IFPRI project "Priorities of Public Investments in Chinese Agriculture," sponsored by the Australian Center for International Agricultural Research (ACIAR), Canberra, Australian, Sept. 2001.

Gilbert, John and Wahl, Thomas, "Applied General Equilibrium Assessments of Trade Liberalization in China." *World Economy* **25**, 5:697–731, May 2002.

Hertel, Thomas and Walmsley, Terrie, "China's Accession to the WTO: Timing Is Everything." *World Economy* **24**, 8:1019–49, Aug. 2001.

Kanbur, Ravi and Zhang, Xiaobo, "Which Regional Inequality? The Evolution of Rural–Urban and Inland–Coastal Inequality in China from 1983 to 1995." *Journal of Comparative Economics* **27**, 4:686–701, Dec. 1999.

Kanbur, Ravi and Zhang, Xiaobo, "Fifty Years of Regional Inequality in China: A Journey Through Revolution, Reform and Openness." London, UK: Center for Economic Policy Research (CEPR) Discussion Paper 2887, July, 2001.

Lejour, Arjan, "China and the WTO: The Impact on China and the World Economy." Paper presented for the Third GTAP Annual Conference, Melbourne, Australia, June 2000.

Martin, Will, Dimaranan, Betina, and Hertel, Thomas, "Trade Policy, Structural Change and China's Trade Growth." Memo, World Bank, 1999.

Ministry of Agriculture (MOA), *China Agricultural Development Report* (English translation.) Beijing: China Agricultural Press, 2000.

Ministry of Agriculture, *China's Agricultural Statistical Materials* (English translation.) Beijing: China Agricultural Publishing House, 1988.

Ministry of Agriculture, *China's Agricultural Yearbook* (English translation.) Beijing: China Agricultural Publishing House, 1980–2000.

Ministry of Agriculture, *China's Rural Statistical Yearbook* (English translation.) Beijing: China Agricultural Publishing House, 1980–2000.

National Bureau of Statistics of China, *China Statistical Yearbook* (English translation.) Beijing: China Statistics Press, 1988–2000.

National Bureau of Statistics of China, *China's Commodity Price Yearbook* (English translation.) Beijing: China Statistics Press, 1980–2000.

National Bureau of Statistics of China, *Collections of Provincial Historical Statistical Materials* (English translation.) Beijing: China Statistics Press, 1988–2000.

Rozelle, Scott, "Rural Industrialization and Increasing Inequality: Emerging Patterns in China's Reforming Economy." *Journal of Comparative Economics* **19**, 3:363–392, Sept. 1994.

Tuan, Francis, Somwaru, Agapi, and Diao, Xinshen, "Rural Labor Migration, Characteristics, and Employment Patterns: A Study Based on China's Agricultural Census." Trade and Macroeconomic Division (TMD) Discussion Paper No. 63, Washington, DC: International Food Policy Research Institute, Nov. 2000, available on web site: www.ifpri.org.

U.S. International Trade Commission (USITC), *Assessment of the Economic Effects on the United States of China's Accession to the WTO*. Washington, DC: USITC Publication 3229, 1999.

Wang, Zhi, "The Impact of China's WTO Entry on the World Labor-Intensive

Export Market: A Recursive Dynamic CGE Analysis." *The World Economy* **22**, 3:379–405, Aug. 1999.

Wang, Zhi and Schuh, Edward G., "The Emergence of a Greater China and Its Impact on World Trade: A Computable General Equilibrium Analysis." *Journal of Comparative Economics* **30**, 3:531–566, Sept. 2002.

Wei, Shang-Jin and Wu, Yi, "Globalization and Inequality: Evidence from Within China." Cambridge, MA: National Bureau of Economic Research (NBER) Working Paper No. w8611, Nov. 2001.

Zhang, Xiaobo and Fan, Shenggen, "Estimating Crop-Specific Production Technology in Chinese Agriculture: A Generalized Maximum Entropy Approach." *American Journal of Agricultural Economics* **83**, 2:378–388, May 2001.

10 Infrastructure and regional economic development in rural China [1]

Shenggen Fan and Xiaobo Zhang

Abstract

Infrastructure affects rural development through many channels such as improved agricultural productivity, increased rural non-farm employment, and rural migration into urban sectors. However, the role of infrastructure in rural development has not been paid enough attention in the literature. One of the thornier problems in analyzing the role of rural infrastructure is the lack of reliable data on various infrastructure indicators. By using newly available detailed data on rural infrastructure from the Agricultural Census combined with data from other official sources, this paper evaluates the current situation of infrastructure and analyzes its role in agriculture and non-farm economies in rural China. We use a traditional source accounting approach to identify the specific role of rural infrastructure and other public capital in explaining productivity difference among regions, shedding new lights on how to allocate limited public resources for both growth and regional equity purposes.

10.1 Introduction

Rapid growth in Chinese agriculture after the reforms has triggered numerous studies to analyze the sources of the rapid growth. These studies include McMillian, Whalley, and Zhu (1989), Fan (1990 and 1991), Lin (1992), Huang and Rozelle (1996), Zhang and Carter (1997), and Fan and Pardey (1997). Most of these studies attempted to analyze the impact of institutional changes and the increased use of inputs on production growth during the reform period from the end of the 1970s to the beginning of the 1990s.

Fan and Pardey (1997) and Fan (2000) were among the first to point out that omitted variables such as research and development (R&D) investment would bias the estimate of the sources of production growth. To address this concern, they included a research stock variable in the production function to account for the contribution of R&D investment to rapid production growth, in addition to the increased use of inputs and institutional changes. They found that by ignoring the R&D variable in the production function estimation, the effects of institutional change would be overestimated to a large extent.

In addition to R&D investment, government investments in roads, electrification, education, and other public investment in rural areas may have also contributed to the rapid growth in agricultural production. It is highly likely that omitting these variables will bias the estimates of the production function for Chinese agriculture as well.

One of the most important features in rural China is the rapid development of rural nonfarm economies since the economic reform in 1978. But very few have analyzed the sources of growth in this sector. The only exception is Fan, Zhang, and Robinson (2003), who decomposed the growth in the non-farm sector into growth in labor and capital. But they failed to include public capital as an input in their source accounting, partly due to the lack of reliable public capital data.

Associated with the rapid economic growth, regional disparity in productivity has also increased for China for the last two decades. The regional difference in productivity is a major determinant of income disparity, an increasing concern by policymakers and many scholars alike. The uneven regional development in nonfarm activities in the rural sector, in particular in the non-farm sector, has been regarded as one major driving force behind the changes in rural regional inequality (Rozelle, 1994; Zhang and Fan, 2003). However, despite a large body of literature on the sources of growth, few studies have attempted to account for the sources of regional difference in productivity of both the agricultural and non-farm sectors (one exception is Fan (1990)), and no studies have systematically assessed the roles of public investment in such differences in regional development.

The motivation of this study is to include these public investment variables that are newly available from the Census to estimate the production functions for both agricultural and non-agricultural economies in rural China and to decompose the sources of difference in productivity among regions. In particular, the specific role of infrastructure in explaining the difference in productivity among regions will be evaluated. There are several advantages in using the Agricultural Census data. First, the Census reports detailed infrastructure information at the country level, which is more disaggregate than the provincial level data commonly seen in the official statistical yearbooks. Second, the arable land area and labor force data are more accurately measured than the previous official sources (Ash and Edmonds, 1998; Smil, 1999).

The paper is organized as follows: Section 10.2 reviews the regional distribution of public capital in rural China. Section 10.3 develops a conceptual framework and model for the purpose of our analysis. Section 10.4 describes the data, and Section 10.5 discusses our estimated results. We conclude the paper, and point out the limitations of the current study and future research directions in the final section.

10.2 Regional dimension of rural infrastructure

The Agricultural Census provides a unique opportunity to analyze the regional dimension of rural infrastructure in China. Table 10.1 presents the selected infrastructure indicators by province in 1996 when the Census was conducted. First, we compare the newly available Census data with the official data which are published previously in various *China Statistical Yearbooks* by the State Statistical Bureau (SSB) or other government agencies. For road

Table 10.1 Regional difference in rural infrastructure (1996)

Province	Road density			Electricity use kw per person	Rural telephone	
	km/10,000 km²	km/10,000 labor	km/10,000 person		Set per 10,000 labor	Set per 10,000 people
Beijing	6,310	48	28	709	1,024	933
Tianjin	5,258	27	17	844	625	555
Hebei	3,021	18	11	252	222	207
Shanxi	3,578	40	24	309	205	183
Inner Mongolia	484	64	42	150	229	199
Liaoning	2,985	31	21	375	502	487
Jilin	2,136	48	29	184	286	266
Heilongjiang	1,200	54	35	177	388	345
Shanghai	17,676	36	26	1,771	2,767	2,760
Jiangsu	6,863	19	13	453	604	573
Zhejiang	3,505	15	10	525	596	582
Anhui	4,905	20	13	113	160	156
Fujian	4,305	35	21	383	735	594
Jiangxi	3,529	29	19	115	109	102
Shandong	6,358	21	14	287	242	206
Henan	4,382	15	9	195	111	106
Hubei	4,199	31	20	182	319	296
Hunan	4,633	30	20	129	171	160
Guangdong	3,843	25	14	625	1,258	1,222
Guangxi	2,287	24	15	114	97	91
Hainan		51	29	63	163	158
Chongqing		22	16	159	121	111
Sichuan	2,050	25	17	165	88	74
Guizhou	3,172	29	18	78	54	42
Yunnan	2,840	51	32	268	108	96
Tibet	344	339	199	22	65	54
Shaanxi	3,210	37	23	172	101	95
Gansu	1,300	42	26	190	81	71
Qinghai	207	72	46	273	247	244
Ningxia	1,082	32	19	161	104	103
Xinjiang	277	90	52	159	172	166

Note: When calculating road density, Hannan and Chongqing are included in Guangdong and Sichuan, respectively.

Source: Calculated from the Agricultural Census.

density, the Census reported 1,679 kilometers per 10,000 square kilometers, which is 34 percent higher than the official data, released from the Ministry of Transportation. Therefore, the data from the Ministry of Transportation may have understated the road density in rural areas. With respect to rural telephones, the Census reported 283 sets per 10,000 rural residents which is 43 percent higher than 197 sets reported by the SSB *Statistical Yearbook*. For rural electricity consumption, the Census reported 260 kw per person for 1996, while the SSB *Statistical Yearbook* reported 200 kw per person in rural China, a 30 percent difference.

In terms of the illiteracy rate, the Census data reported 14 percent for the rural population over the age of seven years. This percentage is comparable to 11 percent in 1996 for agricultural labor reported by the SSB *Rural Statistical Yearbook, 1997*. The higher rate for the general population than agricultural labor may be due to the fact that the general population may have a higher illiteracy rate than the total labor force.

With respect to R&D spending and personnel, the data are not easily comparable. The Census reports such data only for the township level, while official SSB or Ministry of Science and Technology reports the data above the county level. Nevertheless, the Census data provides unique and valuable information about science and technology at the lower level which has never been reported before by other official sources.

The regional data reveals that the infrastructure development is highly correlated with the economic development level. Road density measured as length of rural town roads per 10,000 square kilometers has very large regional variation. If we exclude Beijing, Shanghai, and Tianjin in our analysis, Jiangsu has the highest road density, and Shandong has the second. Not surprisingly, Inner Mongolia, Tibet, Qinghai, and Xinjiang have the lowest road densities among all provinces. However, if we use the length of roads per rural resident, it is the Western provinces or regions that per capita length of roads are the highest, due to their relatively lower population density.

In terms of rural electricity, again it is the Coastal region that has the highest per capita consumption. For example, Guangdong, Jiangsu, and Zhejiang have more than 400 kw per person per year, while in Inner Mongolia, Tibet, Xinjiang, Guizhou, and surprisingly some Central provinces such as Anhui, Jiangxi, and Guangxi, per capita electricity consumption in 1996 is less than 200 kw.

The difference in rural telephone possession is the largest among all types of rural infrastructure. In Guangdong, Jiangsu, Zhejiang, and Fujian, for every 10,000 residents, there are more than 500 telephone sets. But in Gansu, Tibet, Guizhou, Sichuan, and Guangxi, less than 100 sets are possessed for every 10,000 rural residents.

The education data reveals that in the Western region the Census reported a much higher illiteracy rate than the official SSB *Rural Statistical Yearbook, 1997* (Table 10.2). For example, in Tibet and Qinghai, the Census recorded 76 percent and 45 percent for Tibet and Gansu, compared to 61 percent and

Table 10.2 Percentage of rural population with different education levels (1996)

	Illiterate and semi-illiterate	Primary school	Junior middle school	Senior middle school	Special secondary school	College and above
National	14.01	42.15	38.04	5.07	0.57	0.16
Beijing	6.28	21.04	59.08	10.67	2.23	0.70
Tianjin	7.15	37.54	48.30	6.21	0.64	0.16
Hebei	10.03	39.11	43.87	6.45	0.44	0.09
Shanxi	8.81	35.74	48.41	6.20	0.62	0.22
Inner Mongolia	17.26	39.66	36.54	5.66	0.70	0.18
Liaoning	6.31	41.29	47.22	4.08	0.79	0.30
Jilin	8.27	45.47	40.75	4.56	0.77	0.19
Heilongjiang	8.67	43.54	41.95	4.77	0.84	0.24
Shanghai	13.83	28.39	49.38	6.37	1.44	0.60
Jiangsu	12.53	36.94	42.49	7.12	0.63	0.29
Zhejiang	13.85	44.26	36.30	5.07	0.37	0.15
Anhui	16.32	42.52	37.18	3.28	0.55	0.14
Fujian	7.01	51.53	35.83	4.86	0.61	0.16
Jiangxi	11.67	48.90	34.29	4.51	0.52	0.12
Shandong	9.80	40.65	43.09	5.63	0.66	0.15
Henan	13.57	33.41	46.26	6.13	0.49	0.14
Hubei	14.63	40.97	38.21	5.49	0.60	0.10
Hunan	9.65	43.76	39.42	6.37	0.65	0.15
Guangdong	7.93	42.87	41.39	6.81	0.75	0.24
Guangxi	10.42	47.98	35.77	5.00	0.71	0.12
Hainan	17.73	35.60	38.76	7.20	0.59	0.12
Chongqing	11.87	52.03	32.44	3.20	0.37	0.10
Sichuan	15.67	48.60	32.42	2.88	0.35	0.08
Guizhou	29.95	45.47	22.23	1.76	0.50	0.08
Yunnan	28.09	49.11	20.25	2.12	0.38	0.06
Tibet	75.71	22.93	1.21	0.09	0.05	0.01
Shaanxi	16.35	35.21	40.88	6.90	0.50	0.15
Gansu	35.57	34.40	24.12	5.25	0.51	0.15
Qinghai	46.04	31.82	19.10	2.77	0.21	0.06
Ningxia	31.16	33.37	29.68	4.70	0.86	0.22
Xinjiang	15.73	53.69	25.24	3.78	1.18	0.39

Source: Calculated from the Agricultural Census.

34 percent reported by the *Rural Statistical Yearbook*, respectively. The gap in the education level between the Eastern and Western regions may have been higher than previously believed.

The Census data on science and technology personnel and spending uncovers a striking phenomenon (Table 10.3). It is the Western region, for example Xinjiang, and Inner Mongolia, that have the highest ratios of science and technology personnel to rural population or labor. But in terms of science and technology spending, the region has the lowest. This implies that the science and technology personnel in less-developed areas experience a severe shortage of operation funds compared to their Eastern cohorts.

Table 10.3 Sciences and technology personnel and expenses (1996)

	Number of ST personnel per 10,000 rural labor	Number of ST personnel per 10,000 rural residents	ST spending in yuan per rural labor	ST spending in yuan per rural residents
National	90.89	58.41	0.81	0.52
Beijing	200.16	115.69	0.90	0.52
Tianjin	253.67	155.73	0.38	0.23
Hebei	147.87	90.82	0.33	0.20
Shanxi	81.39	48.94	0.47	0.28
Inner Mongolia	344.24	224.39	0.24	0.16
Liaoning	88.93	58.88	1.38	0.92
Jilin	126.34	77.55	0.43	0.26
Heilongjiang	166.80	107.64	0.40	0.26
Shanghai	150.28	107.68	5.93	4.25
Jiangsu	81.50	55.64	1.12	0.77
Zhejiang	57.80	39.10	1.11	0.75
Anhui	54.56	35.04	0.46	0.30
Fujian	92.89	55.40	1.62	0.97
Jiangxi	47.77	30.90	0.22	0.14
Shandong	92.89	61.33	1.26	0.83
Henan	123.86	79.42	0.25	0.16
Hubei	84.61	54.11	0.77	0.49
Hunan	79.70	52.38	0.88	0.58
Guangdong	80.93	45.99	2.76	1.57
Guangxi	66.82	42.16	0.38	0.24
Hainan	143.37	82.08	1.10	0.63
Chongqing	37.32	26.49	0.39	0.28
Sichuan	64.45	44.86	0.91	0.64
Guizhou	27.10	17.12	0.43	0.27
Yunnan	35.05	22.32	0.61	0.39
Tibet	44.86	26.41	0.02	0.01
Shaanxi	104.83	64.08	0.15	0.09
Gansu	104.42	64.93	0.07	0.04
Qinghai	68.40	43.59	0.00	0.00
Ningxia	48.42	28.99	0.14	0.08
Xinjiang	345.98	199.60	0.24	0.14

Source: Calculated from the Agricultural Census.

In summary, the Census data reveals a higher level of rural infrastructure development than previously thought. But it also uncovers a larger regional difference not only in the development of rural infrastructure, but also in the development of education and science and technology. This may explain why the Western region has lagged behind despite rapid economic growth for the nation as a whole.

10.3 Conceptual framework and model

There have been numerous studies on the estimation of production functions for both agricultural and nonfarm sectors. One significant feature in these previous studies is the use of a single-equation approach. There are at least two disadvantages to this approach. First, many production determinants are generated from the same economic process. In other words, these variables are also endogenous variables, and ignoring this characteristic leads to biased estimates of the production functions. Second, certain economic variables affect the rural economy through multiple channels. For example, improved rural infrastructure will not only contribute growth in agricultural production, but also affect nonfarm production. It is very difficult to capture these different effects in a single equation approach.

This study uses a simultaneous equations model to estimate the effects of rural infrastructure on both farm and nonfarm production.

$$AY = f(LAND, AGLABOR, FERT, MACH, IR, RD, SCHY, \\ ROADS, RTR), \tag{1}$$

$$NAY = f(RILABOR, ELEC, SCHY, ROADS, RTR). \tag{2}$$

Equation (1) models the agricultural production function. The dependent variable is gross agricultural output value (AY). Land ($LAND$), labor ($AGLABOR$), fertilizer ($FERT$), machinery ($MACH$) are included as conventional inputs. We include the following variables in the equation to capture the impact of technology, infrastructure, and education on agricultural production: percentage of irrigated cropped area in total cropped area (IR); number of agricultural researchers and extension staff (RD), road density ($ROADS$), number of rural telephone sets per thousand rural residents (RTR), and average years of schooling for population over the age of seven years old ($SCHY$).[2]

Equation (2) is a production function for nonagricultural activities in rural areas. The dependent variable is gross value of the township and village enterprises (NAY). Labor input used in the nonfarm sector ($RILABOR$), infrastructure, and the labor education level are independent variables included in the function.[3] The electricity consumption ($ELEC$) is used to proxy for fixed and current capital used in the nonfarm sector.

Following Fan (1991), Lin (1992), and Fan and Pardey (1997), we use the traditional Cobb-Douglas form for both agricultural and nonfarm equations. In this form, the coefficients of independent variables are simply their elasticities with respect to the dependent variable. Regional dummies are also added to capture the impact of other factors that are not included in the equations.

To account for the sources of difference in productivity, we choose labor productivity in our analysis. Labor productivity is one of the most important indicators in economic development and is one of the major determinants of rural income. Following Hayami and Ruttan (1985) and Fan (1990), we use the following accounting formula:

$$\frac{\Delta \dfrac{Y}{L}}{\left(\dfrac{Y}{L}\right)^0} = \sum_i a_i \frac{\Delta \dfrac{X_i}{L}}{\left(\dfrac{X_i}{L}\right)^0} + \sum b_i \frac{\Delta P_i}{P_{i0}} \qquad (3)$$

We use the average productivity at the national level ($Y/L)_0$ as our base for comparison, i.e., we try to explain the difference in productivity between each region and the national average.[4] In (3), labor productivity difference is explained by the difference in the use of conventional inputs X_i such as labor, land, fertilizer, machinery all measured on a per labor basis, and the difference in rural infrastructure, education, and science and technology capacity, denoted by P_i. If we divide every term on the right hand side by the productivity difference (on the left hand side), then the difference in productivity can be explained by right hand side variables in terms of percentages.

10.4 Data explanations

Our analysis is based at the county level. Most of infrastructure, education and technology variables are available in the Agricultural Census. However, Agricultural Census does not report detailed information on agricultural and nonfarm output. Input uses are also not available. Therefore, in this analysis, we combine the Census data with the data from other SSB sources such as *China Statistical Yearbooks* and *China's Rural Statistical Yearbooks*.

Agricultural output – Agricultural output is measured as gross agricultural production value. The data is taken from the SSB official statistical source.

Nonfarm output – Nonfarm output is measured as gross output value of township and village enterprises. The sources of the data are official SSB and Ministry of Agriculture publications.

Agricultural labor – Agricultural labor is measured in stock terms as the number of persons engaged in agricultural production at the end of each year. They are taken from the Census.

Nonfarm labor – Nonfarm labor is measured as number of employees in the township and village enterprises reported by the Agricultural Census.

Land – land is total arable land used for agricultural production. The data is taken from the Census.

Machinery – Machinery input is measured as horsepower of machinery used in agricultural production. Since the Census does not report horsepower of machinery, we use the data from the SSB *Statistical Yearbook*.

Irrigation – Irrigation services used in agriculture are proxied by the ratio of irrigated area. Since the published Census data do not report irrigated areas by county, we use the data from official sources of SSB and Ministry of Agriculture.

Fertilizer – It is measured as pure nutrients of chemical fertilizer. The data are taken from official sources of SSB and Ministry of Agriculture.

Roads – The length of township roads is reported by the Census. We divided the road length by the geographic areas to obtain the road density variable for our analysis.

Rural telephone – Number of rural telephone sets is available from the Census. We use the number of telephone sets per 10,000 rural residents as our telephone variable.

Education – For the education variable, we use the percentage of population with different education levels to calculate the average years of schooling as our education variable, assuming 0 year for a person who is illiterate and semi-illiterate, 5 years with primary school education, 8 years with junior high school education, 12 years with high school education, 13 years with professional school education, and 16 years with college and above education. The Agricultural Census reports the percentages of population with different education levels who are above the age of seven.

Electricity consumption – Electricity consumption in the nonfarm and agricultural sectors are reported by various issues of *China Rural Statistical Yearbooks*.

Science and technology – We use the number of science and technology personnel per 10,000 rural labor at the township level to represent the capacity of science and technology. The data are taken from the Census.

10.5 Results

Table 10.4 presents the estimated results of production functions for agriculture and nonfarm economies. Only 15 provinces or regions reported county level data in recent SSB provincial publications on the Agricultural Census. They are: Beijing, Tianjin, Shanxi, Heilongjiang, Shanghai, Jiangsu, Zhejiang, Fujian, Jiangxi, Shandong, Hunan, Sichuan, Tibet, Shaanxi, and Ningxia. Although they cover roughly half of the provinces, the number of observations covers only 45 percent of the total number of counties. Therefore, the sample we used in our regression may not represent the whole of China.

Most coefficients in both agricultural and nonfarm production functions are statistically significant. The coefficients for conventional inputs in the agricultural production function such as those for labor, land, fertilizer, and machinery are in the same ranges of other studies (Fan 1991, Fan and Pardey 1997, Zhang and Carter 1997). The labor and electricity variables (as a proxy for both fixed and current capitals) are also statistically significant. One notable feature is that the coefficients for infrastructure and education variables are more significant in the nonfarm production equation than those in the agricultural production function. The fitness of both equations is exceptionally good with R^2 of 0.865 for the agricultural production function, and 0.813 for the nonfarm production function, despite the fact that cross-sectional data are used. The road variable in the nonfarm sector is insignificant due to its high correlation with the telephone variable, therefore we drop it in the final estimation.

Table 10.5 presents the results of accounting. The numbers in parentheses below the first row are the difference in labor productivity level between each

Table 10.4 Estimation of the equation system

	Agricultural output	Non-farm output
Labor	0.262	0.510
	(3.14)*	(16.84)*
Land	0.228	
	(8.47)*	
Fertilizer	0.150	
	(4.55)*	
Machinery (or electricity)	0.115	0.480
	(6.34)*	(15.89)*
Research	0.104	
	(3.42)*	
Irrigation	0.260	
	(9.48)*	
Roads	0.032	
	(2.25)*	
Years of Schooling	0.275	0.792
	(1.81)*	(1.94)*
Telephone	0.056	0.119
	(6.41)*	(6.51)*
R^2	0.865	0.813

Notes: Regional dummies are added to capture the provincial fixed effect, but the coefficients are not reported here. Total number of observations is 1,104.

The subscript * indicates statistically significant at the 5 percent level.

region and the national average. By assuming this difference as 100 percent, we can explain the productivity difference in terms of the percentages by various factors shown in the rest of the rows in the table.[5]

The sources of difference in agricultural labor productivity vary sharply among regions. The higher labor productivity in the Eastern region is primarily explained by higher fertilizer use, better infrastructure, and the residual, which accounts for other missing variables. This residual is particularly large, implying that other factors rather than those included in the equation may have played an even bigger role in explaining its higher productivity. For the Central region, higher productivity is mainly explained by more use of land per labor together with more fertilizer, machinery, and irrigation use. In the Western region, the lower productivity is due to lower land use per labor (and therefore lower fertilizer use), poorer infrastructure and human capitals, and more limited science and technology capacity. The residual that has not been accounted for by the variables included is also quite large, indicating other factors may have also contributed to lower productivity in the region.

For labor productivity in the nonfarm economy, roads and telephone together explained more than 60 percent of the difference between the regional and the national average in the Eastern region. For the Western region, nearly 40 percent of the productivity difference (lower than the

Table 10.5 Accounting for the sources of labor productivity difference among regions

	Agriculture			Nonfarm			Total rural		
	Eastern	Central	Western	Eastern	Central	Western	Eastern	Central	Western
Productivity	100.00	100.00	100.00	100.00	100.00	100.00	100.00	100.00	100.00
	(47.06)	(2.35)	(−35.29)	(38.08)	(17.22)	(−47.35)	(41.32)	(10.82)	(−40.08)
Land	−0.96	230.35	15.36				−0.35	99.08	9.26
Fertilizer	7.45	46.27	10.63				2.69	19.90	6.41
Machinery	0.72	121.43	9.87	−11.46	3.62	−5.92	−7.07	54.29	3.60
Irrigation	−3.44	103.20	7.45				−1.24	44.39	4.50
S&T	−0.08	4.58	0.16				−0.03	1.97	0.10
Roads	−2.16	−30.85	−4.25	0.00	0.00	−0.00	−0.78	−13.27	−2.56
Telephone	20.50	−210.14	10.66	53.83	−61.02	16.88	41.82	−125.16	13.13
Education	1.57	21.04	6.35	5.68	8.41	13.84	4.20	13.84	9.32
Residual	76.39	−185.88	43.78	51.95	148.99	75.20	60.76	4.95	56.25

national average) can be attributed to the physical infrastructure and lower educational level. Large residual in the accounting for nonfarm productivity indicates that many other factors may also play a very important role in the nonfarm economy.

For the overall rural economy (aggregation of both agricultural and non-farm economies), public capital such as roads, telecommunications, and education explained about 45 percent of the higher productivity in the Eastern region. In the Western region, lower public capital accounted for 26 percent of the lower productivity. In the Central region, however, since its productivity is very close to the national level, it is not obvious how public capital has affected its productivity difference when compared to the national average.

10.6 Conclusions

The 1996 Agricultural Census provides a unique data set to analyze various issues on rural development in China. In particular, it provides very detailed data on rural infrastructure, education, and science and technology. This paper is an early attempt to use this data set. Partly due to the limited access, the data we have is not complete, covering only 45 percent of the country. We will pursue more detailed and more thorough analyses once we have a complete data set for all counties.

Despite the crudeness of the data and model we used, the results do shed new lights. First, rural infrastructure and education play a more important role in explaining the difference in rural nonfarm productivity than agricultural productivity. Since the rural nonfarm economy is a major determinant of rural income, investing more in rural infrastructure is key to increasing over-all income of rural population. Second, the lower productivity in the Western region is explained by its lower level of rural infrastructure, education, and science and technology. Therefore, improving both the level and efficiency of public capital in the West is a must to narrow its difference in productivity with other regions.

This research merely serves as a touchstone for future research. One of the urgent future research topics is to search different policy options to mobil-ize resources to support public investment provisions for the less developed Western region. Under the current fiscal decentralization scheme, financing infrastructure in regions with a small nonfarm sector faces a great challenge. Lack of local revenues causes under-investment in the less developed Western region.

Notes

1 The funding from FAO to the first author for his travel to Beijing to participate in the International Seminar on Chinese Census Results, September 19–22, 2000, Beijing, and the funding from ACIAR for all the authors in data collection, data compiling and paper preparation are acknowledged.

2 The electricity variable is excluded mainly because it is highly correlated with road and telephone variables.
3 Ideally, the capital variable should also be included in the function. But there is no such data available at county level.
4 This decomposition implicitly assumes a constant return to scale, i.e., $\Sigma\, a_i = 1$. This assumption is not too realistic, as evidenced by Fan (1991) and Zhang and Carter (1997).
5 Because the development level in the Central region is close to the national average, the absolute difference in labor productivity is rather small. However, the decomposition analysis is based on relative percentage terms. Therefore, the results for the Central regions could be very sensitive.

References

Ash, R.F., and R.L. Edmonds (1998) "China's Land Resources, Environment and Agricultural Production," *China Quarterly*, 156: 836–879.

Fan, Shenggen (1990) *Regional Productivity Growth in China's Agriculture*, Westview Press, Boulder.

Fan, Shenggen (1991) "Effects of Technological Change and Institutional Reform on Production Growth in Chinese Agriculture," *American Journal of Agricultural Economics*, 73(2): 266–275.

Fan, Shenggen (2000) "Research Investment and the Economic Returns to Chinese Agricultural Research," *Journal of Productivity Analysis*, 14(92): 163–180.

Fan, Shenggen, and Philip Pardey (1997) "Research, Productivity, and Output Growth in Chinese Agriculture," *Journal of Development Economics*, 53: 115–137.

Fan, S., X. Zhang, and S. Robinson (2003) "Structural Change and Economic Growth," *Review of Development Economics* 7(3): 360–377.

Hayami, Y., and Vernon Ruttan (1985) *Agricultural Development: An International Perspective*, Johns Hopkins University Press, Baltimore.

Huang, J., and S. Rozelle (1996) "Environmental Stress and Grain Yields in China," *American Journal of Agricultural Economics*, 77: 853–864.

Huang, J., and S. Rozelle (1997) "Technological Change: Rediscovering the Engine of Productivity Growth in China's Agricultural Economy," *Journal of Development Economics*, 49: 337–369.

Kanbur, Ravi, and Xiaobo Zhang (1999) "Which Regional Inequality? The Evolution of Rural–Urban and Inland–Coastal Inequality in China, 1983–1995," *Journal of Comparative Economics* 27, 686–701.

Lin, Justin Yifu (1992) "Rural Reforms and Agricultural Growth in China," *American Economic Review*, 82(1): 34–51.

McMillan, John, John Whalley, and Lijing G. Zhu (1989) "The Impact of China's Economic Reforms on Agricultural Productivity Growth," *Journal of Political Economy*, 97: 781–807.

Rozelle, Scott (1994) "Rural Industrialization and Increasing Inequality: Emerging Patterns in China's Reforming Economy," *Journal of Comparative Economics* 19, 3: 362–391.

Smil, V. (1999) "China's Agricultural Land," *China Quarterly*, 158: 414–429.

Zhang, B., and C.A. Carter (1997) "Reforms, the Weather, and Productivity Growth in China's Grain Sector," *American Journal of Agricultural Economics* 79, 1266–1277.

Zhang, X., and S. Fan (2003) "Public Investment and Regional Inequality in Rural China," *Agricultural Economics*, forthcoming.

11 Public investment and regional inequality in rural China

Xiaobo Zhang and Shenggen Fan[1]

Abstract

This paper develops a method for decomposing the contributions of various types of public investment to regional inequality and applies the method to rural China. Public investments are found to have contributed to production growth in both the agricultural and rural non-agricultural sectors, but their contributions to regional inequality have differed by type of investment and the region in which they are made. All types of investment in the least-developed western region reduce regional inequality, whereas additional investments in the coastal and central regions worsen regional inequality. Investments in rural education and agricultural R&D in the western region have the largest and most favorable impacts on reducing regional inequality.

11.1 Introduction

There has been a long debate on the role of public investment in economic growth (Aschauer, 1989; Barro, 1990; Munnell, 1992; Tatom, 1993; Gramlich, 1994; Holtz-Eakin, 1994; Evans and Karras, 1994; Garcia-Mila, McGuire, and Porter, 1996). Public investments can be allocated to promote growth directly by providing various public goods, such as research and development (R&D), infrastructure and education, or indirectly by creating an environment to attract private investment. Different public goods have different characteristics and externalities and may, therefore, have different impacts on growth and equity. However, most theoretical and empirical studies focus on either just one type of public investment or on total public investment, and ignore differences between types of public investment. Considering just one type of public investment often leads to overestimation of its returns (Antle, 1988; Griliches, 1988), while using aggregate government investment masks important policy information about which public investments deserve highest priority.

Apart from their role in growth, different types of public investment are also key instruments for governments to use in reducing regional inequality (World Bank, 1994). But except for Martin (1999) and Jacoby (2000), few studies have attempted to investigate both the regional equity and growth impacts of public investments. Jacoby (2000) found that investments in rural roads have a positive impact on growth but an ambiguous effect on regional inequality in rural Nepal. Using a two-region endogenous growth model, Martin (1999) explored the link between road infrastructure and regional inequality. Since both studies only consider roads, they have limited relevance for policy makers who must choose between different types of investment as well as investment levels.

Understanding the marginal effects of different types of government expenditure is crucial for developing countries to adopt pro-poor growth strategies. Due to budget constraints, significant increases in public investment in rural areas seem unlikely. Therefore, the government must give greater emphasis to using their public investment resources more efficiently. Reliable information on the marginal effects of various types of spending will help governments to hone future investment priorities to achieve the goals of equity and growth.

In this study, we develop a framework to assess the impact of various forms of public investment on growth and regional inequality using China as an example. The key hypothesis we test is that different types of public investment have different impacts on regional inequality. We consider six major types of public investment in this study: Roads, education, electrification, telephones, irrigation, and agricultural R&D. These six types of investment are the major instruments used by the government for growth and poverty reduction. In addition, these measures are readily available at the provincial level and consistently compiled for a reasonably long period.[2]

There are two reasons for our choice of China as an example. First, the Chinese economy has grown rapidly over the past two decades at an average annual rate of about 10 percent while regional inequality has increased significantly (SSB, 1998). Second, due to huge regional differences in geography and resource endowments, China has made significant public investments in some regions in an attempt to overcome natural constraints and reduce regional inequality. The dramatic increase in regional inequality despite rapid growth and an active public investment strategy in China provide a good test for our hypothesis. Since over 60 percent of the total population in China is still rural, and since most of the poor are concentrated in rural areas, we focus our study on the rural sector. Although numerous studies attempt to describe and explain China's regional inequality (Lyons, 1991; Tsui, 1991; Yang, 1999; and Kanbur and Zhang, 1999), previous studies have not systematically examined the role of public investment in changing regional inequality.

One constraint to assessing the distributional impact of public investment is the lack of a suitable analytical framework to distinguish between the contributions of production factors and public investment to regional inequality. In the literature, inequality is decomposed based on either exogenous population groups or income sources (Shorrocks, 1982, 1984). Since the distributional effect of production factors and public investment cannot be directly analyzed with these frameworks, we develop a new approach based on Shorrocks' decomposition methods. Specifically, we first assume both agricultural and non-agricultural production functions are of Cobb-Douglas form, which implies no interdependence among different types of public investment. After expressing the production function in double log-linear form, we can apply Shorrocks' decomposition method.[3]

The paper is organized as follows. Section 11.2 describes recent trends in growth and regional inequality in China. Section 11.3 develops our conceptual framework. Section 11.4 provides our estimates of the agricultural and non-agricultural production functions needed to decompose the sources of regional inequality. A simulation is conducted in section 11.5 to evaluate the marginal impacts of public investments on inequality amongst three regions. Section 11.6 highlights our conclusions and policy implications.

11.2 Growth and regional inequality in China

During the past two decades, Chinese agriculture has experienced phenomenal economic growth. This rapid growth followed the policy reforms of the early 1980s and has stimulated numerous studies that analyze its sources (e.g. McMillan, Whalley, and Zhu, 1989; Fan, 1991; Lin, 1992; Fan and Pardey, 1997). Following the traditional growth accounting approach (Solow, 1957; Denison, 1962), most of these studies attempt to analyze the impact of institutional changes in addition to increases in the use of inputs on production growth during the reform period.

Fan and Pardey (1997) were the first to point out that omitted variables such as agricultural R&D investment would bias estimates of the sources of production growth. To address this concern, they included a research stock variable in the production function to account for the contribution of R&D investment to rapid production growth, in addition to inputs and institutional changes. They found that ignoring the R&D variable in the production function leads to a significant overestimation of the impact of institutional change.

In addition to R&D investment, government investment in roads, electrification, education, and other public goods and services in rural areas may have also contributed to rapid growth in agricultural production. Omitting these variables will also likely bias estimates of the production function for Chinese agriculture.

Despite the phenomenal development of the rural nonfarm sector in China, very few researchers have analyzed the sources of growth of this increasingly important sector. The only exception is Fan, Zhang, and Robinson (2002), who decomposed the sources of growth into growth in capital and labor. But they failed to include public investment directly as a source of growth. One of the motivations of this study is to include these public investment variables when estimating the production functions for agriculture and non-agriculture, and to calculate the differential impact of these investments on regional inequality.

Table 11.1 presents data on six types of government spending from 1978 to 1995. The average annual growth rate of total investment is 8.3 percent, which is in line with the annual growth rate of GDP. The weights of the six types of spending has changed significantly. The share of agricultural R&D expenditure has declined at an annual rate of 3.9 percent, while government spending on communication has experienced a dramatic increase (11.9 percent per year). The changes in levels and composition of government spending are likely to affect both regional growth and equity.

Another feature of the Chinese economy is that the gains from the policy reforms have not been evenly distributed across regions. The difference in the growth rates between the coastal and inland regions has been as high as 3 percentage points during the past two decades and regional inequality for China as a whole has increased significantly (Kanbur and Zhang, 1999). Since the late 1970s, China has implemented a coastal development policy. Special zones and open economic areas were enacted in coastal cities and granted tax breaks and other preferential investment policies. As a result, a large portion of foreign direct investment and public investment has been concentrated in the coastal region. As shown the last column in Table 11.1, the ratio of per capita government spending in the coastal region relative to other regions has increased from 0.9 in 1978 to 1.7 in 1995. It is legitimate to speculate that the skewed distribution of public investment might be an important factor behind the increase in regional inequality.

In order to better analyze these issues, we divide China into three zones: the east or coastal zone which includes Hebei, Liaoning, Shandong, Jiangsu, Zhejiang, Fujian, Guangdong, and Guangxi provinces; the central zone comprising Shanxi, Inner Mongolia, Anhui, Jiangxi, Henan, Hubei, and Hunan provinces; and the west zone comprising all remaining provinces. Tibet is excluded due to lack of data. Hainan is included in Guangdong Province. Beijing, Shanghai and Tianjin are excluded because of their small share of rural areas and population.

Table 11.2 compares key characteristics of the three zones in 1978 and 1995, using the western region in 1978 as a base. Labor productivities in the agricultural and non-agricultural sectors were higher in the coastal and central regions than in the western region in 1978. In addition, the productivity gaps between the western and other regions increased significantly between 1978 and 1995. For instance, the difference in agricultural labor productivity between the coastal and western zones rose from 1.03 to 1.76 (2.75/1.56).

Not only has the gap in labor productivity increased, but also has the disparity in input use. For example, the capital-labor ratio for non-agricultural production was 20 percent higher in the coastal zone than in the western zone in 1978. By 1995, the capital-labor ratio was 116 percent higher than the level in the western region in 1978, and more than two times higher than the western region's level in 1995. The most notable gap is the difference in the number of rural telephones per rural resident. In 1978, the coastal region had 126 percent more telephones per hundred households than the

Table 11.1 Public spending in rural China, 1978–1995

Year	Total (billions of 1990 yuan)	R&D (%)	Irrigation (%)	Education (%)	Roads (%)	Power (%)	Communication (%)	Coastal/Non-coastal
1978	19.3	5.9	44.5	39.1	3.5	5.4	1.5	0.9
1979	22.4	5.9	44.0	41.0	3.3	4.7	1.2	1.0
1980	21.3	6.1	35.0	50.0	3.2	4.6	1.1	1.0
1981	19.4	6.3	26.8	58.2	2.0	5.5	1.2	1.1
1982	21.3	5.7	26.8	58.5	2.0	5.8	1.2	1.1
1983	23.8	6.4	25.9	58.1	1.9	6.5	1.3	1.1
1984	26.6	6.6	21.8	60.9	1.8	7.3	1.5	1.1
1985	30.2	5.8	17.1	62.9	4.1	8.5	1.5	1.2
1986	35.3	5.0	15.6	63.4	3.9	10.3	1.7	1.3
1987	41.2	4.0	14.9	64.1	3.9	11.0	2.1	1.3
1988	41.9	4.4	14.0	64.4	4.6	10.7	2.0	1.3
1989	37.5	4.7	15.3	61.0	5.5	11.1	2.4	1.3
1990	42.4	3.8	16.9	59.0	6.0	11.7	2.5	1.4
1991	50.1	3.6	19.6	56.9	5.9	11.2	2.8	1.4
1992	62.8	3.4	21.9	51.4	8.3	11.3	3.8	1.6
1993	72.1	3.1	19.9	52.8	5.3	12.0	6.9	1.5
1994	72.4	3.2	18.8	47.9	6.8	12.3	11.1	1.7
1995	74.9	3.0	20.6	45.6	7.6	12.8	10.4	1.7
Annual growth rate (%)	8.3	3.9	−4.4	0.9	4.6	5.2	11.9	3.7

Source: Fan, Zhang and Zhang (p. 19, 2002). Total public spending is the sum of the six types of spending listed in the table. The last column is calculated by the authors.

Table 11.2 Productivity and public capitals by zone

Year and characteristics	Coastal	Central	Western
1978			
Agricultural GDP / labor	1.03	1.12	1.00
Rural non-agricultural GDP / labor	1.53	1.29	1.00
Capital/labor			
for agricultural production	0.69	0.55	1.00
for non-agricultural production	1.20	1.75	1.00
Road density	2.97	1.93	1.00
Education level	1.79	1.27	1.00
Electrification	1.46	1.45	1.00
Phone (rural communication)	2.26	1.52	1.00
The percentage arable land irrigated	1.54	1.12	1.00
Agricultural R&D per capita	0.40	0.41	1.00
1995			
Agricultural GDP / labor	2.75	2.34	1.56
Rural non-agricultural GDP / labor	12.90	11.49	7.39
Capital/labor			
for agricultural production	1.14	0.99	1.01
for non-agricultural production	2.16	0.92	0.67
Road density	4.88	2.26	1.23
Education level	1.54	1.55	1.25
Electrification	13.83	5.61	4.11
Phone (rural communication)	40.78	9.50	3.91
The percentage arable land irrigated	1.63	1.15	1.12
Agricultural R&D per capita	0.28	0.19	0.36

Note: Authors' calculations.
1. The coastal zone includes the provinces Hebei, Liaoning, Shandong, Jiangsu, Zhejiang, Fujian, Guangdong, and Guangxi. The central zone contains Shanxi, Inner Mongolia, Anhui, Jiangxi, Henan, Hubei, and Hunan. The remaining provinces are classified as the western zone. Tibet is excluded due to the lack of data. Hainan is included in Guangdong Province.
2. All numbers are expressed as ratios of the corresponding value for the western region.

western region. In 1995, the gap was more than 40 times the level in the western region in 1978, and ten times the western level in 1995. Comparing public capital stocks among different regions, only the gaps in education and irrigation levels have narrowed between the coastal and western regions. In comparison, the differences in public capital stocks between the central and western regions have changed rather modestly. It appears that the increased disparity in output levels among regions might have been caused in large part by differences in public investment. However, we need a more formal model to quantify the contributions of various investments on overall inequality.

11.3 Conceptual framework

We assume that each region has the same agricultural and non-agricultural production functions at a given time but that they lie on different points on the production surfaces. Following standard procedures in the literature, we assume that the agricultural and non-agricultural production functions are of Cobb-Douglas form, with k conventional inputs and m public inputs as follows:[4]

$$Y = A \prod_{i=1}^{k} X_i^{\beta_i} \prod_{j=1}^{m} P_j^{\gamma_j} \tag{1}$$

where Y = total Gross Domestic Product (GDP),
A = intercept,
X_i = conventional inputs such as labor, capital and land,
P_j = public investments such as roads and R&D,
β_i = output elasticity with respect to conventional input i, and
γ_j = output elasticity with respect to public investment j.

The logarithm form of equation (1) is given by:

$$y = a + \sum_{i=1}^{k} \beta_i x_i + \sum_{j=1}^{m} \gamma_j p_j + \varepsilon, \tag{2}$$

where lower cases indicate logarithms. An error term ε is added to represent stochastic shocks to output and is assumed to be unrelated to the other variables.

Following Shorrocks (1982), the variance of y in equation (2) can be decomposed as:[5]

$$\sigma^2(y) = \sum_{i=1}^{k} \mathrm{cov}(y, \beta_i x_i) + \sum_{j=1}^{m} \mathrm{cov}(y, \gamma_j p_j) + \mathrm{cov}(y, \varepsilon)$$

$$= \sum_{i=1}^{k} \beta_i \, \mathrm{cov}(y, x_i) + \sum_{j=1}^{m} \gamma_j \, \mathrm{cov}(y, p_j) + \sigma^2(\varepsilon), \tag{3}$$

where $\sigma^2(y)$ is the variance of y and $\mathrm{cov}(y, \bullet)$ represents the covariance of y with other variables. Since all the right-hand side variables in equation (2) are not correlated with the error term, the covariance of y and ε is equal to the variance of ε. Considering that y is in logarithmic form, $\sigma^2(y)$ is a standard inequality measure known as the logarithmic variance (Cowell, 1995). It has the property of invariance to scale. According to Shorrocks (1982), the co-variance terms on the right-hand-side of (3) can be regarded as the contributions of the factor components to total inequality.

Using estimates from (2) and applying the decomposition in (3), we are able to quantify the contributions of various public investments to regional inequality in agricultural GDP and non-agricultural GDP. Moreover, it is also possible to calculate the impact of public investment on regional inequality in total GDP. For this purpose, we assume a Cobb-Douglas aggregation over sectors, and then regress the logarithms of agricultural GDP and non-agricultural GDP on the logarithm of total GDP as follows:

$$y = a_1 y_1 + a_2 y_2 \qquad (4)$$

where y, y_1, and y_2 are GDP, agricultural GDP, and non-agricultural GDP in logarithms, respectively; and a_1 and a_2 are the elasticities of y_1 and y_2 with respect to y. After estimating y_1 and y_2 based on (2), we can substitute the estimates into the aggregate GDP function (4) and then decompose the contributions of different inputs and investments on inequality in total GDP, again using equation (3).

11.4 Data and empirical results

11.4.1 Data

A panel data set including 25 provinces over the period 1978–1995 was constructed from various governmental data sources. We divided total rural GDP into agricultural GDP and rural non-agricultural GDP to reflect differences in their underlying production structures. Both nominal GDP and real GDP growth indices for various sectors are available from *The Gross Domestic Product of China 1952–95* (State Statistical Bureau (SSB), 1997a). The data sources and method of construction of national GDP estimates are published by the State Statistical Bureau (SSB, 1997b). This publication indicates that the SSB has used the UN standard SNA (system of national accounts) definitions to estimate GDP in Mainland China for the period of 1952–1995. This is the first time that the SSB has published historical GDP information at the provincial level for such a long period of time. We assume prices were the same for all provinces in 1980. Under this assumption, real GDP estimates for the whole period can be derived from nominal GDP data for 1980 and the published annual growth rates in real GDP.

In the empirical analysis, we consider both agricultural and non-agricultural production. Our specification of the agricultural production function includes conventional inputs (land, labor, and capital) and public investment goods such as roads, education, irrigation, electrification, rural telephones, and agricultural R&D capital generated by government investment. Additionally, we include annual rainfall to reflect regional differences in natural production conditions. Our specification of the non-agricultural production function includes all the same variables except land, irrigation, agricultural R&D, and rainfall.

Since the data sources for the above input variables can be found in Fan, Zhang, and Zhang (2002), we only briefly introduce the definitions of these variables. Labor is measured in stock terms as the number of persons at the end of each year. Capital stocks are calculated based on gross capital formation and annual fixed asset investment and adjusted with appropriate price indices and depreciation rates. Land refers to arable land area. The average years of schooling among the rural population is used as the measure of education. The irrigation variable is expressed as the ratio of irrigated area to total arable land. Roads are measured in density form, i.e. road length in kilometers per thousand square kilometers of geographic area. Electricity and rural telephones are the average electricity consumption and number of rural telephones per rural resident.

R&D is measured in stock form, and is defined as a function of past government expenditures on agricultural R&D. For simplification, we assume that the R&D stock follows a polynomial distributed lag (PDL) of degree 2. Based on available data and econometric tests, the lag length is set at 17 years. This means we only need estimate three parameters to obtain all the parameters of a 17-year lag structure. For additional details on the method, see Davidson and MacKinnon (1993) and Fan, Zhang, and Zhang (2002).

11.4.2 Results

Agricultural and non-agricultural GDP functions were estimated based on equation (2) and the results are presented in Table 11.3. For each production function, we present three different specifications: fixed effects, random effects, and regional dummy method. In all the specifications, year dummies are included to capture time-specific effects common to all provinces. But the specifications differ in how region-specific effects are dealt with. In the first specification, a standard fixed effects model, all the province dummies are included. The second specification assumes the individual constant terms are randomly distributed across cross-sectional units. In the third specification, only two regional dummies (one is set as default) are included to capture systematic difference across the coastal, central and western regions.

Overall, because this specification includes more variables than the other two specifications, it has the highest R^2. After adjusting the degree of freedom, the *AIC* shows that the fixed effects model has a better fit than the regional dummy model. However, under this specification, the independent variables are highly correlated to each other. The variable "road" in particular has a serious problem as shown in the last row with a VIF value of 202 and 169 for agricultural and non-agricultural production functions (a value over 20 indicates the existence of multicollinearity).

The random effects model is less costly in terms of degrees of freedom than the fixed effects model. But it assumes the cross-sectional units are chosen randomly from a large population and the individual effects are uncorrelated with the other regressors. Because the data set covers all the provinces, it is inappropriate to assume the cross-sectional units are randomly drawn from a larger population. To check the second point of no correlation, we present

Table 11.3 Production function estimations

Variables	Agricultural GDP			Rural non-agricultural GDP		
	(1) Fixed	(2) Random	(3) Zone dummy	(1) Fixed	(2) Random	(3) Zone dummy
Labor	0.198*	0.431*	0.364*	0.045	0.222*	0.485*
	(0.063)	(0.053)	(0.042)	(0.048)	(0.046)	(0.042)
Capital	0.030	0.043	0.068*	0.250*	0.426*	0.494*
	(0.038)	(0.033)	(0.017)	(0.073)	(0.061)	(0.040)
Land	0.028	0.343*	0.561*			
	(0.065)	(0.050)	(0.039)			
Roads	0.172*	0.081*	0.012	−0.669*	0.237*	0.134*
	(0.073)	(0.047)	(0.026)	(0.198)	(0.097)	(0.037)
Education	−0.077	0.073	0.340*	1.169*	0.876*	0.324*
	(0.084)	(0.087)	(0.089)	(0.244)	(0.228)	(0.174)
Electricity	0.014	0.093*	0.055*	0.291*	0.013	0.104*
	(0.030)	(0.028)	(0.027)	(0.096)	(0.078)	(0.040)
Telephones	−0.007	0.018	0.110*	0.212*	0.187*	0.216*
	(0.014)	(0.014)	(0.017)	(0.041)	(0.041)	(0.033)
Irrigation	0.023	0.260*	0.318*			
	(0.058)	(0.044)	(0.025)			
Research	0.019	0.036*	0.032			
	(0.020)	(0.017)	(0.023)			
Rainfall	0.053*	0.082*	0.225*			
	(0.019)	(0.020)	(0.027)			
R^2	0.992	0.934	0.969	0.979	0.931	0.951
AIC	−883.21	n.a.	−344.062	92.185	n.a.	437.581
Hausman test (p-value)		0.000			0.000	
VIF for roads	202.48		6.63	168.76		2.62

Note:
1. The data used are from 1978 to 1995. All variables are in logarithms. Year dummies were included in the model.
2. * indicates statistical significance at 10 percent. Figures in parentheses are standard errors.

the Hausman test in the second to last row. The small p-values strongly reject the null hypothesis of orthogonality underlying the random effects model and suggest there are some individual effects. As a compromise, the third specification includes only regional dummies. In so doing, we not only reduce the extent of multicollinearity inherent in the fixed effects model (the largest VIF is below 20), but also to a certain degree capture systematic individual effects as suggested by the Hausman test. We therefore use the third specification as a basis for the inequality decomposition.

Regarding the third specification, most of the coefficients for the year and region dummy variables (which are not reported in the table) are statistically significant. The adjusted R^2s for the agricultural and non-agricultural GDP functions are high at 0.966 and 0.949, respectively, implying good fits. All the coefficients in the estimated agricultural GDP function are positive and, except for roads, statistically significant at the 5 percent level. The summation of the coefficients for conventional inputs – labor, capital and land, is 0.993, suggesting constant returns to scale. In China, labor is abundant and land is scarce, hence one should expect that the elasticity of land would be larger than that of labor. This is confirmed in Table 11.3; the elasticity of land is 0.56 while the elasticity of labor is 0.36. The coefficient for irrigation – a land-enhancing technology – is also significant at 0.318. These results are consistent with the induced innovation hypothesis (Hayami and Ruttan, 1985). Because arable land is a rather scarce production factor, land is usually cultivated more intensively to increase yield through land-enhancing technologies, such as irrigation. Among the six types of public investment goods, education and irrigation have the largest and second largest output elasticities. The elasticities for roads and agricultural R&D are relatively small.

Turning to the rural non-agricultural GDP function, all coefficients are significant and positive. The sum of the coefficients for the conventional inputs (capital and labor) is also roughly one, suggesting that there are no economies or diseconomies of scale. Education is the most significant contributing public investment to rural non-agricultural GDP. Rural telephone services and roads have the second and third largest effects on non-agricultural output, respectively.

Figure 11.1 shows the time paths of regional inequality, measured in log variance, in agricultural GDP rural non-agricultural GDP, and total GDP from 1978 to 1995. Regional inequality in agricultural GDP changed rather modestly from 0.681 to 0.727 over this period, but inequality in non-agricultural GDP doubled from 1.107 to 2.322. Inequality in total GDP doubled from 0.751 in 1978 to 1.510 in 1995, and this was almost entirely due to increased inequality in non-agricultural GDP. This confirms similar findings by Rozelle (1994).

Given the estimated coefficients for the two GDP functions, we can now apply the inequality decomposition method outlined in equation (3). Tables 11.4 through 11.6 report the contributions of each factor to regional inequality for agricultural GDP, non-agricultural GDP and total GDP,

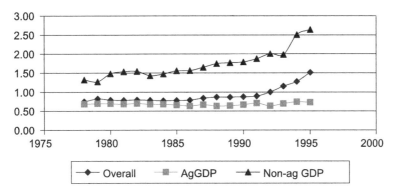

Figure 11.1 Regional inequality from 1978 to 1995 (lag variance).

respectively. The contributions of the three conventional inputs (capital, labor and land) to regional inequality in agricultural GDP have declined, while the contributions of most public investments, especially R&D, electrification, and telephones, have increased (Table 11.4). Public investment's total contribution to regional inequality in agricultural GDP increased from 0.074 in 1978 to 0.161 in 1995.

The results are similar for changes in regional inequality in non-agricultural GDP (Table 11.5). Capital and labor have contributed little to growing inequality, while public investment in roads, electricity, and telephones in total has increased regional inequality. Public investment's contribution to regional inequality in non-agricultural GDP increased from 0.139 in 1978 to 0.510 in 1995.

Turning to total GDP, capital's contribution to growing regional inequality increased from 0.070 in 1978 to 0.383 in 1995, even though its shares in the inequality of agricultural GDP and non-agricultural GDP changed little (Table 11.6). This is probably due to a structural shift in capital from agricultural to non-agricultural production in the economy because rural industry is more capital intensive than agriculture. For the same reason, land and land enhancing technologies, especially irrigation, which are mainly used in agricultural production, have accounted for a decreasing share of overall inequality. The contributions of roads, agricultural R&D, electricity, and telecommunications have increased significantly. All this suggests that public investment has pursued a regionally biased strategy over the past two decades. As discussed earlier, the coastal region has enjoyed the most favorable investment policy granted by the central government.

11.5 Marginal effects of public investment on inequality

Using the estimated coefficients in Table 11.3 and 1995 values for all relevant variables, we are able to calculate the marginal impacts of different types of public investments on regional inequality. Table 11.7 reports the percentage

Table 11.4 Contributions of input factors to regional inequality in agricultural GDP

Year	Inequality	Capital	Labour	Land	Education	Irrigation	Roads	R&D	Electricity	Phones	Public investment
1978	0.729	0.036	0.260	0.226	0.029	0.064	0.005	−0.008	−0.006	0.002	0.086
1979	0.800	0.037	0.270	0.238	0.022	0.071	0.005	−0.008	−0.005	0.005	0.090
1980	0.769	0.038	0.264	0.228	0.019	0.071	0.006	−0.006	−0.005	0.003	0.087
1981	0.748	0.037	0.258	0.233	0.019	0.070	0.005	−0.007	−0.003	0.005	0.090
1982	0.756	0.037	0.260	0.230	0.016	0.072	0.005	−0.006	−0.001	0.004	0.090
1983	0.729	0.035	0.248	0.243	0.018	0.061	0.005	−0.005	0.003	0.002	0.084
1984	0.718	0.035	0.244	0.239	0.019	0.063	0.005	−0.007	0.003	0.001	0.084
1985	0.696	0.035	0.242	0.232	0.018	0.068	0.005	−0.008	0.003	0.000	0.086
1986	0.673	0.034	0.235	0.228	0.020	0.061	0.005	−0.008	0.004	0.001	0.083
1987	0.691	0.033	0.237	0.230	0.022	0.061	0.005	−0.008	0.003	0.001	0.084
1988	0.663	0.032	0.230	0.227	0.027	0.058	0.005	−0.007	0.003	0.004	0.090
1989	0.662	0.031	0.235	0.219	0.025	0.064	0.005	−0.005	0.003	0.002	0.094
1990	0.653	0.030	0.231	0.231	0.028	0.056	0.005	−0.002	0.002	0.005	0.094
1991	0.648	0.029	0.230	0.222	0.029	0.059	0.004	0.001	0.003	0.008	0.104
1992	0.664	0.030	0.230	0.223	0.029	0.056	0.005	0.004	0.004	0.012	0.109
1993	0.668	0.031	0.227	0.223	0.026	0.058	0.005	0.006	0.005	0.008	0.108
1994	0.676	0.032	0.223	0.224	0.028	0.059	0.005	0.006	0.006	0.045	0.149
1995	0.719	0.035	0.227	0.229	0.027	0.062	0.005	0.007	0.009	0.045	0.156

Note: The public investment column is the summation of the columns for education, irrigation, roads, R&D, electricity, and telephones.

Table 11.5 Contributions of input factors to regional inequality in non-agricultural GDP

Year	Inequality	Capital	Labour	Education	Roads	Electricity	Phone	Public investment
1978	1.102	0.520	0.417	0.034	0.074	−0.005	0.018	0.121
1979	1.130	0.529	0.503	0.026	0.075	0.001	0.025	0.127
1980	1.096	0.528	0.556	0.022	0.072	0.003	0.025	0.121
1981	1.255	0.576	0.611	0.023	0.082	0.009	0.031	0.144
1982	1.269	0.586	0.607	0.021	0.079	0.014	0.032	0.146
1983	1.380	0.620	0.617	0.024	0.084	0.020	0.029	0.159
1984	1.333	0.623	0.598	0.025	0.085	0.021	0.029	0.159
1985	1.417	0.645	0.646	0.028	0.089	0.029	0.035	0.180
1986	1.566	0.689	0.660	0.032	0.096	0.034	0.039	0.200
1987	1.784	0.752	0.713	0.038	0.100	0.038	0.043	0.219
1988	1.940	0.785	0.751	0.047	0.107	0.041	0.059	0.254
1989	1.941	0.794	0.740	0.047	0.107	0.041	0.064	0.259
1990	2.009	0.814	0.754	0.047	0.111	0.037	0.073	0.267
1991	2.033	0.838	0.759	0.047	0.112	0.041	0.086	0.286
1992	2.262	0.913	0.815	0.049	0.122	0.047	0.106	0.324
1993	2.509	0.966	0.869	0.048	0.131	0.050	0.089	0.318
1994	2.581	1.041	0.873	0.051	0.134	0.057	0.245	0.488
1995	2.761	1.012	0.905	0.052	0.143	0.050	0.245	0.490

Note: The public investment column is the summation of the columns for education, roads, electricity, and telephones.

Table 11.6 Contributions of input factors to regional inequality in total GDP

Year	Inequality	Capital	Labour	Land	Education	Irrigation	Roads	R&D	Electricity	Phones	Public investment
1978	0.752	0.070	0.274	0.208	0.030	0.061	0.011	-0.008	-0.006	0.003	0.091
1979	0.822	0.075	0.290	0.219	0.023	0.067	0.011	-0.007	-0.005	0.006	0.094
1980	0.792	0.079	0.291	0.207	0.019	0.067	0.012	-0.006	-0.005	0.005	0.092
1981	0.783	0.079	0.287	0.210	0.019	0.067	0.012	-0.006	-0.002	0.007	0.097
1982	0.796	0.083	0.289	0.208	0.017	0.068	0.012	-0.006	0.000	0.006	0.097
1983	0.783	0.086	0.280	0.216	0.019	0.058	0.012	-0.005	0.004	0.004	0.094
1984	0.774	0.093	0.279	0.208	0.020	0.060	0.013	-0.006	0.004	0.004	0.095
1985	0.780	0.114	0.291	0.192	0.020	0.060	0.016	-0.006	0.006	0.005	0.100
1986	0.790	0.123	0.291	0.187	0.022	0.055	0.017	-0.006	0.008	0.007	0.103
1987	0.844	0.138	0.304	0.187	0.025	0.055	0.018	-0.006	0.008	0.009	0.109
1988	0.869	0.154	0.313	0.181	0.032	0.053	0.020	-0.005	0.010	0.015	0.124
1989	0.870	0.160	0.319	0.175	0.030	0.054	0.021	-0.004	0.010	0.015	0.127
1990	0.878	0.160	0.318	0.183	0.032	0.052	0.021	-0.002	0.009	0.019	0.132
1991	0.898	0.173	0.324	0.173	0.033	0.054	0.022	0.001	0.011	0.026	0.146
1992	1.007	0.215	0.354	0.164	0.035	0.051	0.027	0.003	0.015	0.038	0.168
1993	1.166	0.282	0.396	0.147	0.033	0.049	0.036	0.004	0.019	0.036	0.177
1994	1.286	0.357	0.426	0.132	0.036	0.047	0.043	0.004	0.025	0.118	0.274
1995	1.522	0.394	0.486	0.152	0.040	0.054	0.051	0.006	0.028	0.130	0.309

Note: The public investment column is the summation of the columns for education, irrigation, roads, R&D, electricity, and telephones.

changes in regional inequality in agricultural GDP, non-agricultural GDP, and total GDP, as a result of a 1 percent increase in each type of public investment (measured in physical units) within a particular region. Two results are of special interest. First, additional investments of all types in the western areas reduce regional inequality. Additional education in the western region is much more effective in reducing regional inequality in agricultural, non-agricultural and total GDP than any other investment (with elasticities of −0.218, −0.127, and −0.172, respectively). Irrigation has the second largest impact on regional inequality in agricultural GDP with an elasticity of −0.203. For non-agricultural production, development of the rural telephone system in the western region is another important way of reducing regional inequality.

Second, if the government's current coast-biased development strategy continues, regional disparities will worsen. The positive numbers in the second column of Table 11.7 indicate that additional public investment of all types in the coastal area will worsen regional inequality. One percent increases in education, telephones and electricity in the coastal area will lead to 0.116, 0.056, and 0.027 percent increases, respectively, in overall regional inequality. Compared with the western and coastal regions, the marginal effects of public investment in the central region on inequality are less striking.

We can regress each public investment variable against historical government expenditure data following the method developed by Fan, Zhang and Zhang (2002) to obtain a dynamic relationship between the stocks of public goods and past government expenditures. Based on the above information in Table 11.7 and the estimated stock-expenditure relationships, we can further calculate the marginal impact or regional inequality of an additional 100 Yuan (about 12 US$) of public investment per rural resident in each of the three regions (Table 11.8).

A positive number in Table 11.8 implies that increasing public investment in that region will widen regional inequality. The results show large regional variations in the impact of different public investments on regional inequality. Additional investments of all types in the western region reduce regional inequality, whereas additional investments of all types in the coastal and central regions increase regional inequality. Education has the largest impact of any investment and, again, additional investment in the western region reduces regional inequality, whereas additional education investments in the central and coastal regions increase it. Investment in the less developed region not only increases labor productivity there, but also enhances labor mobility across regions both of, which contribute to the reduction in regional inequality. These results are true for agricultural, non-agricultural and total GDP.

Additional investments in rural telephones also have large impacts on regional inequality, and follow much the same pattern as investments in education. In particular, additional investment in rural telephones in the coastal regions has a large inequality enhancing effect. The large marginal effects of

Table 11.7 Changes in regional inequality as a result of additional public investments in each region

Public investment	Coastal	Central	Western
Agricultural GDP			
Roads	0.004	0.002	−0.008
Education	0.136	0.081	−0.218
Electricity	0.022	0.013	−0.036
Telephones	0.044	0.026	−0.071
Irrigation	0.127	0.075	−0.203
Agricultural R&D	0.017	0.010	−0.028
Rural non-agricultural GDP			
Roads	0.036	0.016	−0.053
Education	0.088	0.039	−0.127
Electricity	0.028	0.012	−0.041
Telephones	0.059	0.026	−0.085
Total rural GDP			
Roads	0.024	0.012	−0.036
Education	0.116	0.057	−0.172
Electricity	0.027	0.013	−0.041
Telephones	0.056	0.027	−0.083
Irrigation	0.058	0.028	−0.086
Agricultural R&D	0.008	0.004	−0.012

Note: The entries are percent changes in regional inequality as a result of a 1 percent increase in a type of public investment in a specific region. All calculations take 1995 as the base year.

telephone are directly related to the fact that telephone investment has a large fixed cost. Once it is in place, the additional marginal cost is very low compared to the benefit. From Table 11.2, it can be seen that the number of telephones per hundred households is already much higher in the coastal regions than elsewhere.

11.6 Conclusions

This paper provides a framework for applying Shorrocks' method for decomposing the distributional consequence of various types of public investment on regional inequality. Using a provincial level data set for the period 1978 to 1995 in rural China, a model was estimated that enables the impacts on regional inequality of different types of public investments in each of three regions to be quantified.

Conventional and public inputs have contributed to growth in both agricultural and non-agricultural production, but have played different roles in contributing to changes in overall inequality. In general, the government has pursued a coast-biased investment strategy, and this has been an important factor contributing to the rapid increase in regional inequality.

Regional variations in the impact of public investments on regional

Table 11.8 The marginal impact of public investments by region on regional inequality

Public investment	Coastal	Central	Western
Agricultural GDP			
Roads	0.046	0.046	−0.115
Education	2.121	2.761	−8.984
Electricity	0.265	0.316	−0.753
Telephones	2.174	0.811	−0.892
Irrigation	0.722	0.619	−1.278
Agricultural R&D	3.881	3.308	−4.282
Rural non-agricultural GDP			
Roads	1.520	1.267	−2.785
Education	5.267	5.150	−20.189
Electricity	1.330	1.208	−3.293
Telephones	11.255	3.175	−4.108
Total rural GDP			
Roads	0.559	0.515	−1.050
Education	3.809	4.105	−15.002
Electricity	0.708	0.711	−1.794
Telephones	5.885	1.830	−2.206
Irrigation	0.693	0.491	−1.140
Agricultural R&D	0.681	0.397	−2.820

Note: The entries are percentage changes in regional inequality as a result of an additional 100 yuan (about 12 US$) per capita public investment in a specific region. Calculations are based on the most recent year for which data are available, except for telephones that are based on 1988 to 1993 averages.

inequality are large. Increasing public investment in the less-developed western region will lead to a decline in regional disparity. In contrast, if the government continues to favor the coastal region in its investment strategy, regional disparities will widen further. The magnitude of the impact of different types of public investment differs as well. Among the six types of public investment considered in this paper, additional investments in education and agricultural R&D in the western region are the two most powerful ways of reducing regional inequality.

Prioritizing investment in the less developed region will also have a positive impact on poverty reduction. In China, most poor are concentrated in the western region (Fan, Zhang, and Zhang, 2002). The poor own little physical capital and their most important resources are their own human capital. Therefore building human capital through education in the less developed region will enhance labor productivity and improve workers' mobility to seek better job opportunities, thereby benefiting the vast poor population residing in the region. Because the rural poor depend primarily on agriculture and related activities for their livelihood, output and yields of food staples affect the trend of poverty directly. Increasing investment in agricultural

R&D is one of the most efficient ways to boost agricultural productivity, which in turn will help reduce rural poverty. In general, the pro-poor growth investment strategy is not only good for promoting growth but also helps to reduce regional inequality and poverty.

Further research is needed on public investment and regional inequality. One of the most important research topics is why there is under-investment in poor rural areas. An analysis of the political and institutional context of public investments and conditions for efficient provision of public goods and services is much needed to improve the efficiency of public investment. In particular, how can the government design a mechanism (policies, regulations, and fiscal systems) to mobilize public resources to invest in rural areas? How to evaluate interdependencies between investments across regions and of different types is another area for future research.

Notes

1 The authors would like to acknowledge helpful comments by Peter Hazell and seminar participants at Beijing University, IFPRI and the World Bank.
2 In a similar study, Zhang and Fan (2000) use county-level production data to analyze regional inequality and find that within-province inequality accounts for about 50 percent of overall regional inequality and the uneven county distribution of nonfarm activities is the major cause. Lacking public investment variables at the county level, Zhang and Fan include only education and rural communications in their analysis, and find that they have important effects on the growth and distribution of the nonfarm sector.
3 The Cobb-Douglas type is a rather restrictive form for a production function since it assumes that there is no interdependence among different types of input. However, under the Cobb-Douglas specification, the logarithmic production value is a summation of linear terms, to which Shorrocks' decomposition formulae can be applied.
4 Governance varies across regions, which may in turn influence the allocation and efficiency of public inputs. However, due to lack of systematic data to capture this variable, the role of governance is not considered in the model.
5 Fields and Yoo (2000) use a similar method to account for labour income inequality in Korea.

References

Antle, J.M., 1988. "Dynamics, Causality, and Agricultural Productivity," in Susan M. Capalbo and John M. Antle (eds) *Agricultural Productivity: Measurement and Explanation*, pp. 332–365. Washington, DC: Resource for the Future.
Aschauer, D., 1989. "Is Public Expenditure Productive?" *Journal of Monetary Economics* 23: 177–220.
Barro, J.R., 1990. "Government Spending in a Simple Model of Endogenous Growth." *Journal of Political Economy* 20(2): 221–247.
China State Statistics Bureau (SSB), 1978–1996. *China Population Statistics*. Beijing: China Statistical Press.
China State Statistics Bureau (SSB), 1978–1996. *China Rural Statistical Yearbook*. Beijing: China Statistical Press.

China State Statistics Bureau (SSB), 1978–1996. *China Transportation Yearbook.* Beijing: China Statistical Press.

China State Statistics Bureau (SSB), 1997a. *The Gross Domestic Product of China, 1952–95.* Dalin: Dongbei University of Finance and Economics Press.

China State Statistics Bureau (SSB), 1997b. *Calculation Methods of China Annual GDP.* Beijing: China Statistical Publishing House.

China State Statistics Bureau (SSB), 1998. *China Development Report.* Beijing: China Statistical Press.

Cowell, F., 1995. *Measuring Inequality.* 2nd ed., London, New York: Prentice Hall/ Harvester Wheatsheaf.

Davidson, R., and MacKinnon, J., 1993. *Estimation and Inference in Econometrics.* New York and London: Oxford University Press.

Denison, E.F., 1962. *The Sources of Economic Growth in the United States and the Alternatives Before Us*, Washington DC, Committee for Economic Development.

Evans, P., and Karras, G., 1994. "Are Government Activities Productive? Evidence from a Panel of U.S. States," *Review of Economics and Statistics*, February 76(1): 1–11.

Fan, S., 1991. "Effects of Technology Change and Institutional Reform on Production Growth in Chinese Agriculture." *American Journal of Agriculture Economics* 73(2): 266–275.

Fan, S., and Pardey, P., 1997. "Research, Productivity, and Output Growth in Chinese Agriculture." *Journal of Development Economics* 53: 115–137.

Fan, S., Zhang, X., and Robinson, S., 2002. "Structural Change and Economic Growth in China," *Review of Development Economics*, 7(3): 360–377.

Fan, S., Zhang, L., and Zhang, X., 2002. *Growth and Poverty in Rural China: The Role of Public Investments.* International Food Policy Research Report No. 125. Washington, DC.

Fields, G., and Yoo, G., 2000. "Falling Labour Income Inequality in Korea's Economic Growth: Patterns and Underlying Causes," *Review of Income and Wealth* 46(2): 139–159.

Garcia-Mila, T., McGuire, T.J., and Porter, R.H., 1996. "The Effect of Public Capital in State-level Production Functions Reconsidered," *Review of Economics and Statistics*, 177–180.

Gramlich, E.M., 1994. "Infrastructure Investment: A Review Essay." *Journal of Economic Literature*, 32: 1176–1196.

Griliches, Z., 1988. "Productivity Puzzles and R&D." *Journal of Economic Perspectives*, 2(4): 9–21.

Hayami, Y., and Ruttan, V., 1985. *Agricultural Development: An International Perspective.* Baltimore: Johns Hopkins University Press.

Holtz-Eakin, D., 1994. "Public-Sector Capital and the Productivity Puzzle," *Review of Economics and Statistics*, 76(1): 12–21.

Jacoby, H., 2000. "Access to Markets and the Benefits of Rural Roads." *Economic Journal*, 110: 713–737.

Kanbur, R., and Zhang, X., 1999. "Which Regional Inequality? The Evolution of Rural-Urban and Inland-Coastal Inequality in China, 1983–1995." *Journal of Comparative Economics* 27: 686–701.

Lin, J.Y., 1992. "Rural Reforms and Agricultural Growth in China." *American Economic Review*, 82(1): 34–51.

Lyons, T.P., 1991. "Interprovincial Disparities in China: Output and Consumption, 1952–1987." *Economic Development and Cultural Change*, 39(3): 471–506.

McMillan, J., Whalley, J., and Zhu, L.G., 1989. "The Impact of China's Economic Reforms on Agricultural Productivity Growth." *Journal of Political Economy*, 97: 781–807.

Martin, P., 1999. "Public Policies, Regional Inequalities and Growth." *Journal of Public Economics*, 73: 85–105.

Munnell, A.H., 1992. "Infrastructure Investment and Economic Growth." *Journal of Economic Perspective*, 6(4): 189–198.

Rozelle, S., 1994. "Rural Industrialization and Increasing Inequality: Emerging Patterns in China's Reforming Economy." *Journal of Comparative Economics*, 19(3): 362–391, Dec.

Shorrocks, A.F., 1982. "Inequality Decomposition by Factor Components." *Econometrica*, 50(1): 193–211.

Shorrocks, A.F., 1984. "Inequality Decomposition by Population Subgroups." *Econometrica*, 52(6): 1369–1385.

Solow, R.M., 1957. "Technical Change and the Aggregate Production Function." *Review of Economics and Statistics*, 39: 312–320.

Tatom, J.A., 1993. "Paved with Good Intentions: The Mythical National Infrastructure Crisis." Policy Analysis, Cato Institute, August 12.

Tsui, K., 1991. "China's Regional Inequality, 1952–1985." *Journal of Comparative Economics*, 15(1): 1–21.

World Bank, 1994. *World Development Report 1994: Infrastructure for Development.* New York: Oxford University Press.

Yang, D., 1999. "Urban-Biased Policies and Rising Income Inequality in China." *American Economic Review* (Paper and Proceedings), 89(2): 306–310.

Zhang, X., and Fan, S., 2000. "The Profile of China's Regional Inequality: The Importance of Nonfarm Sector and Public Inputs." A Report of Australian Centre for International Agricultural Research (ACIAR) funded project on public investment in Chinese agriculture.

12 Reforms, investment, and poverty in rural China

Shenggen Fan, Linxiu Zhang, and Xiaobo Zhang

12.1 Introduction

China is one of the few countries in the developing world that has made progress in reducing its total number of poor during the past two decades (World Bank, 2000). Numbers of poor in China fell precipitously, from 250 million in 1978 to 30 million in 2000.[1] A reduction in poverty on this scale and within such a short time is unprecedented in history and is considered by many to be one of the greatest achievements in human development in the twentieth century. Contributing to this success are policy and institutional reforms, promotion of equal access to social services and production assets, and public investments in rural areas.

The literature on Chinese agricultural growth and rural poverty reduction is extensive. But few have attempted to link these topics to public investment.[2] We argue that even with the economic reforms that began in the late 1970s it would have been impossible to achieve rapid economic growth and poverty reduction without the past several decades of government investment. Prior to the reforms, the effects of government investment were inhibited by policy and institutional barriers. The reforms reduced these barriers, enabling investments to generate tremendous economic growth and poverty reduction. Similarly, public investment may have played a large role in reducing regional inequality, an issue of increasing concern to policymakers. The primary purpose of this study is to develop an analytical framework for examining the specific role of different types of government expenditure on growth and poverty reduction in rural China by controlling other factors such as institutional and policy changes.

Using provincial-level data for the past several decades, we construct an econometric model that permits calculation of economic returns, the number of poor people raised above the poverty line, and impact on regional inequality for additional units of expenditure on different items. The model enables us to identify the different channels through which government investments impact growth, inequality, and poverty. For instance, increased government investment in roads and education may reduce rural poverty not only by stimulating agricultural production, but also by creating improved employment opportunities in the nonfarm sector. Understanding these different effects provides useful policy insights to improve the effectiveness of government poverty alleviation strategies. Moreover, the model enables us to calculate growth, inequality, and poverty-reduction effects from the regional dimension. Specific regional information helps government to better target its limited resources and achieve more equitable regional development, a key objective debated in both academic and policymaking venues in China.

The rest of the paper is organized as follows. Section 12.2 details the evolution of reforms, growth and poverty in rural China over the past several decades. Section 12.3 describes trends of government spending in technology, education, and infrastructure, as these have long-term effects on growth and poverty reduction. Section 12.4 develops the conceptual framework to track multiple poverty effects of these expenditures. Section 12.5 describes the data and estimation strategy and presents the estimation results. Section 12.6 concludes the report with policy implications. Data description is provided in the appendix.

12.2 Reform, growth and poverty

China is one of the few countries in the developing world that has made progress in reducing its total number of poor during the past two decades (World Bank, 2000). Numbers of poor in China fell precipitously, from 250 million in 1978 to 30 million in 2000. A reduction in poverty on this scale and within such a short time is unprecedented in history and is considered by many to be one of the greatest achievements in human development in the twentieth century. Contributing to this success are policy and institutional reforms, promotion of equal access to social services and production assets, and public investments in rural areas.

Per capita income in rural China was extremely low prior to the reforms. In 1978, average income per rural resident was only about 220 yuan per year, or about US $150 (Table 12.1).[3] During the 29 years from 1949 to 1978, per capita income increased by only 95 percent, or 2.3 percent per annum. China was one of the poorest countries in the world. Most rural people struggled to survive from day to day. In 1978, 250 million residents in rural China, or 33 percent of the total rural population, lived below the poverty line, without access to sufficient food or income to maintain a healthy and productive life.

This changed dramatically directly after the initiation of rural reforms in 1978. Per capita income increased to 522 yuan in 1984 from 220 yuan in 1978, a growth rate of 15 percent per annum (Table 12.1). This rapid growth in agricultural income came from both productivity improvement and higher agricultural prices.[4] The income gains were shared widely enough to cut the number of poor, hence the rate of poverty, by more than half. By 1984, only 11 percent of the rural population was below the poverty line. Because of the equitable distribution of land to families, income inequality, measured as Gini coefficient, increased only slightly.

Table 12.1 Per capita income and incidence of poverty in rural China

Year	Per capita income		Poverty incidence		Gini coefficient
	Yuan per person	% of urban residents	Official	World Bank (one dollar per day)	
	1990 prices	%	%	%	
1978	220	42	32.9		0.21
1980	306	44	27.1		0.23
1981	349	49	24.3		0.24
1982	414	55	17.5		0.23
1983	467	59	15.2		0.25
1984	522	58	11.1		0.26
1985	593	58	11.9		0.26
1986	612	51	12.0		0.29
1987	644	51	11.1		0.29
1988	685	49	10.4		0.30
1989	674	44	12.4		0.30
1990	686	49	11.5	31.3	0.31
1991	700	42	11.1	31.7	0.31
1992	741	39	10.6	30.1	0.31
1993	765	39	9.4	29.1	0.32
1994	803	38	8.2	25.9	0.33
1995	846	41	7.6	21.8	0.34
1996	922	44	6.7	15.0	n.a.
1997	964	40	5.8	13.5	n.a.
1998	1,122	40	4.8	11.5	n.a
1999	1,147	38	3.9		n.a
2000	1,169	36	3.7		n.a

Source: The *China Statistical Yearbook*, *China Agricultural Development Report* (various years), and World Bank (2000).

During the second stage of reforms (1985–89), rural income continued to increase, but at the much slower pace of 3 percent per annum (Table 12.1). This was due mainly to the stagnation of agricultural production after the reforms. The effects of fast agricultural growth on rural poverty were largely exhausted by the end of 1984. Over this same period, rural income distribution became less egalitarian, and the Gini index rose from 0.264 to 0.301 (SSB, 1990). The changes in income distribution probably resulted from the changed nature of income gains and the growing differential in rural nonfarm opportunities among regions (Rozelle, 1994).

With real crop prices stagnating, rural income gains had to come from increased efficiency in agricultural production and marketing or from employment outside of agriculture.[5] Although the poor had increased access to modern inputs, their generally adverse production conditions kept gains low. With nonfarm income an increasingly large proportion of rural income, regional variations in nonfarm income played a growing role in worsening income distributions. Development of the nonfarm sector was concentrated mostly in the coastal areas, where per capita income was already high and poverty incidence much lower than elsewhere. The large areas in the west and border provinces, home to most of the rural poor, lagged far behind. As a result, the number of poor increased from 89 million in 1984 to 103 million in 1989, a net gain of 14 million in five years (Table 12.1).

Only in 1990 did rural poverty begin to decline once again. The number of rural poor dropped 9 percent per annum, from 103 million in 1989 to 30 million in 2000. Even using a higher poverty line of one dollar per day, the number of poor declined from 280 million in 1990 to 106 million in 1998, or a reduction of poverty rate from 31.3 percent to 11.5 percent (World Bank, 2000).

Rural residents earned less than half their urban cohorts in 1978, with rural income 42 percent of that in urban areas (Table 12.1). Due to the success of rural reforms, that percentage increased to 59 percent in 1984. But it declined again to 36 percent in 2000, mainly owing to fast growth in urban areas and relatively sluggish increases in rural earnings. Poverty in China is therefore still mainly a rural phenomenon. Urban poor have been relatively few in number in China, although income distribution in the cities was less egalitarian in recent years (Park, Wang, and Wu, 2002; World Bank, 1992). Nevertheless, the size and severity of urban poverty remains of a much lesser scale than in the rural areas.

12.3 Government spending

This section of the paper describes the trend and composition of government spending over the last several decades in rural China. As shown in Figure 12.1,

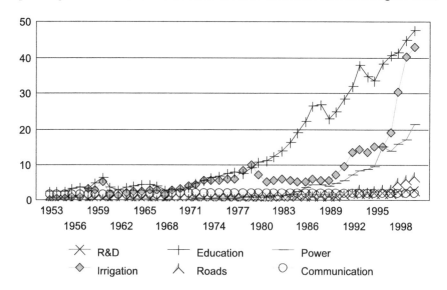

Figure 12.1 Public investment in rural China, 1990 billion yuan.

rural education spending accounted for 33 percent of total expenditures in rural areas in 2000. Irrigation is next, accounting for 30 percent. The irrigation spending considered in this study was only that directly related to irrigation, not including urban water supply, navigation, and hydropower generation. Investment in rural infrastructure took about 33 percent of total government spending in rural areas, with 15 percent for rural power, 5 percent for rural roads, and 14 percent for rural telecommunications. Agricultural research accounted for only a small fraction of total government investment in rural areas, at 2.2 percent.

12.3.1 R&D

China's agricultural research system expanded rapidly during the past four decades and is now one of the largest public systems in the world. By the early 1990s, for which comparative figures are available, the Chinese system accounted for over 40 percent of the less-developed world's agricultural researchers and 35 percent of its research expenditures.

However, the Chinese agricultural research system has experienced many ups and downs for the last several decades. Right after the foundation of the country in 1949, China's investments in agricultural research was minimal, but grew rapidly since 1960 (Figure 12.1). The growth in the 1960s was relatively small due to the three-year natural disaster (1959–61) and the Cultural Revolution (1966–76). Investment increased steadily during the 1970s, but this growth slowed down during the 1980s, and grew only by 23 percent during the entire ten-year period. In the 1990s, agricultural research expenditures began to rise again, largely due to government efforts of boosting grain production through science and technology.

12.3.2 Irrigation

The government assigned top priority to irrigation immediately after 1949. In 1953 the government spent 177 million yuan in irrigation investment, 10 times larger than research investment in agriculture (Figure 12.1). The investment in irrigation continued to increase until 1966. Under the commune system, it was rather easy for the government to mobilize a large amount of rural laborers to involve in large irrigation projects. As a result of this increased investment, more than 10 million hectares of land was brought under irrigation. However, the investment increased very little from 1976 to 1995. In fact, it declined from 1976 to 1989. In 1989, irrigation investment was only 44 percent of that of 1976. During this period, there was no increase in irrigated areas in Chinese agricultural production. In response to the grain shortfall and large imports in 1995, the government increased investment in irrigation sharply in 1997–99. But further expansion would be difficult because of the competing industrial and residential uses. As a result, the returns to investment in irrigation may decline in the future.

12.3.3 Education

Education level of the general population was one of the lowest in the world four decades ago. In 1956, it was still the case that less than one-half of primary and secondary aged children were in school. The periods of the Great Leap Forward (1958–61) and the subsequent Cultural Revolution (1966–76) were very disruptive times for Chinese society in general and its education in particular. The educational infrastructure was decimated as a result of the revolutionary struggles, and students suffered because of a vastly watered-down or non-existent curricula.

Since 1978, China has promoted the education policy of "nine-year compulsory schooling system," which requires all children to attend school for at least nine years to finish both the primary and junior middle-school programs. But the policy was never seriously implemented, particularly in rural areas. In 1986, an education law of nine years compulsory schooling was formally issued. By 2000, the enrollment ratio of school-aged children had risen to over 98 percent, and the percentage of primary school entering junior high school to 85 percent in rural China (SSB, 2000). Consequently, labor quality has improved substantially, with a decline of the illiteracy rate of agricultural labor from 28 percent in 1985 to 10 percent in 1997. This improved human capital in rural areas provided great opportunity for farmers to use modern farming technology, and to engage in non-farm activities in both rural township enterprises and urban industrial centers.

Despite these successes, government investment in education is still not sufficient. In terms of expenditures, the government has spent roughly 2.6 percent of the total national GDP on education, which is lower than most developing countries with exceptions such as Bangladesh, Indonesia, and Myanmar. In particular, many poor were not reached by the government efforts. Official provincial-level data reveals astonishing differences among provinces in illiteracy rates of rural laborers (*China Statistical Yearbook*, 2000). Not only was illiteracy higher in the western region, but its rate of decline there was the lowest of all provinces. The disparity can be even greater within a single province or county. According to official statistics, in the poorer half of the townships of 35 counties supported by a World Bank project in Yunnan, Guizhou, and Guangxi, average enrollment was at least 10 percentage points lower than the national average for the same age group (Piazza and Liang, 1998). Special household surveys document even greater disparities at the village level. The State Statistical Bureau's (SSB) 1994 survey of 600 households in the poorest townships of these 35 counties showed that the average enrollment rate for children ages 6–12 was only 55 percent. It is therefore unsurprising that official statistics in these counties indicate an average literacy rate for the total population of only 35 percent (Piazza and Liang, 1998).

12.3.4 *Infrastructure*

The mountainous topography in many parts of China has hindered the development of roads. In 1953, total length of roads was only about 137,000 kilometers, and the road density was about 14 kilometers per thousand square kilometers, much lower than that of India at the time. Moreover, the government investment in road construction increased very little from 1953 to 1976 (Figure 12.1). Nevertheless, the length of roads has increased gradually. Since 1985, the government has geared up its investment in roads, particularly high-quality roads such as highways connecting major industrial centers in coastal areas. Rural roads, usually of lower quality, account for about 70 percent of total road length.

In contrast to road development, one of the greatest achievements in rural China has been the rapid electrification during the past several decades. The introduction of electricity often profoundly affects village life. Electric lighting expands the productive and social hours in the day. Radio and television provide accessible, affordable entertainment and education. Power machinery can raise productivity and improve working conditions. Most important, electrification brings with it expectations for progress and a better future.

For the past several decades, China has given higher priority in electricity than in road development in its investment portfolio (Figure 12.1). Investment in power has increased 90 fold. Electricity consumption in rural areas increased from almost zero to 242 billion kw in 2000. The rapid growth occurred in the 1970s and 1980s. The percentage of villages that have access to electricity is 98 percent in 1998, and more than 97 percent of the households have the electricity connection. This percentage is much higher than that of India in the same year.

During most of the time of the pre-1980 period, growth in government investment in telecommunication was very slow (Figure 12.1). The investment increased from 166 million yuan to 738 million yuan in 1980. However, large-scale development happened in the last several years when the number of rural telephone sets increased from 3.4 million in 1992 to 51.7 million in 2000. This is in large a result of both public and private investments in the sector. From 1989 to 2000, public investment alone increased more than 20 fold.

12.4 Conceptual framework and model

This study develops a simultaneous equations model to estimate the various effects of government expenditure on production and poverty through different channels. There are at least two advantages to this method. First, many poverty determinants, such as income, production or productivity growth, prices, wages, and nonfarm employment, are generated from the same economic process as inequality and poverty. In other words, these variables are also endogenous variables. Ignoring this characteristic leads to biased estimates of the poverty and inequality effects. Second, certain economic variables affect poverty through multiple channels. For example, improved rural infrastructure reduces rural poverty not only through improved growth in agricultural production but also through improved wages and opportunities for nonfarm employment. It is very difficult to capture these different effects using a single-equation approach.

Equations (1) to (11) give the formal structure of the system. Table 12.2 presents the definition of variables. Equation (1) models the determinants of rural poverty (P).[6] Determinants include agricultural GDP per agricultural laborer $(AGDPPC)$, the rural nonfarm daily wage $(WAGE)$, nonagricultural employment $(NAGEMPLY)$, the domestic terms of trade for agriculture (TT), percentage of urban population in total population $(URBANP)$, and a three-year lagged moving average of per capita government spending on poverty alleviation loans $(PLOAN)$. Agricultural GDP per worker is included as a variable in the poverty equation because agricultural income still accounts for a substantial share of total income among rural households.

Table 12.2 Definition of exogenous and endogenous variables

Exogenous variables

LANDPC:	Land area per worker
AKPC:	Agricultural capital per worker
NAKPC:	Capital per worker in rural nonagricultural sector
URBANP	Percentage of urban population in total population
UGDPPC:	Per capita GDP produced by the urban sector
IRE:	Government expenditure on irrigation, both from revenue and capital accounts
RDE:	Government spending (both revenue and capital) on agricultural R&D
ROADE:	Government investment and spending on rural roads
EDE:	Government spending on rural education
RTRE:	Government spending on rural telecommunications
PWRE:	Government spending on rural power
PLOAN:	Government expenditures for poverty alleviation per capita, measured as last three years moving average

Endogenous variables

P:	Percentage of rural population below poverty line
SCHY:	Average years of schooling of rural population 15 years and older
ROADS:	Road density in rural areas
IR:	Percentage of total cropped area that is irrigated
ELECT:	Electricity consumption
RTR:	Rural telephone
WAGE:	Wage rate of nonagricultural labor in rural areas
NAGEMPLY:	Percentage of nonagricultural employment in total rural employment
AGDPPC:	Agricultural GDP per laborer
AGDPPCn:	Agricultural productivity growth at the national level
NAGDPPC	Nonagricultural GDP per worker in rural area
TT:	Terms of trade, measured as agricultural prices divided by a relevant nonagricultural GNP deflator

$$P = f(AGDPPC, WAGE, NAGEMPLY, TT, URBANP, PLOAN) \quad (1)$$

$$AGDPPC = f(LANDPC, AKPC, RDE, RDE_{-l}, \ldots RDE_{-l}, IR, SCHY, ROADS, ELECT, RTR, X) \quad (2)$$

$$NAGDPPC = f(NAKPC, SCHY, ROADS, ELECT, RTR) \quad (3)$$

$$WAGE = f(ROADS, SCHY, RTR, ELECT, AGDPPC_{-l}, UGDPPC_{-l}) \quad (4)$$

$$NAGEMPLY = f(ROADS, SCHY, ELECT, RTR, AGDPPC_{-l}, UGDPPC_{-l}) \quad (5)$$

$$IR = f(IRE, IRE_{-l}, \ldots, IRE_{-j}) \quad (6)$$

$$ROADS = f(ROADE, ROADE_{-l}, \ldots, ROADE_{-k}) \quad (7)$$

$$SCHY = f(EDE, EDE_{-l}, \ldots, EDE_{-m}) \quad (8)$$

$$RTR = f(RTRE, RTRE_{-l}, \ldots RTRE_{-l}) \quad (9)$$

$$ELECT = f(PWRE, PWRE_{-l}, \ldots, PWRE_{-n}) \quad (10)$$

$$TT = f(AGDPPC, AGDPPCn) \quad (11)$$

Nonfarm employment income is the second most important source of income after agricultural production for rural residents in China. The wage and number of nonfarm laborers are good proxies for nonfarm income. Moreover, we can distinguish the differential impacts of changes in wages and number of workers in the nonfarm sector on rural poverty reduction. These differential impacts may have important policy implications for further poverty reduction. If improvement in rural wages reduces rural poverty more than increased rural nonfarm employment does, then government resources should be targeted to improve rural wages, or vice versa.

The terms-of-trade variable measures the impact on rural poverty of changes in agricultural prices relative to nonagricultural prices. Price policy can have a large effect on the rural poor. We hypothesize that in the short run the poor may suffer from higher agricultural prices if they are usually net buyers of food grains. But they may gain from higher prices if they are net sellers of agricultural products. In the long run, however, increased agricultural prices may induce government and farmers to invest more in agricultural production, shifting the supply curve outward.

Public spending on rural poverty loans has been a major policy instrument for the government to reduce poverty. For example, in 1996 such loans accounted for 82 percent of total government spending on poverty alleviation. Since these funds often take time to affect rural poverty, we use a moving average of the past three years' spending in our regression.

For the agricultural productivity function (equation 2), labor productivity is the dependent variable, while independent variables include land and capital per worker (*LANDPC* and *AKPC*) as conventional inputs. The following supply shifter variables capture the direct impact of technology, infrastructure, and education on agricultural labor productivity growth: current and lagged government spending on agricultural research and extension (RDE, RDE_{-l}, ... RDE_{-i}), percentage of irrigated cropped area in total cropped area (IR), average years of schooling of rural population ($SCHY$), road density ($ROADS$), per capita agricultural electricity consumption ($ELECT$), and number of rural telephone sets per thousand rural residents (RTR). The impact of rural reforms on agricultural productivity is captured by the variable X. In this case, we use the year dummies to capture the year-specific policy reforms on growth in agricultural productivity.

For the nonagricultural productivity function (equation 3), the dependent variable is nonagricultural (township and village enterprise) GDP labor productivity ($NAGDPPC$). Independent variables are capital per worker ($NAKPC$), workers' years of schooling, and infrastructure.

Equations (4) and (5) are wages and employment determination functions in the rural nonfarm sector. These equations are reduced forms of labor supply and demand, where equilibrium wages clear the labor market. The derived labor and wages are a function of labor productivity. Labor productivity in turn is a function of capital/labor ratio and production shifters such as infrastructure and improvements in education. Therefore, final labor and wage equations are functions of capital/labor ratios and production shifters. However, when we include capital/labor ratio in our model, the coefficients are not statistically significant. We therefore drop them from the equations. This may be because TVEs may have difficulties in raising capital to expand production due to lack of credit support or well-developed capital market. Growth in the urban sector ($UGDPPC_{-l}$) is included to control for the effects of urban growth on rural wages and nonfarm employment.

Equations (6) to (10) model the relationships between physical infrastructure levels and past government expenditures for different items. Equation (6) defines the relationship between the share of cropped areas irrigated and current and past government spending on irrigation (IRE, IRE_{-l}, ... IRE_{-j}); equation (7) defines the relationship between road density and current and past government spending on rural roads ($ROADE$, $ROADE_{-l}$, ... $ROADE_{-k}$); equation (8) defines the relationship between average years of schooling of rural population and current and past government expenditures on education (EDU, EDU_{-l}, ... EDU_{-m}); equation (9) models the relationship between the number of rural telephones and government expenditures on telecommunications ($RTRE$, $RTRE_{-l}$, ... $RTRE_{-l}$); and equation (10) models the relationship between the consumption of electricity ($ELECT$) and government spending on power ($PWRE$, $PWRE_{-l}$, ... $PWRE_{-n}$).

Equation (11) determines the agricultural terms of trade. Growth in agricultural productivity at the province and national level ($AGDPPCn$) increases the supply of agricultural products and thus reduces agricultural prices. The inclusion of national productivity growth reduces any upward bias in the estimation of the poverty alleviation effects of government spending within each province, since production growth in other provinces will also contribute to lower food prices through the national market. Initially, we also included some demand-side variables in the equation such as population and income growth. But they were not significant and so were dropped.

Institutional changes and policy reforms made large contributions to the rapid growth in agricultural and nonagricultural production and to poverty reduction in China's rural areas. This study does not aim to quantify these effects, as previous studies have already done so (Lin, 1992). However, in order to reduce or eliminate the estimation bias from omitting these effects in our model estimation, we add year dummies in all equations to capture the year-specific institutional and policy changes on growth in agricultural and non-agricultural production and on poverty reduction. Regional dummies are also included to control for region-specific fixed effects.

12.5 Estimation and results

This section discusses the estimation technique and estimation results. It further details the calculation and analysis of the marginal returns derived from additional units of expenditure on various types of public spending and in different regions.

12.5.1 Model estimation

We use double-log functional forms for all equations in the system. More flexible functional forms such as translog or quadratic impose fewer restrictions on estimated parameters, but many coefficients are not statistically significant due to multicollinearity problems among various interaction variables. For the system equations, we use the full information maximum-likelihood estimation technique.

Since our provincial poverty data are only available for seven years (1985–89, 1991, and 1996) a two-step procedure is used in estimating the full equations system. The first step involves estimating all the equations except for the poverty equation using the provincial-level data from 1970 to 1997. Then the values of *AGDPPC*, *WAGE*, and *NAGEMPLY* and *TT* at the provincial level are predicted using the estimated parameters. The second step estimates the poverty equation using the predicted values of the independent variables at the provincial level based on the available poverty data for 1985–89, 1991, and 1996. The advantage of this procedure is to fully use the information available for all non-poverty equations, therefore increasing the reliability of estimates and avoiding the endogeneity problem of the poverty equation.

Government investments in R&D, roads, education, power, telecommunications, and irrigation can have long lead times in affecting agricultural production and poverty reduction, and their effects can be long term once they kick in. Thus, one of the thornier problems to resolve when including government investment variables in a production or productivity function concerns the choice of appropriate lag structure. Most past studies use stock variables, which are usually weighted averages of current and past government expenditures on certain investments such as R&D. But what weights and how many years' lag should be used in the aggregation are under debate. Since the shape and length of these investments are largely unknown, we use a free-form lag structure in our analysis; that is, we include current and past government expenditures on certain investment items such as R&D, irrigation, roads, power, and education in the respective productivity, technology, infrastructure, and education equations. Then we use statistical tools to test and determine the appropriate length of lag for each investment expenditure.

Various procedures have been suggested for determining the appropriate lag length. The adjusted R^2 and Akaike's Information Criteria (AIC) are often used by economists (Greene 1993). This report simply uses the adjusted R^2. Since R^2 estimated from the simultaneous system does not provide the correct information on the fitness of the estimation, we use the adjusted R^2 estimated from the single equation. The optimal length is determined when adjusted R^2 reaches a maximum. The AIC is similar in spirit to the adjusted R^2 in that it rewards good fit but penalizes the loss of degrees of freedom. The lags determined by the adjusted R^2 approach are 17, 14, 16, 12, and 17 years for R&D, irrigation, education, power, and roads.

Another problem related to the estimation of lag distribution is that independent variables (for example, RDE, RDE_{-1}, RDE_{-2}, ... and RDE_{-i} in the productivity function) are often highly correlated, making the estimated coefficients statistically insignificant. A number of ways to tackle this problem have been proposed. The most popular is to use what are called *polynomial distributed lags*, or *PDLs*. In a polynomial distributed lag, the coefficients are all required to lie on a polynomial of some degree *d*. This analysis uses *PDLs* with degree 2. In this case, we only need to estimate three instead of *i* + 1 parameters for the lag distribution. For more detailed information on this subject, refer to Davidson and MacKinnon (1993). Once the lengths of lags are determined, we estimate the simultaneous equation system with the *PDLs* and appropriate lag length for each investment.

12.5.2 Estimation results

Table 12.3 presents the results of the systems equation estimation. Most of the coefficients in the estimated system are statistically significant at the 10 percent confidence level (one-tail test). Since we use the double-log functional form, the estimated coefficients are elasticities in their respective equations.

The estimated poverty equation (equation 1) supports the findings of many previous studies. Improvements in agricultural productivity, higher agricultural wages, and increased nonagricultural employment opportunities have all contributed significantly to reducing poverty. The coefficient of the

Table 12.3 Estimates of the simultaneous equation system

(1) $P = -1.219\,AGDPPC - 0.371\,WAGE - 0.937\,NAGEMPLY - 1.15TT - 0.051PLOAN - 0.389URBANP$ $\quad R^2 = 0.655$
$\qquad\quad (-2.99){*}\qquad\quad (-1.22)\qquad\quad (-3.82){*}\qquad\quad (-1.62)\quad (-0.81)\qquad (-0.87)$

(2) $AGDPPC = +0.438\,LANDPC + 0.113\,AKPC + 0.079\,RDE + 0.099\,ROAD + 0.481\,IR + 0.301\,SCHY$ $\quad R^2 = 0.914$
$\qquad\qquad\quad (9.36){*}\qquad\quad (5.16){*}\qquad (2.47){*}\qquad (3.43){*}\qquad (12.51){*}\quad (2.62){*}$
$\qquad\qquad\quad 0.079\,RTR\qquad 0.010\,ELECT$
$\qquad\qquad\quad (4.40){*}\qquad\quad (0.32)$

(3) $NAGDPPC = +0.576\,NAKPC + 0.173\,ROADS + 0.581\,SCHY + 0.011\,ELECT + 0.079\,RTR$ $\quad R^2 = 0.810$
$\qquad\qquad\qquad (17.83){*}\qquad\quad (4.26){*}\qquad (3.71){*}\qquad (0.21)\qquad (1.78){*}$

(4) $WAGE = +0.090\,ROADS + 0.112\,ELECT + 0.035\,RTR + 0.690\,SCHY + 0.587\,AGDPPC_{-1} - 0.148UGDPPC$ $\quad R^2 = 0.541$
$\qquad\qquad\quad (2.05){*}\qquad\quad (1.70)\qquad\quad (2.21){*}\qquad (2.40){*}\qquad (8.79){*}\qquad\qquad (-1.49)$

(5) $NAGEMPLY = +0.100\,ROADS + 0.036\,RTR + 0.406\,SCHY + 0.112\,ELECT - 0.063\,AGDPPC_{-1} + 0.112\,UGDPPC$ $\quad R^2 = 0.995$
$\qquad\qquad\qquad (3.16){*}\qquad\quad (1.90){*}\qquad (3.04){*}\qquad (2.04){*}\qquad (-1.36)\qquad\qquad (2.19){*}$

(6) $IR = 0.247\,IRE$ $\quad R^2 = 0.976$
$\qquad (3.374){*}$

(7) $ROADS = 0.120\,ROADE$ $\quad R^2 = 0.959$
$\qquad\qquad (1.752){*}$

(8) $SCHY = 0.409\,EDE$ $\quad R^2 = 0.975$
$\qquad\qquad (1.768){*}$

(9) $RTR = 0.270\,RTRE$ $\quad R^2 = 0.976$
$\qquad\quad (2.13){*}$

(10) $ELECT = 0.328\,PWRE$ $\quad R^2 = 0.976$
$\qquad\qquad (5.56){*}$

(11) $TT = -0.142\,AGDPPC - 0.041\,AGDPPCn$ $\quad R^2 = 0.932$
$\qquad\quad (-2.15){*}\qquad (-1.87){*}$

Notes: Region and year dummies are not reported. Asterisk indicates that coefficients are statistically significant at the 10 percent level. The coefficients for the technology, education, and infrastructure variables are the sum of those for past government expenditures.

terms-of-trade variable is negative and statistically significant, meaning that higher agricultural prices are good for the poor. This is explained by the fact that most poor farmers in China are net sellers of agricultural products. When agricultural prices rise, their incomes rise. Government spending on poverty alleviation loans helps to reduce rural poverty, but the coefficient of the variable is not statistically significant.

The estimated agricultural labor productivity function (equation 2) shows that agricultural research and extension, roads, irrigation, and education have contributed significantly to growth in agriculture. But the coefficient for the electricity variable is not statistically significant. The coefficient reported here for agricultural research and extension is the sum of the past 17 years' coefficients from the *PDLs* distribution. The significance test is the joint *t* test of the three parameters of the *PDLs*.

The estimated equation (3) shows that improved roads, education, and rural telecommunications have all contributed to the development of the rural nonfarm sector. Similar to the equation (2) estimation, in the agricultural productivity function the access to electricity variable is not statistically significant, although the sign of its coefficient is positive.

The estimates for equation (4) show that rural nonfarm wages are determined mainly by government investments in roads, education, and telecommunications. An important finding in this equation is that agricultural labor productivity affects rural nonfarm wages significantly. But urban growth has no statistically significant impact on rural wages.

The estimates for equation (5) show that improved rural roads, telecommunications, electrification, and education have contributed to growth in nonfarm employment. Growth in the urban sector has also contributed significantly to the development of rural nonfarm employment. In contrast to the wage equation, agricultural labor productivity had no significant impact on rural nonfarm employment.

The estimated results for equations (6) to (10) show that government investments in irrigation, roads, education, rural telecommunications, and power have contributed to the improvement of irrigation, to the development of roads, to rural education, to rural communication, and to the increased use of electricity. All the coefficients are statistically significant.

Finally, the estimated terms-of-trade equation (equation 11) confirms that increases in agricultural productivity at local and national levels exerted a downward pressure on agricultural prices, worsening the terms of trade for agriculture.

12.5.3 *Effects of institutional reforms and government spending*

Using equations (1) to (11) and the estimates in Table 12.3, we can derive the sources of growth and poverty reduction, and the marginal returns to different types of government expenditures in growth and reduction of rural poverty as shown in Appendix 12.2.

Table 12.3 shows the sources of agricultural growth and poverty reduction. From 1978 to 1984, rural reforms accounted for more than 60 percent of total production growth in Chinese agriculture. This share confirms the findings of (1992) that the implementation of the household responsibility system has led to rapid growth in Chinese agriculture. More important is its tremendous contribution to rural poverty reduction. More than 51 percent of poverty reduction can be attributed to these reforms. Public investment also played a significant role in both growth in agricultural production and poverty reduction as it accounted for 12 percent of growth and 45 percent of poverty reduction during this reform period of 1978–84.

From 1985 to 2000, the impact of institutional reforms on agricultural productivity growth is not significant. In fact, it is slightly negative. The contribution of public investment has increased to 63 percent, more than five times of its share during 1978–84. More important is its large contribution to poverty reduction, accounting for 94 percent. Similarly, the institutional reforms in the agricultural sector had no impact on poverty reduction during the post reform period.

We calculate marginal returns by different types of investments in three regions[7]. Table 12.4 shows the marginal effects of government spending on agricultural and nonagricultural production and rural poverty for the three regions and for China as a whole. Effects are measured as the returns in yuan or the number of poor brought out of poverty per unit of spending in 2000. For example, the returns to investments in irrigation are measured as yuan of additional production or number of persons brought out of poverty per one additional unit spent on irrigation.[8] These measures provide useful information for comparing the relative benefits of additional units of expenditure on different items in different regions, particularly for setting future priorities for government expenditure to further increase production and reduce rural

Table 12.4 Accounting for sources of agricultural growth and poverty reduction

	1978–84	1985–2000
Agricultural production growth		
Institutional reforms	60.08	−0.84
Public investment	12.43	63.25
Others	27.49	37.59
Poverty reduction		
Institutional reforms	51.25	−0.43
Public investment	45.45	94.17
Others	3.30	6.26

Notes: The institutional reform affects reduction in rural poverty through increased agricultural productivity. The other channels such as through improved labor market is not captured here.

poverty. Since the official poverty data by region is not available after 1996, we use Xian and Sheng's estimates of rural poverty rates by province in calculating the returns to poverty reduction.[9] There are two advantages in using these data. First the rates are for 1998, therefore they are more relevant for the current policy debate. Second, the income poverty line used is 836 yuan per year per person, which is close to the one dollar per day commonly used by the World Bank.

An important feature of the results in Table 12.4 is that all production-enhancing investments reduce poverty while at the same time increasing agricultural and nonagricultural GDP. However, there are sizable differences in production gains and poverty reductions among the various expenditure items and across regions. For the country as a whole, government expenditure on education had the largest impact in reducing poverty. In addition, it had the largest return to nonfarm GDP and overall rural GDP, and second largest return to AgGDP. Therefore, investing more in education is the dominant "win-win" strategy. For every 10,000 yuan investment, some 12 people are brought out of poverty.

Investment in agricultural R&D had the second largest impact on poverty, and its impact on AgGDP ranks first. Agricultural R&D is thus another very favorable investment. Government expenditure on rural infrastructure also made large contributions to poverty reduction. These impacts were realized through growth in both agricultural and nonagricultural production. Among the three infrastructure variables considered, the impact of roads is particularly large. For every 10,000 yuan invested, 6.6 poor are lifted above the poverty line. Roads, thus, rank third in poverty-reduction impact, after education and R&D. In terms of impact on growth, for every yuan invested in roads, 6.57 yuan in rural GDP is produced, only slightly less than the return to education investments. This stems from high returns to nonagricultural GDP, second largest return at 4.88 yuan for every yuan invested.[10]

For rural telephony, investments had favorable returns to both agricultural and nonagricultural GDP, and the impact on rural poverty was similar to that of road investments.

Although electricity investment showed low returns to both agricultural and nonagricultural GDP, its poverty reduction impact is significant. For every 10,000 yuan investment, 4.9 people were brought out of poverty. This is because access to electricity is essential to the expansion of nonfarm employment (Table 12.5).

For the nation as a whole, irrigation investment had relatively little impact on rural poverty reduction, although its economic returns were still positive. This is because irrigation affects poverty reduction solely through improved agricultural productivity.

One striking result from our study is the very small and statistically insignificant impact of government poverty alleviation loans. For every 10,000 yuan invested, only slightly more than 3 poor is brought out of poverty.

Regional variation is large in the marginal returns to government spending

Table 12.5 Returns of public investment to production and poverty reduction, 2000

	Coastal	*Central*	*Western*	*Average*
Returns to total rural GDP		*yuan per yuan expenditure*		
R&D	5.54	6.63	10.19	6.75
Irrigation	1.62	1.11	2.13	1.45
Roads	8.34	6.90	3.39	6.57
Education	11.98	8.72	4.76	8.96
Electricity	3.78	2.82	1.63	2.89
Telephone	4.09	4.60	3.81	4.22
Returns to agricultural GDP		*yuan per yuan expenditure*		
R&D	5.54	6.63	10.19	6.75
Irrigation	1.62	1.11	2.13	1.45
Roads	1.62	1.74	1.73	1.69
Education	2.18	2.06	2.33	2.17
Electricity	0.81	0.78	0.88	0.82
Telephone	1.25	1.75	2.49	1.63
Returns to nonfarm GDP		*yuan per yuan expenditure*		
Roads	6.71	5.16	1.66	4.88
Education	9.80	6.66	2.43	6.79
Electricity	2.96	2.04	0.75	2.07
Telephone	2.85	2.85	1.32	2.59
Returns to poverty reduction		*no. of poor reduced per 10,000 yuan expenditure*		
R&D	3.72	12.96	24.03	10.74
Irrigation	1.08	2.16	5.02	2.31
Roads	2.68	8.38	10.03	6.63
Education	5.03	13.90	18.93	11.88
Electricity	2.04	5.71	7.78	4.85
Telephone	1.99	8.10	13.94	6.17
Poverty loan	3.70	3.57	2.40	3.03

Note: We use the parameters from the productivity functions to calculate the returns to GDP (Table 12.3). Under the assumption of constant return to scale, coefficients for nonlabor parameters in the production function should be the same as those in the labor productivity function. The marginal returns can be easily derived and calculated by multiplying production elasticities by partial productivity of each spending item. Since only two coefficients (on electricity) are not statistically significant, the results are little different when we use the only statistically significant coefficients in the calculation. The number of poor used in the calculation is from Xian and Sheng (2002). Most of estimates are statistically significant at the 10 percent level. The only exceptions are returns in agricultural GDP, nonfarm GDP, and overall GDP to electricity investment.

in both GDP growth and poverty reduction. In terms of poverty-reduction effects, all kinds of investments had high returns in the western region. For example, for every 10,000 yuan invested in agricultural R&D, education, roads, telecommunications, and electricity, the respective numbers of poor reduced were 24, 19, 10, 14, and 8. These effects are 6.4, 3.7, 3.7, 7.0, and 3.8 times higher than the coastal areas. Even for irrigation, every 10,000 yuan additional investment was sufficient to bring five people out of poverty, four times higher than the coastal area.

With respect to returns to growth in agriculture, most investments had the largest returns in the western areas. On the other hand, most government expenditures had their largest impact on rural nonfarm GDP in the coastal areas.

12.6 Conclusions

Using provincial-level data for 1953–2000, this study developed a simultaneous equations model to estimate the effects of different types of government expenditure on growth, regional inequality, and rural poverty in China. The results show that government spending on production-enhancing investments, such as agricultural R&D and irrigation, rural education, and infrastructure (including roads, electricity, and telecommunications) all contributed to agricultural productivity growth and reduced rural poverty. But variations in their marginal effects on productivity were large, among the different types of spending as well as across regions. During 1978–84, institutional and policy reforms were the dominant factor in promoting both growth and in reducing rural poverty. But during 1985 to 2000, it is public investment that has become the largest source of production growth and poverty reduction.

Government expenditure on education had the largest impact on poverty reduction and very high returns to growth in agriculture and the nonfarm sector, as well as to the rural economy as a whole.

Government spending on agricultural research and extension improved agricultural production substantially. In fact, this type of expenditure had the largest returns to growth in agricultural production and overall in the rural economy. Since China is a large country, growth in agriculture is still much needed to meet the increasing food needs of its richer and larger population. Agricultural growth also trickled down in large benefits for the rural poor. The impact of R&D on poverty ranked second only to education investments.

Government spending on rural telecommunications, electricity, and roads also had substantial marginal impact on rural poverty reduction. These poverty-reduction effects came mainly from improved nonfarm employment and increased rural wages. Specifically, road investment had the second largest return to GDP growth in the nonfarm economy and the second largest return to the overall rural economy.

Irrigation investment had only modest impact on growth in agricultural production and even less impact on rural poverty reduction, even after trickle-down benefits were allowed for. This is consistent with the results of Fan, Hazell, and Thorat (1999) for India. Another striking result is that government spending on loans specifically targeted for poverty alleviation had the least impact on rural poverty reduction. Neither did this type of spending have any obvious productivity effect. Again this is consistent with the Indian findings of Fan, Hazell, and Thorat (*ibid.*).

Additional investments in the western region contribute most to reducing poverty, because this is where most of the poor are now concentrated. The poverty-reduction effect of spending in education, agricultural R&D, and infrastructure is especially high in the region.

The results of this study have important policy implications for future priorities in government expenditure. The study reveals large differential impacts of various types of government spending on growth, poverty reduction, and regional inequality. Potential gains from reallocating government resources are enormous. Based on the results of our study, we offer the following policy suggestions:

1. The government should continue efforts to increase its overall investment in rural areas. Government spending in rural areas accounted for only 20 percent of total government expenditures in 2000, but rural residents account for 69 percent of China's total population. Moreover, almost 50 percent of national GDP was produced by the rural sector (agriculture and rural township and village enterprises) in 2000. Government's rural spending as a percentage of rural GDP is only about five percent compared with 16.4 percent for the whole economy. China has implemented an urban- and industry-biased investment policy for the past several decades. As a result, the rural-urban income gap is gigantic and has increased over time. Any policies against the rural sector will aggravate the existing disparity and should be discontinued.

2. There is an urgent need to increase investment in agricultural R&D. Agricultural research expenditure as percentage of AgGDP is only 0.3 percent. This is extremely low in comparison to the 2 percent spent in many developed countries; it is even lower than in most developing countries (0.5 percent–0.8 percent). Various evidence, including this study, shows that agricultural research investment not only has high economic returns (Fan, 2000), but it also has large impact in reducing rural poverty and regional inequality. Moreover, new evidence has revealed that agricultural research contributes to a large drop in urban poverty through lowered food price (Fan, Fang, and Zhang, 2001). Without agricultural research, China would have many more urban poor today. Finally, increased agricultural research investment is one of the most efficient ways to solve China's long-term food-security problem (Huang, Rozelle, and Rosegrant, 1999). All this suggests that increased investment in agricultural research is a "win-win-win" (growth, poverty and equity, food security) national development strategy.

3. The government should gear up its investment in rural education, even though its current rural education spending is already the largest of all rural expenditures. Improved education helps farmers access and use new technologies generated by the research system, thereby promoting agricultural growth. But more importantly, education helps farmers to gain and improve the skills they need for nonfarm jobs in rural enterprises and for migration to the urban sector. Our results show that rural education investment has the largest poverty-reduction effect per unit of spending. Therefore, continued

increases in rural education investment, particularly in the less-developed western region, are a very effective means of promoting growth in agriculture and rural nonfarm employment and reducing rural poverty and regional inequality.

4. Rural infrastructure should receive high priority in government's investment portfolio. Like rural education, investments in infrastructure contribute to reduce rural poverty and regional inequality mainly by spurring nonfarm employment and growth in agricultural production. Among all rural infrastructures, roads should receive special attention, as they have the largest poverty-reduction and growth impact (compared with telecommunications and electricity).

5. China invested heavily in irrigation in the past. Large-scale irrigation facilities were built, and a high percentage of the country's arable land is now under irrigation. The marginal returns from further investment may therefore be small and declining, and future investments should be geared to improving the efficiency of existing public irrigation systems.

6. The low returns of rural poverty alleviation loans to poverty reduction indicate that these loans should be better targeted. Studies show that a large part of the funds have gone to the nonpoor regions and to nonpoor households, and many rural poor do not benefit from them at all. The funds are also often used for purposes such as covering administrative costs of local governments instead of for poverty alleviation. Although government has realized the seriousness of the problem, more efforts are needed to better target the funds to the poor, or otherwise use the moneys to improve rural education and infrastructure, which promote long-term growth and thereby offer a long-term solution to poverty reduction.

7. The highest returns in the western region to all kinds of investment in reducing both rural poverty and regional inequality, as evidenced in this study, are consistent with the national strategy to develop the western region. In particular, investment in agricultural research, education, and rural infrastructure there should be the government's top priority. Considering China's decentralized fiscal system and the western region's small tax base, fiscal transfers from the richer coastal region are called for to develop the vast west.

Appendix 12.1: Data sources and explanations

Poverty

There are several estimates of rural poverty in China. Official statistics indicate that the number of poor declined to about 50 million by 1997 (MOA, *China Agricultural Yearbook*, 1998). World Bank (2000) estimates are similar to Chinese official statistics. A third set of estimates, based on a much higher poverty line (Ravallion and Chen, 1997), shows a far greater proportion of the total population subject to poverty, with a poverty incidence of 60 percent in 1978 and 22 percent in 1995. However, the declining trend of rural poverty in this last set of estimates is steeper than that in the official Chinese statistics. Khan (1997), using samples of the household survey, obtained 35.1 percent for 1988 and 28.6 percent for 1995.[11] Although these poverty rates are higher than the official rates, the change over time differs little from the official statistics.

The present study uses provincial-level poverty data from official sources. Few scholars have reported their estimates by province. Khan estimated provincial poverty indicators (both head count ratio and poverty gap index) for 1988 and 1995 using the household survey data. To test the sensitivity of our estimated results, we first used both official statistics and Khan's estimates, obtaining similar results, largely because the two sets of poverty figures share similar trends. Our final results are based on the official data simply because poverty data are available by province for more years.

Agricultural and nonagricultural GDP

Both nominal GDP and real GDP growth indices for various sectors are available from *The Gross Domestic Product of China, 1952–95* (SSB 1997a). Data sources and construction of national GDP estimates were also published by the State Statistical Bureau in *Calculation and Methods of China's Annual GDP* (SSB 1997b). According to this publication, the SSB used the UN standard SNA (system of national accounts) definitions to estimate GDP for 29 provinces by three economic sectors (primary, secondary, and tertiary) in mainland China for the period 1952–95. Since 1995, the *China Statistical Yearbook* has published GDP data every year for each province by the same three sectors. Both nominal and real growth rates are available from SSB publications.

The agricultural sector is equivalent to the primary sector used by the SSB. We use the following procedures to construct GDP for the nonagricultural sector in rural areas: Until 1996, China published the value of annual gross production for rural industry and services. In 1996, it began to publish value-added figures. The definition of value added is equivalent to the GDP data. The Ministry of Agriculture published data on both gross production value and value added for rural industry (including construction) and services in *China's Agricultural Yearbook 1996*. The data on nominal value added for rural industry and services prior to 1995 were estimated using the growth rate of gross production value and 1995 value-added figures, assuming no change in the ratio of value added to gross production value.

GDP for rural industry was subtracted from GDP for industry as a whole (or the secondary sector as classified by the SSB) to obtain GDP for urban industry. Similarly, GDP for rural services was subtracted from the aggregate service sector GDP (or the tertiary sector as classified by the SSB) to obtain GDP for the urban service sector. GDP for rural enterprise is the sum of GDP for rural industry and rural services.

The implicit GDP deflators by province for the three sectors are estimated by dividing nominal GDP by real GDP. These deflators are then used to deflate nominal GDP for rural industry and services to obtain their GDP in real terms.

Labor

Agricultural labor is measured in stock terms as the number of persons engaged in agricultural production at the end of each year. The data prior to 1978 were available in the SSB's *Historical Statistical Materials for Provinces, Autonomous Regions and Municipalities (1949–1989)*. The data after 1977 were taken from various issues of *China Agricultural Yearbook*, *China Statistical Yearbook*, and *China Rural Statistical Yearbook*.

The labor input for the nonfarm sector is calculated simply by subtracting agricultural labor from total rural labor.

Capital stock

Capital stocks for the agricultural and nonagricultural sectors in rural areas are calculated from data on gross capital formation and annual fixed asset investment. For the three sectors classified, the SSB (1997) published data on gross capital formation by province after 1978. Gross capital formation is defined as the value of fixed assets and inventory acquired minus the value of fixed assets and inventory disposed. To construct a capital stock series from data on capital formation, we use the following procedure: define the capital stock in time t as the stock in time $t-1$ plus investment minus depreciation,

$$K_t = I_t + (1 - \delta)K_{t-1}, \qquad (A1)$$

where K_t is the capital stock in year t, I_t is gross capital formation in year t, and δ is the depreciation rate. *China Statistical Yearbook* (SSB 1995) reports the depreciation rate of fixed assets of state-owned enterprises for industry, railways, communications, commerce, and grain for the period 1952–92. We use the rates for grain and commerce for agriculture and services, respectively. After 1992, the SSB ceased to report official depreciation rates. For the years after 1992 we used the 1992 depreciation rates.

To obtain initial values for the capital stock, we used a procedure similar to Kohli (1982). That is, we assume that prior to 1978 real investment grew at a steady rate (r), which is assumed to be the same as the rate of growth of real GDP from 1952 to 1977. Thus,

$$K_{1978} = \frac{I_{1978}}{(\delta + r)}. \qquad (A2)$$

This approach ensures that the 1978 value of the capital stock is independent of the 1978–95 data used in our analysis. Moreover, given the relatively small capital stock in 1978 and the high levels of investment, the estimates for later years are not sensitive to the 1978 benchmark value of the capital stock.

Estimates of capital stocks for rural industry and services are constructed using the annual fixed asset investment by province from 1978 to 1995. These are from the annual *China Statistical Yearbook* and the *China Fixed Asset Investment Statistical Materials, 1950–95*. Initial values are calculated using equation (A2), but the growth rate of real investment prior to 1978 is assumed to be 4 percent. Again, the initial capital stock is low so the estimated series is not sensitive to the benchmark starting value.

Capital stock for rural industry is subtracted from that of total industry (or secondary industry as classified by the SSB) to obtain capital stock for the urban industrial sector. Similarly, capital stock for rural services is subtracted from the aggregate service sector (or tertiary sector as classified by the SSB) to obtain the capital stock for the urban service sector. Finally, capital stock for rural enterprise is the sum of capital stocks for rural industry and services.

Prior to constructing capital stocks for each sector, annual data on capital formation and fixed asset investment was deflated by a capital investment deflator. The SSB began to publish provincial price indices for fixed asset investment in 1987. Prior to 1987, we use the national price index of construction materials to proxy the capital investment deflator.

R&D expenditure

Public investment in agricultural R&D is accounted for in the total national science and technology budget. The sources of agricultural R&D investment are different government agencies. Science and technology commissions at different levels of government allocate funds to national, provincial, and prefectural institutes, primarily as core support. These funds are mainly used by institutes to cover researchers' salaries, benefits, and administrative expenses. Project funds come primarily from other sources, including departments of agriculture, research foundations, and international donors. Recently, revenues generated from commercial activities (development income) became an important source of revenue for the research institutes. The research expenditures reported in this study include only those expenses used to directly support agricultural research. The data reported here are from Fan and Pardey (1997) and various publications from the Government Science and Technology Commission and the State Statistical Bureau. Research expenditures and personnel numbers include those from research institutions at national, provincial, and prefectural levels, as well as agricultural universities (only the research part).

When calculating returns to R&D investment, expenditures on agricultural research as well as extension at the national and sub-national levels are used as total R&D spending. This implicitly assumes that research conducted at the national level affects each province's production in proportion to the province's research expenditures, and the impact of extension conducted in each province is proportional to research impact.

Irrigation expenditures

Provincial irrigation expenditures refer to total government fiscal expenditures in construction of reservoirs, irrigation and drainage systems, and flood and lodging prevention, as well as maintenance of these systems. However, government reports of such data are available only after 1980 in the *China Water Conservancy Yearbook* (various issues). Prior to 1979, the Ministry of Water Conservancy reported total expenditure (not by item) on reservoirs, irrigation and drainage systems, flood and lodging prevention, water supply, and hydropower (Ministry of Water Conservancy, 1980). This spending item is much broader than irrigation, as it also includes urban water supply, flood control, and hydropower generation. To calculate the cost solely of irrigation prior to 1979, we use the percentage of irrigation spending in total expenditures on water conservancy in 1980.

Education expenditures

Provincial expenditures for primary- and middle-school education in rural areas after 1990 are reported in various issues of the *China Education Yearbook* (Ministry of Education) and the *China Education Expenditure Yearbook* (SSB). Expenditures prior to 1990 are extrapolated using the percentage of rural students in total students. Since education expenditure per student in urban areas is higher than that in rural areas, we use the cost difference in 1990 to adjust down the total education expenditures in rural areas.

Road expenditures

Road expenditures are reported in *China Fixed Asset Investment Statistical Materials, 1950–95* (SSB, 1996) and various issues of the *China Transportation Yearbook* (Ministry of Transportation). However, there is no breakdown between rural and urban road expenditures. We use the percentage of the length of rural roads in total length of roads to extrapolate the cost of rural roads by assuming the unit cost of rural road construction is one third that of urban roads (Ministry of Transportation, 1995).

Power expenditures

Provincial power expenditures are available in *China Fixed Asset Investment Statistical Materials, 1950–95* (SSB, 1996) and various issues of the *China*

Power Yearbook (Ministry of Electric Power). We use the unit cost of electricity per kilowatt to calculate power expenditures for rural areas.

Telecommunications expenditures

Telecommunications expenditures by province are available in *China Fixed Asset Investment Statistical Materials, 1950–95* (SSB, 1996) and various issues of the *China Transportation Yearbook* (Ministry of Transportation). However, similar to expenditures on roads and power, there is no breakdown between rural and urban expenditures. We use the number of telephones in rural and urban areas to extrapolate the cost of rural telecommunications.

Rural education

We use the percentage of population with different education levels to calculate the average years of schooling as our education variable, assuming 0 years for a person who is illiterate or semi-illiterate, 5 years for primary-school education, 8 years for a junior high-school education, 12 years for a high-school education, 13 years for a professional-school education, and 16 years for college and above education. The population census and the Ministry of Education report education levels for population above age seven.

Roads

The road variable is measured as road density, road length in kilometers per thousand square kilometers of geographic area. The length of total roads by province is reported in various issues of the *China Statistical Yearbook* and the *China Transportation Yearbook*, while the length of rural roads in the 1980s is reported in various issues of the *China Rural Statistical Yearbook*. In more recent years, the *China Rural Statistical Yearbook* stopped reporting rural roads. We therefore use the trend of total length of roads (except highways) to extrapolate the length of rural roads for the years in which data are not available.

Electricity

Total rural electricity consumption for both production and residential uses by province are available in various issues of the *China Rural Statistical Yearbook* and the *China Agricultural Yearbook*. In more recent years, the *China Rural Energy Yearbook* (MOA 1995–2000) began publishing the use of electricity separately for residential and production purposes by province. We use this newly available information to review the different use by province for earlier years.

Rural Telephony

Number of rural telephones is used as a proxy for the development of rural telecommunications. The number of rural telephones by province is published in various issues of the *China Rural Statistical Yearbook*, the *China Statistical Yearbook*, and the *China Transportation Yearbook*.

Appendix 12.2 Marginal impact on growth and poverty reduction

By totally differentiating equations (1) to (11), we can derive the marginal impact and elasticities of different types of government expenditures on growth in agricultural and nonfarm productivity and on reductions in regional inequality and rural poverty.

As an example, the marginal impact on agricultural productivity growth of R&D investment in year $t - i$ on agricultural labor productivity in year t can be derived as

$$dAGDPPC/dRDE_{-i} = \partial AGDPPC/\partial RDE_{-i}. \tag{A3}$$

Equation (A3) measures the direct impact of investment in research on agricultural productivity growth. By aggregating the total effects of all past government expenditures over the lag period, the sum of marginal effects is obtained for any particular year. The marginal impact of government spending on nonfarm labor productivity can be derived similarly.

As an example, the impact of government investment in rural roads in year $t - k$ on poverty in year t is derived as

$$dP/dROADE_{-k} =$$

$$(\partial P/\partial AGDPPC)\,(\partial AGGDPC/\partial ROADS)\,(\partial ROADS/\partial ROADE_{-k}) +$$

$$(\partial P/\partial WAGE)\,(\partial WAGE/\partial AGDPPC)\,(\partial AGDPPC/\partial ROADS)\,(\partial ROADS/\partial ROADE_{-k}) +$$

$$(\partial P/\partial NAGEMPLY)\,(\partial NAGEMPLY/\partial AGDPPC)\,(\partial AGDPPC/\partial ROADS)\,(\partial ROADS/\partial ROADE_{-k}) +$$

$$(\partial P/\partial TT)\,(\partial TT/\partial AGDPPC)\,(\partial AGDPPC/\partial ROADE_{-i}) +$$

$$(\partial P/\partial WAGE)\,(\partial WAGE/\partial ROADS)\,(\partial ROADS/\partial ROADE_{-k}) +$$

$$(\partial P/\partial NAGEMPLY)\,(\partial NAGEMPLY/\partial ROADS)\,(\partial ROADS/\partial ROADE_{-k}). \tag{A4}$$

The first term on the right side of equation (A4) measures the direct effects on poverty of improved productivity attributable to greater road density.[12] Terms 2, 3, and 4 are the indirect effects of improved productivity through changes in rural nonfarm wages, employment, and prices. Terms 5 and 6 capture the direct effects on poverty of higher nonfarm wages and greater nonagricultural employment opportunities arising from government investment in roads. We can similarly derive the impact on rural poverty of increased investment in telecommunications, electricity, and education.

Using these elasticities, we can also analyze the sources of growth and poverty reduction. We first assume the total growth and poverty reduction is equal to 100 percent over a certain period of time. The relative contribution of one particular input (for example public investment or institutional reforms) are its elasticity multiplied by its annual average growth rate of the respective variable. For more details, refer to Fan (2000).

Notes

1 The number of rural poor for each year is reported in the *China Agricultural Development Report*, a white paper of the Ministry of Agriculture. The poverty line is defined as the level below which income (and food production in rural areas) are below subsistence levels for food intake, shelter, and clothing.
2 Some studies link public investment to food security and agricultural growth (Fan and Pardey, 1992; Huang, Rosegrant, and Rozelle, 1997; Huang, Rozelle and Rosegrant, 1999; Fan, 2000). But very few link these investments to poverty reduction in a systematic way. Chapter 4 presents a more detailed literature review.
3 Total and per capita incomes are all measured in 1990 constant prices.
4 Agricultural output grew at 6.69 percent per year when using a more appropriate aggregation and adjusted output (Fan and Zhang, 2002), while the official rate of growth is 7.73 percent (SSB). The productivity growth was 3.16 percent per annum during the period. The rest of the growth (or 53 percent) is from increased input use induced by higher output prices (Fan and Zhang, 2002).
5 Agricultural procurement prices increased at only 1.5 percent per annum over 1984–89 compared to 4.5 percent over 1978–84.
6 All variables without subscripts indicate observations in year t at the provincial level. For presentation purposes, we omit the subscript. The variables with subscript "$-1, \ldots -j$" indicate observations in year $t-1, \ldots t-j$.
7 The coastal region includes the following provinces: Hebei, Liaoning, Shandong, Jiangsu, Zhejiang, Fujian, Guangdong, and Guangxi. The central region contains Shanxi, Inner Mongolia, Anhui, Jiangxi, Henan, Hubei, and Hunan. The remaining provinces are classified as the western region. Tibet is excluded due to the lack of data. Hainan is included in Guangdong Province. Beijing, Shanghai, and Tianjin are excluded because of their small share of rural areas and population.
8 To convert the cost-benefit ratios to the rates of returns, simply use the following formula: CBR=IRR/R, where CBR is cost-benefit ratio, IRR is a rate of returns, and R is real interest rate (or social discount rate). For a developing country like China, the common practice is to use 10 percent social discount rate. In this case, a cost/benefit ratio of 9.75 means a rate of return of 97.5 percent. Or in other words, if one invests one yuan today, he will get 0.975 yuan in return every year after this year forever.
9 Xian, Zude and Sheng Laiyun, "PRC's Rural Residents with Consumption Less Than 860 Yuan:Targeting Group and Characteristics". Memos, National Statistical Bureau, Beijing, China.
10 The return to road investment may be overstated due to understated cost. A male laborer is required to contribute about 20 days for road construction without pay.

However, we do not have any viable statistical data to adjust the cost. Nevertheless, even if we increase the road cost by 30 percent, the ranking of the road effect on poverty is still the same.

11 The dataset included 10,258 rural households in 1998 and 7,998 in 1995.

12 The terms are separated by "+".

References

Barro, J. R. 1990. Government spending in a simple model of endogenous growth. *Journal of Political Economy*, 20 (2): 221–247.

Davidson, R. and J. MacKinnon. 1993. *Estimation and inference in econometrics.* New York and London: Oxford University Press.

Devarajan, S., V. Swaroop, and H. Zou. 1996. The composition of public expenditure and economic growth. *Journal of Monetary Economics*, 37: 313–344.

Fan, S. 2000. Research investment and the economic returns to Chinese agricultural research. *Journal of Productivity Analysis* 14 (92): 163–180.

Fan, S. and P. G. Pardey. 1997. Research, productivity, and output growth in Chinese agriculture. *Journal of Development Economics* 53: 115–137.

Fan, S. and X. Zhang. 2002. Production and productivity growth in Chinese agriculture: New regional and national measures. *Economic Development and Cultural Change*, 50 (4): 819–838.

Fan, S., C. Fang, and X. Zhang. 2001. *How agricultural research affects urban poverty in developing countries: The case of China.* EPTD Discussion Paper # 80. Washington, DC: International Food Policy Research Institute.

Fan, S., P. Hazell, and S. Thorat. 1999. Linkages between government spending, growth, and poverty in rural India. IFPRI Study: Washington.

Greene, W. H. 1993. *Econometric analysis.* Hemel Hempstead: Prentice-Hall, Inc.

Gustafsson, B. and S. Li. 1998. The structure of Chinese poverty, 1988. *The Developing Economies* 36 (4): 387–406.

Huang, J., M. Rosegrant, and S. Rozelle. 1997. Public investment, technological change, and agricultural growth in China. Working Paper. Stanford, CA: Food Research Institute, Stanford University.

Huang, J., S. Rozelle, and M.W. Rosegrant. 1999. China's food economy to the twenty-first century: Supply, demand, and trade. *Economic Development and Cultural Change* 47 (4): 737–66.

Jalan, J. and M. Ravallion. 2000. Geographic poverty traps? A micro model of consumption growth in rural China. Washington, DC: World Bank (Mimeo).

Khan, A. R. 1997. Poverty in China in the period of globalization. (Mimeo).

Kohli, Ulrich. 1982. A gross national product function and the derived demand for imports and supply of exports. *Canadian Journal of Economics* 18: 369–386.

Lin, J. Yi. 1992. Rural reforms and agricultural growth in China. *American Economic Review* 82 (1): 34–51.

Ministry of Agriculture. 1980–2000. *China Agricultural Yearbook.* Beijing: China Agricultural Publishing House.

Ministry of Agriculture. 1995–2000. *China Rural Energy Yearbook.* Beijing: China Agricultural Publishing House.

Ministry of Education. 1984–2000. *China Education Yearbook.* Beijing: People's Education Press.

Ministry of Electric Power. 1990–2000. *China Power Yearbook.* Beijing: China Electric Power Publishing House.

Ministry of Transportation. 1984–2000. *China Transportation Yearbook*. Beijing: China Statistical Publishing House.

Ministry of Water Conservancy. 1980. *Thirty Years of Water Conservancy Statistical Materials*. Beijing: Water and Power Publishing House.

Park, A., S. Wang, and G. Wu. 2002. Regional poverty targeting in China. *Journal of Public Economics*, 86 (1): 123–153.

Piazza, A. and E. Liang. 1998. Reducing absolute poverty in China: Current status and issues. *Journal of International Affairs* 52 (1): 253–273.

Ravallion, M. and S. Chen. 1997. What can new survey data tell us about recent changes in distribution and poverty? World Bank Policy Research Working Paper 1694.

Rozelle, S. 1994. Rural industrialization and increasing inequality: Emerging patterns in China's reforming economy. *Journal of Comparative Economics* 19 (3): 362–391.

State Statistical Bureau (SSB). 1996. *China Fixed Asset Investment Statistical Materials, 1950–95*. Beijing: China Statistical Publishing House.

——. 1980. *National Agricultural Statistical Materials for 30 years, 1949–1979*. Beijing: State Statistical Bureau

——. 1990. *Historical Statistical Materials for Provinces, Autonomous Regions and Municipalities (1949–1989)*. Beijing: China Statistical Publishing House.

——. 1997a. *The Gross Domestic Product of China, 1952–95*. Dalin: Dongbei University of Finance and Economics Press.

——. 1997b. *Calculation and Methods of China's Annual GDP*. Beijing: State Statistical Bureau.

——. 1982–2000. *China Statistical Yearbook*. Beijing: China Statistical Publishing House.

——. 1987–2000. *China Education Expenditure Yearbook*. Beijing: China Statistical Publishing House.

——. 1985–99. *China Agricultural Development Bank Yearbook*. Beijing: China Statistical Publishing House.

Tanzi, V. and H. Zee. 1997. Fiscal policy and long-run growth. *IMF Staff Papers* 44 (2): 179–209.

World Bank. 1992. China: Strategies for reducing poverty in the 1990s. Country Study. Washington, DC: World Bank.

World Bank. 2000. *China: Overcoming rural poverty*. Washington, DC: World Bank.

13 Fiscal decentralization and political centralization in China

Implications for growth and inequality

Xiaobo Zhang

Abstract

China's current fiscal system is largely decentralized while its governance structure is rather centralized with strong top-down mandates and a homogenous governance structure. Due to large differences in initial economic structures and revenue bases, the implicit tax rate and fiscal burdens to support the functioning of local government vary significantly across jurisdictions. Regions initially endowed with a broader non-farm tax base do not need to rely heavily on pre-existing or new firms to finance public goods provision, thereby creating a healthy investment environment for the non-farm sector to grow. In contrast, regions with agriculture as the major economic activity have little resources left for public investment after paying the expenses of bureaucracy. Consequently, differences in economic structures and fiscal burdens may translate into a widening regional gap.

13.1 Introduction

Transferring authority to lower levels of government, which have better knowledge of the local conditions and preferences and are under closer scrutiny by their constituencies, is expected to improve the provision of local public goods and services (Dethier, 1999; Bardhan, 2002). Tiebout (1956) argues that under fiscal decentralization and inter-jurisdictional competition, citizens can vote with their feet to allocate themselves according to their preference to a package of local public goods and taxes. In other words, fiscal decentralization can prompt more efficient provisions of local public goods if individuals can freely move across localities. In addition to the sorting and matching role, Qian and Roland (1998, QR for short hereafter) emphasize that fiscal decentralization can also serve as a disciplinary device to preserve market incentives. These theories highlight the positive role of fiscal decentralization and inter-jurisdictional competition on the efficiency of public goods provision. In the past two decades, decentralization has become a global trend. However, empirical evaluation on the impact of decentralization on growth and distribution in developing countries is still in its infancy (Bardhan, 2002).

China, like many developing countries, has undergone a process of fiscal decentralization.[1] The sheer size of China provides a good ground to test the predictions of the theories in the context of development. Using provincial data up to 1993, Lin and Liu (2000) provide empirical evidence that decentralization is conducive to growth. Zhang and Zou (1998), however, have found a negative relationship between growth and decentralization. Jin, Qian, and Weingast (2005) reach a more optimistic finding that decentralization is not only good for growth but also for equity based on data up to 1992. Using data at more micro levels, a few other studies (West and Wong, 1995; Park et al. 1996; Knight and Li, 1999) show that decentralization has a negative distributional effect. These studies are all based on data up to the early 1990s. Since then, more in-depth fiscal reforms have taken place and more comprehensive data have become publicly available. Therefore, it is important to extend the work to cover a longer period and more spatial units so as to reconcile the differences.

Compared to the decentralized fiscal system, China's political system is rather centralized and can be described as a multidivisional-form hierarchy structure (M-structure) (Maskin, Qian, and Xu, 2000). Under this structure, the government can create a yardstick competition among local officials by rewarding or publishing them on the basis of economic performance. By examining the turnover data of top provincial leaders in China, Li and Zhou (2005) show that the internal political market also serves as a disciplinary mechanism for local officials to promote economic growth. Their finding suggests that governance structure matters to economic growth in China.

In this study, we use a nationwide panel data set at the county level to more systematically investigate the distributional impact of decentralization by taking into account both the fiscal and governance structures. To our knowledge, this study is one of the first attempts done with panel data at the county level.[2] The panel data set at the county level covering a more recent period provides a vehicle to reconcile the differences of empirical research on China's fiscal decentralization. The work is also a contribution to the literature. As Bardhan (2002) points out, few studies have empirically examined performance of fiscal decentralization at the micro level in developing countries.

The next section provides descriptive statistics of the data set used. Section 13.3 discusses the major theoretical arguments on decentralization. Section 13.4 presents empirical analysis and shows why the results are seemingly in contrary to the theoretical predictions. The last section ends with conclusion and policy implications.

13.2 Data and discriptive analysis

Through the 1980s and the early 1990s, China implemented a series of reforms to decentralize its fiscal system so as to provide more incentives for local government to promote economic growth (Lin and Liu, 2000). However, the decentralization led to widening fiscal disparity and shrinking central government revenues (World Bank, 2002). In 1994, the government introduced the tax sharing reform in order to boost the central revenues and enhance intergovernmental transfers.

In this study, we make use of a county-level public finance data set for our analysis. Since 1993, the China Statistical Bureau has published the *China County Public Finance Statistical Yearbook*. The yearbook contains detailed revenue, expenditure, gross value of industrial and agricultural output (GVIAO), population, and the size of public sector at the county level. There are over 2,000 rural counties in China. Between 1993 and 2000, several hundred counties have changed their names or judiciary boundaries. We make an effort to match these counties, relying mainly on the official declarations on judiciary changes posted in the Ministry of Civil Affairs website. Because data for Tibet are largely missing, we drop Tibet in our analysis. In total, we have a panel of 1,860 observations in 1993 and 2000.

Table 13.1 reports per capita revenues and expenditures as well as their compositions in percentage in the coastal, inland, and for China as a whole in

Table 13.1 Revenues and expenditures at the county level, 2000

	Coastal	*Inland*	*China*
Revenues (yuan per capita)	*488.86*	*326.14*	*387.32*
Value-added tax	11.34	5.71	8.38
Business tax	9.37	7.04	8.15
Personal income tax	4.58	2.91	3.70
Urban maintenance & construction tax	2.53	1.77	2.13
Agricultural taxes	6.47	10.24	8.45
Revenue from enterprises	7.37	4.27	5.74
Tax rebate	18.22	11.50	14.69
Subsidies	17.38	36.00	27.16
Miscellaneous revenues	22.74	20.56	21.59
Expenditures (yuan per capita)	*467.10*	*326.58*	*379.41*
Capital construction	1.84	2.39	2.14
Supporting agricultural production	3.59	3.02	3.28
Operating expenses of agriculture, forestry, water conservancy and meteorology	3.73	5.16	4.50
Education	22.70	22.70	22.70
Social welfare	1.45	2.43	1.97
Administrative expenses	10.71	13.79	12.37
Public security	5.42	5.47	5.45
Original-system remittances	7.36	2.07	4.52
Earmarked remittances	4.08	3.75	3.90
Miscellaneous expenditures	39.12	39.22	39.17

Note: Calculated by the author based on *China County Public Finance Statistical Yearbook*. Except for per capita revenue and expenditure, all the figures are in percentage. The figures in this table may appear to be slightly different from Table 1 in Tsui (2005) due to difference in sample coverage. Our study focuses on rural counties while Tsui (2005) does not separate the rural counties from urban districts. In addition, we have made more concerted effort to match all the counties which have changed names or status from 1993 to 2000.

2000.[3] The per capita revenue and expenditure in the coastal region are 50 percent and 43 percent, respectively, higher than those in the inland region.[4] The difference in the source of revenues between the two regions is more noticeable than that in the shares of expenditures. Under the new tax sharing system local taxes are closely tied to the economic structures. As shown in the upper panel of the table, the more developed regions can retain more revenues from the value-added tax, the business tax, the urban maintenance and construction tax, and the personal income tax which usually accrue to the secondary and tertiary sectors. In addition, the coastal region enjoys a higher percentage of tax rebates. By looking at the same data source, Tsui (2005) concludes that the regional fiscal disparity has worsened since the 1994 fiscal reform.

Table 13.2 presents economic structure and tax rates for the two regions in 1993 and 2000. The agricultural tax rate is defined as the ratio of agricultural tax revenue to the gross agricultural output value, while the implicit industrial rate is measured as the ratio of tax revenues from the industrial sector relative to the gross industrial output value. Land rents include city construction tax and land user fees. Fiscal dependent burden is denoted as the number of public employees per 10,000 yuan (1993 value) of local revenue. We use the national GDP deflator (1.977) to adjust GVIAO per capita, agricultural tax per capita and land rent per capita to ensure they are comparable between the two years.

Several features are apparent from Table 13.2. First, although both regions have experienced fast growth, the eastern region has grown at an annual rate of 3.81 percent, compared to 3.71 percent in the inland region, indicating a widening regional gap. The per capita GVIAO in the coastal region was about three times of that in the inland region in 2000. In addition, the share of agricultural output value in total GVIAO in the coastal areas was twice of that in the inland region.

Second, the tax rates in both agricultural and rural industrial sectors are regressive – the better-off coastal regions enjoy lower tax rates than the less developed inland regions. On a per capita basis, the distribution of agricultural taxes is rather even. However, because of the difference in economic base, the effective tax rates differ across regions. Figure 13.1 presents the implicit industrial tax rate against the logarithmic per capita GVIAO in 1993 and 2000. The downward straight line in the figure again clearly demonstrates that the industrial tax rate is regressive. The richer a county, the lower is its industrial tax rate.

Third, the coastal region benefits more from the rising land value. The local revenue from city construction tax and land development in the coastal region is much higher than that in the inland region (Zhang, 2007). With a lower industrial tax rate, the rich region can attract more investments and migrants, which certainly boosts the value of land. Figure 13.2 illustrates that land revenue is positively related to the level of economic development, being consistent with the results for two regions in Table 13.2.

Table 13.2 Economic structure and taxes, 1993 and 2000

Year/Region	Per capita GVIAO	The percentage of agricultural output value in GVIAO	Agricultural tax rate (yuan per 100 yuan)	Industrial tax rate (yuan per 100 yuan)	Agricultural tax per capita	Land revenue per capita
1993						
Coastal	6,062	20.41	0.81	2.74	11.45	
Inland	2,050	41.54	1.15	5.95	11.18	
China	3,569	27.81	0.99	3.67	11.28	
2000						
Coastal	7,876	19.20	1.06	0.80	37.91	8.01
Inland	2,646	37.21	1.72	1.30	39.12	3.89
China	4,612	25.65	1.40	0.94	38.67	5.44

Note: Calculated by author based on *China County Public Finance Statistical Yearbook*. GVIAO stands for the gross value of industrial and agricultural output. Per capita GVIAO, per capita agricultural taxes, and per capita land revenue are in constant 1993 yuan.

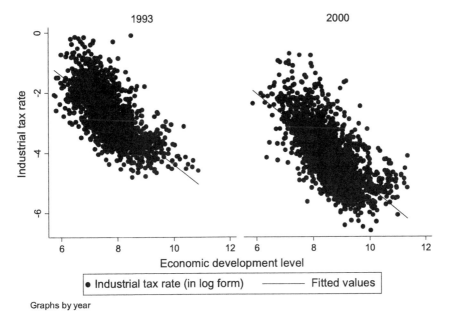

Figure 13.1 Economic development level and effective industrial tax rate.

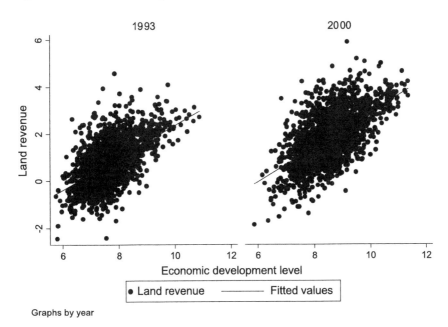

Figure 13.2 Economic development level and rent from land development.

Note: The land revenue includes city maintenance and development tax and land using tax. Because in 1993 the land using tax was not published, the data in the figure are only for 2000. The vertical axis stands for the per capita land revenue in logarithmic form.

The rich regions can capitalize more from the rising land value than the poor regions.

Table 13.3 reports local government sizes and fiscal burdens to support the government. On average there are more than two persons on public payroll per hundred people and the ratio has increased between 1993 and 2000, indicating an inflating government size. The burden is heavier in the inland region than in the coastal region. Because of the difference in tax base, the fiscal burden to support the local government is more unevenly distributed across regions. The number of people on public payroll per unit of local revenue in the inland region is significantly higher than that in the coastal region. As a result, the inland region spent a larger share on the administrative expenses and a smaller amount on productive public investment.

Figure 13.3 further highlights the correlation between fiscal dependent burden and economic development. The negative relationship reveals that the revenue capacity to support the public payroll in poor counties is much weaker than in more developed ones. The government size, which is to a large extent in proportion to total population, is largely determined by the upper level government. The top priorities for the local government are collecting taxes, maintaining social order, and carrying over various tasks, such as agricultural industrialization and urbanization, assigned from the upper level governments (Lin et al., 2002). In the poor regions, the local government has little financial resources to carry over to the task of public goods provision after covering the salaries of public employees.

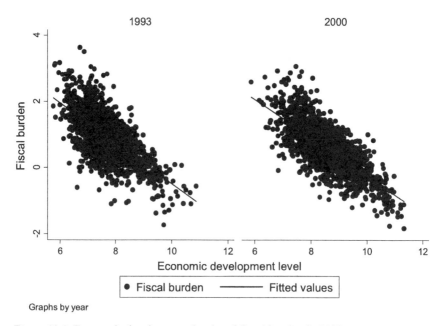

Figure 13.3 Economic development level and fiscal burden in 2000.

Table 13.3 Government size and fiscal burdens, 1993 and 2000

Year/Region	No. of government employees per hundred people	No. of government employees per 10,000 yuan of fiscal revenue (1993 constant)	The percentage of administrative expenditure	The percentage of productive expenditure	Per capita productive public expenditure (1993 constant yuan)
1993					
Coastal	2.08	1.08	9.69	14.39	21.59
Inland	2.24	1.75	14.05	13.55	16.57
China	2.18	1.43	11.99	13.93	18.47
2000					
Coastal	2.45	0.99	10.71	5.43	12.82
Inland	2.72	1.65	13.79	5.41	8.94
China	2.62	1.34	12.37	5.42	10.40

Note: The number of government employees per 10,000 yuan of fiscal revenue and per capita productive public expenditure in 2000 are adjusted using comparable GDP deflator with 1993 as a base year. The definition of the productive public expenditure is not totally comparable between 1993 and 2000. In 1993, it includes capital construction (jiben jianshe zhichu), expenditures for supporting agricultural production (zhiyuan nongcun shengchan zhichu), and expenditures for innovation (waqian gaizao zhichu), while the last term was not listed in the 2000 yearbook.

To examine the dynamics of regional distribution, we further calculate the Gini coefficient of per capita GVIAO, per capita productive public expenditure, and the share of productive investment in total public expenditure, respectively, based on data at the county level and present them in Table 13.4. All the three indicators show rising regional disparity. The Gini coefficient of per capita GVIAO rises from 46.47 to 48.39. Figure 13.4 plots the density distributions of logarithmic per capita GVIAO in 1993 and 2000, which clearly shows a spreading out over the period. Noticeably, inequality in the level and share of productive investment has increased by 7 percent and 27 percent, respectively, during the seven-year period, much higher than that in per capita GVIAO.

Table 13.4 Gini coefficient of three indicators, 1993 and 2001

Year	Per capita GVIAO	Per capita productive public expenditure	Share of productive investment in total public expenditure
1993	46.47	68.28	33.04
2000	48.39	73.34	41.82
Rate of change (%)	4.13	7.41	26.57

Note: Calculated by the author based on *China County Public Finance Statistical Yearbook.* GVIAO stands for the gross value of industrial and agricultural output.

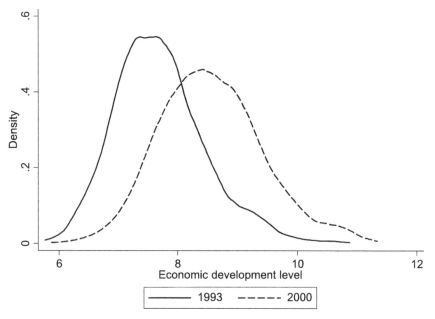

Figure 13.4 The density function of per capita gross industrial and agricultural output (log form).

The uneven regional development in nonfarm activities in the rural sector has been regarded as one of the major driving forces behind the changes in rural regional inequality (Rozelle, 1994; Fan, Zhang, and Zhang, 2004). Wan, Lu, and Chen (2003) and Zhang and Fan (2004) further show that the growing regional disparity in public capital significantly attributes to the rising regional inequality in nonfarm development largely because public capital is complementary to private capital. The evidence here offers an additional explanation: regions with higher implicit industrial tax rate have more difficulty attracting capital inflows than those with lower tax rates, thereby resulting in more fragmentation in capital markets and higher regional disparity.

In short, the descriptive analysis show that along with fiscal decentralization, regional distribution in public finance, in particular in productive public spending, has greatly deteriorated, contrary to what Jin, Qian and Weingast (2005) observed up to 1992. The results seem to be inconsistent with the theoretical predictions by Tiebout (1956) and QR (1998). In the next section, we provide a more quantitative examination on the impact of decentralization.

13.3 Theoretical consideration

Much of the literature on fiscal federalism, represented by Tiebout (1956) and QR (1998), focuses on the economic efficiency aspect of market competition. In essence, the Tiebout model assumes full factor mobility. Bardhan (2002) comments that the assumptions underlying the Tiebout model are often too stringent in developing countries. In the case of China, despite loosening control of migration in recent years, there still exist obstacles to labor movement, in particular from rural areas to cities. Another implicit assumption of the Tiebout model is that local governments are responsive to the needs of voters. However, in China local government officials are in general not elected and their preferences may not be consistent with those of their constituents. In addition, the size of local governments is mainly determined by the upper level government and has much less to do with local needs. All these factors may make the Tiebout model inapplicable.

The QR federalism model has a crucial assumption that all the regions are identical. Within the more developed coastal areas, such as Zhejiang Province, where many counties share similar initial conditions, this assumption may hold. However, for China as a whole, regional differences, in particular between the inland and the coast, are substantial, making this assumption inappropriate.

Moreover, these theories do not take the transaction costs of tax collection and its consequences into account. Adam Smith (1776) regarded fairness and economy in tax collection as fundamental principles. Regarding collection cost, he stated explicitly (page 1044):

> Every tax ought to be so contrived as both to take out and to keep out of
> the pockets of the people as little as possible, over and above what it
> brings into the public treasury of the state.

In particular, he opposed levying a tax if it involves a great number of people
whose salaries eat up a large share of the tax. In a less perfect world, labor
migration involves costs, so do tax collection and policy implementation. In
China's context, regions differ greatly in economic and taxation structures. As
a result, the assumptions underlying the above two theoretical models may not
be valid and the predictions of the above models may not bear out in reality.

Let us begin with a thought experiment. Suppose there are two regions, A
(coastal) and B (inland). Before the fiscal decentralization, Region A is
endowed with a large share of non-farm economy while Region B relies on
agriculture as the major source of revenue. However, the administrative structures in the two regions are the same.[5] In addition, the average cost of collecting each unit of tax from a firm is much lower than from a rural household.
Consequently, both regions prefer to levy taxes on enterprises than on households if possible. After decentralization, both regions must be responsible for
collecting their own revenues and fulfilling the same responsibilities or
mandates.[6]

In Region A, because of the large industrial base, the local government can
obtain most revenues from the industrial sector. Moreover, a large industrial
base means high opportunity cost of labor, making collecting taxes from
rural households rather costly. If the incurred tax collection cost from households outweighs the revenue, it is more cost-effective for the local government
to forego farmers' tax obligations and pay the agricultural taxes to upper
level governments using other revenue sources. When there are many local
enterprises, the implicit taxation burden to each firm is relatively lower, which
in turn help attract more business and enlarge the tax base. In addition, the
current tax sharing scheme favors regions with larger share of the secondary
and tertiary sectors as the value-added taxes and personal income taxes
which are shared with the local government are largely linked to these sectors
(Tsui, 2005).

Moreover, because the local government size is mainly related to the size of
the population instead of the level of economic development, the government
in this region has more local revenues disposable for productive public
investment after covering the salaries of public employees. Better infrastructure and lower tax burdens can offset the relatively higher labor and land
cost in Region A. All these help create an enabling investment and form a
virtuous cycle. In other words, in Region A, the local government tends to
stretch out "helping hands" to business development (Frye and Shleifer,
1997). This is a hypothesis we want to test.

In contrast, in Region B, there are few nonfarm enterprises. Because of
lower tax collection cost on firms relative to agricultural taxes on households,
the existing firms are more prone to be the predatory targets of their local

government's excessive taxes and fees. Therefore, the implicit industrial tax rate tends to be high, which will discourage the entry of potential investment and drive away existing business enterprises, hampering the growth in the nonfarm sector over the long run. However, in China the size of local governments is rather fixed. After paying the salaries of public employees, local governments in poor regions often have little resources remaining to provide public investment. Low levels and quality of public infrastructure and service often result in unfavorable investment environment. Obviously, it is hard for any factories to operate normally and efficiently in an area plagued with irregular power output and unpaved roads. Consequently, Region B may have a worse investment environment despite its lower wage rate and land rent. The large share of the agriculture sector means a higher collection cost of taxes on average because a higher level of manpower is required in the collection activities. Consequently we hypothesize that in Region B, the local governments tend to have "grabbing hands".

All in all, under fiscal decentralization, the transaction cost of tax collection and economic structure may affect the outcome of decentralization. As a result, the relationship between the local government and businesses may differ across regions. Because of the difference in initial economic structure and endowment, two equilibrium, one with "helping hands" and one with "grabbing hands," may evolve as theorized by Cai and Treisman (2005). It is an empirical question to examine whether under fiscal decentralization the heterogeneous revenue structure and homogenous government structure matter to the growth patterns.

13.4 Quantitative analysis

Now we use a more quantitative method to examine the impact of initial economic structure and fiscal dependent burdens on subsequent local economic growth. Following Barro and Sala-I-Martin (1995) on growth convergence, we model the growth rate of per capita GVIAO as a function of its initial value, initial economic structure, fiscal dependent burdens, and a set of other variables:

$$\log\left(\frac{y_{it}}{y_{it-1}}\right) = a + \beta \log(y_{i-1}) + \gamma Z + \delta D + \varepsilon_i$$

where y_{it} is per capita GVIAO. The subscripts t and $t-1$ refer to 2000 and 1993, respectively. The left-hand side variable represents the growth rate of per capita GVIAO over the period. The coefficient β stands for the speed of convergence of per capita GVIAO. A negative value for this coefficient indicates convergence while a positive value implies divergence. It provides useful information on understanding how initial conditions contribute to long-term growth and whether there is convergence or not. Because of diminishing returns to capital, in a perfect market, the returns to capital and labor will equalize across regions and lead to convergence. Z includes the share of the gross value of agricultural output in GVIAO, the ratio of public employee to total local revenue. These two variables are in logarithmic form. γ is the corresponding coefficient for the two variables. D is a set of dummy variables. If a county is nationally designated a poor county, it is assigned a value of 1 and 0 otherwise. In different specifications, we also include prefecture and provincial fixed effects. δ is a vector of coefficients for these fixed effects.

Table 13.5 reports regression results under four specifications. The first three regressions include prefecture, provincial, and regional fixed effects, respectively. The last column excludes any dummy variables. The second to the last row presents the Akaike's information criterion (AIC) for model selection. The model with the smallest value is preferred. The AIC criterion suggests that the first regression with the prefecture fixed effects dominates the other three. Because we do not have county-specific price information, the fixed prefecture effects serve as a good proxy to eliminate the price effect inherent in the nominal growth of per capital GVIAO in the period. Moreover, they may capture other shocks common to a prefecture.

The table also presents the *p*-values of the regression specification error test (RESET) for omitted variables. Only the first specification with prefecture dummies accepts the null hypothesis that there are no missing variables. The

Table 13.5 The effect of initial economic structure and government size on economic growth

Variables	R1	R2	R3	R4
Initial value in 1993	−0.467**	−0.423**	−0.384**	−0.313**
	(0.030)	(0.027)	(0.026)	(0.025)
Economic structure in 1993	−0.340**	−0.209**	−0.211**	−0.244**
(Agricultural gross output value/GVIAO)	(0.084)	(0.083)	(0.080)	(0.081)
Fiscal dependent burdens in 1993	−0.125**	−0.171**	−0.165**	−0.161**
(No. of employee on public payroll /Total local revenue)	(0.025)	(0.025)	(0.023)	(0.023)
Nationally designated poor county status in 1993	−0.227**	−0.243**	−0.233**	−0.233**
	(0.028)	(0.028)	(0.030)	(0.031)
Regional dummies	Prefecture**	Province**	Region**	None
Omission variable test (*p*-value)	0.336	0.037	0.086	0.046
AIC	1681.5	2220.1	2598.8	2653.1
Adjusted R^2	0.536	0.290	0.117	0.090

Note: Coefficients for dummies are not reported here. The figures in parentheses are standard errors. The symbol ** means a significance level of 1%.

other three regressions all reject the null hypotheses. As a result, the first specification is preferable.

The coefficient for the initial value of per capita GVIAO in all the three regressions is negative, suggesting the existence of a mean convergence. The coefficient for the share of agricultural output in the initial year of 1993 is statistically significant in all the three regressions, indicating that the heterogeneous economic structure is an offsetting divergent force. For a region primarily relying on agricultural revenues, the subsequent growth in productive spending is slower than a region endowed with a large nonfarm tax base.

The negative and significant coefficient for the fiscal dependent variable in 1993 suggests that oversized bureaucracy can be a real burden for local economic growth in poor regions. In an ideal Tiebout world where local governments are responsive to the needs of constituents, lower revenues mean lower levels of public service and smaller government. Because of the nature of political centralization in China, the government size is rather inflexible, which leads to relatively heavier burdens in the poorer regions than in the richer regions under the arrangement of fiscal decentralization.

The table also shows that those nationally designated poor counties are growing slower than other counties. This is consistent with the findings by Fan, Zhang, and Zhang (2004) on the performance of China's poverty alleviation program. There are several possible explanations. First, local governments in the poor counties may be more likely to understate their performance indicators so as to retain the "designated-poverty" status and qualify for transfers. Second, in the presence of central transfers, local officials may spend more time building up connections with the upper level governments rather than developing the local economy.

The coefficients for the dummy variables are not presented in the table to save space. They are jointly significant in the first three specifications. In the third specification, the coefficient for the inland coefficient is statistically negative. To check the robustness of the results, Table 13.6 lists the separate

Table 13.6 The effect of initial economic structure and government size on economic growth by region

Variables	Coastal	Inland
Initial value in 1993	−0.418**	−0.503**
	(0.062)	(0.036)
Economic structure in 1993	−0.153	−0.406**
(Agricultural gross output value/GVIAO)	(0.160)	(0.099)
Fiscal dependent burdens in 1993	−0.198**	−0.106**
(No. of employee on public payroll /Total local revenue)	(0.060)	(0.028)
Nationally designated poor county status	−0.229**	−0.238**
	(0.070)	(0.031)
R^2	0.690	0.580

Note: Coefficients for prefecture dummies are not reported here. The figures in parentheses are standard errors. The symbol ** means a significance level of 1%.

regression results for the coastal and inland regions. Except for the economic structure variable, the coefficients for other variables are rather robust. Within a prefecture in a coastal region, the economic structure is more homogenous. This is probably why the coefficient for this variable in the first regression is insignificant.

In short, fiscal decentralization may bring about detrimental distributional consequences when economic structure differs and government sizes are excessive.

13.5 Conclusions and policy implication

Considering the sheer size of China, fiscal decentralization is imperative for the government to tackle the information and incentive problems inherent in the relationship between the central and local governments. However, decentralization is a complex process involving not only fiscal aspects but also governance and mandates. When government sizes are largely independent of the demand of constituencies, the standard Tiebout sorting model is not applicable anymore.

Under the current local-central fiscal arrangement, the large regional variation in production patterns and revenue structures makes the underlying assumption of the QR fiscal federalism model invalid. Moreover, the transaction costs of tax collections become a more serious issue under fiscal decentralization. The high collection cost of agricultural tax plus the excessive government size makes local governments in regions endowed mostly with agricultural production barely able to provide the necessary public goods and services. Farmers and firms in poor regions are paying heavy taxes, while those in rich regions enjoy generous support and lower tax burdens. The regressive nature of the rural taxation system plays a significant role in explaining the divergent regional growth patterns even after controlling for the initial value. Overall, the fiscal decentralization is in favor of the rich localities and exacerbates the regional gap.

In his famous article, Oates (1968) has argued that to ensure the functioning of fiscal federalism, the central government should carry over the functions of stabilization and distribution, while the local government should be mainly responsible for performing the allocation role, i.e. a more efficient provision of public goods and service. In the case of China, however, the local government has to perform both the functions of distribution and allocation. By nature, it is almost impossible for local governments to equalize the fiscal capacity across regions in such a diverse country.

The large and inflexible size of local governments is another major impediment. Without a large reduction in the number of local public employees, especially in areas with agriculture as the major means of revenue, fiscal decentralization alone is not sufficient to deal with the distributional problem. Most theories on federalism assume that size and service of local government are responsive to the needs of local residents. In a democratic society, voters endogenously determine local government size. However, under the current system in China, if the central government grants more power to the local government and lets it determine the staffing level, it is likely that local government sizes in the less developed region will inflate rather than decrease. In a region lacking nonfarm job opportunities, entering the government payroll is one of the most attractive options, which may create a large rent-seeking behavior for officials to hire relatives and friends. Consequently, the size of local government is more likely to rise provided that the constituents do not have much say on local affairs. Therefore, how to control and reduce government sizes under the current political system poses a dilemma for policy makers. Economic decentralization in the reform period has undoubtedly helped prompt China's growth. But under the regime of political centralization, regional disparities have widened significantly. How to achieve balanced regional growth is a delicate task. Considering that China has been rather successful in engineering institutional innovations based on existing institutions, the challenge may induce more institutional innovations on fiscal decentralization and governance.

Notes

1 For detailed description on China's fiscal decentralization, see Tong (1998), Zhang (1999) and World Bank (2002).
2 Using the same data set Shih and Zhang (2004) examine the issue of transfers and subsidies and Tsui (2005) look at the regional fiscal disparity.
3 The coastal zone includes Hebei, Liaoning, Shandong, Jiangsu, Zhejiang, Fujian, Guangdong, and Guangxi provinces; the inland zone comprises of all the remaining provinces. Kanbur and Zhang (1999; 2005) have used the same classification.
4 The extra-budgetary items are not included in the official statistics. If the tax-sharing reform worsens the regressive tax structure, poor regions are more likely to stretch out grabbing hands and the paper's results maybe underestimated. Thank an anonymous referee for this point.
5 Xu Yong (2003) has documented the evolution of administrative units in rural China and shown how excessive they are.
6 Liu and Tao (2004) list a set of central mandates and policy burdens.

References

Bardhan, Pranab, 2002. "Decentralization of Governance and Development," *Journal of Economic Perspective*, 16 (4): 185–205.
Barro, Robert J. and Xavier Sala-I-Martin, 1995. *Economic Growth*. McGraw-Hill Inc.
Cai, Hongbin and Daniel Treisman, 2005. "Does Competition for Capital Discipline Governments? Decentralization, Globalization, and Public Policy," *American Economic Review*, 95 (3): 817–830.
China State Statistical Bureau, various years. *China County Public Finance Statistical Yearbook*. Beijing: China Statistical Publishing House.
Dethier, Jean-Jacques. 1999. "Governance and Economic Performance: A Survey," ZEF Discussion Paper on Development Policy No. 5.
Fan, Shenggen, Linxiu Zhang, and Xiaobo Zhang, 2004. "Reform, Investment and

Poverty in Rural China," *Economic Development and Cultural Change*, 52 (2): 395–422.

Frye Timothy and Andrei Shleifer, 1997. "The Invisible Hand and the Grabbing Hand," *American Economic Review*, 87 (2): 354–358.

Jin, Hehui, Yingyi Qian, and Barry R. Weingast, 2005. "Regional Decentralization and Fiscal Incentives: Federalism, Chinese Style," *Journal of Public Economics*, 89 (9–10): 1719–1742.

Kanbur, Ravi and Xiaobo Zhang, 1999. "Which Regional Inequality: Rural–Urban or Inland–Coastal? An Application to China," *Journal of Comparative Economics* 27: 686–701.

Kanbur, Ravi and Xiaobo Zhang, 2005. "Fifty Years of Regional Inequality in China: A Journey Through Central Planning, Reform and Openness," *Review of Development Economics* 9 (1): 87–106.

Knight, John and Li Shi, 1999. "Fiscal Decentralization: Incentives, Redistribution and Reform in China," *Oxford Development Studies*, 27 (1): 5–32.

Knight, John and Lina Song, 1993. "The Spatial Contribution to Income Inequality in Rural China," *Cambridge Journal of Economics*, 17: 195–213.

Li, Hongbin and Li-An Zhou, 2005. "Political Turnover and Economic Performance: The Incentive Role of Personnel Control in China," *Journal of Public Economics*, 89: 1743–1762.

Lin, Justin Yifu and Zhiqiang Liu, 2000. "Fiscal Decentralization and Economic Growth in China," *Economic Development and Cultural Change*, 49 (1): 1–21.

Lin, Justin Yifu, Ran Tao, Mingxing Liu, and Qi Zhang. 2002. "Urban and Rural Household Taxation in China: Measurement and Stylized Facts," CCER Working Paper.

Liu, Mingxing and Ran Tao, 2004. "Regional Competition, Fiscal Reform and Local Governance in China," paper presented in the conference "Paying for Progress. Public Finance, Human Welfare, and Inequality in China," May 21–23, Institute for Chinese Studies, Oxford.

Maskin, Eric, Yingyi Qian, and Chenggan Xu, 2000. "Incentives, Scale Economies, and Organization Form," *Review of Economic Studies*, 67: 359–378.

Oates, Wallace, 1968. "The Theory of Public Finance in a Federal System," *Canadian Journal of Economics*, 1 (1): 37–54.

Park, Albert, Scott Rozelle, Christine Wong, and Changqing Ren, 1996. "Distributional Consequences of Reforming Local Public Finance in China," *China Quarterly*, 147: 751–778, September.

Qian, Yingyi and Gerard Roland, 1998. "Federalism and the Soft Budget Constraint." *American Economic Review* 88 (5): 1143–1162, December.

Rozelle, Scott, 1994. "Rural Industrialization and Increasing Inequality: Emerging Patterns in China's Reforming Economy," *Journal of Comparative Economics*, 19: 362–91.

Shih, Victor and Zhang Qi, "Who Receives Subsidies: A Look at the County-level before and after the 1994 Tax Reform," paper presented in the conference "Paying for Progress. Public Finance, Human Welfare, and Inequality in China," Institute for Chinese Studies, Oxford, May 21–23, 2004.

Smith, Adam, 1776. *The Wealth of Nations*. Bantam Classic Edition/March 2003, Bantam Dell: New York.

Tiebout, Charles, 1956. "A Pure Theory of Local Expenditures," *Journal of Political Economy*, 64: 416–424.

Tong, James, 1998. "Fiscal Regimes in China, 1971–1998," *Chinese Economy*, 31 (3): 5–21, May–June.

Tsui, Kai-yuen, 2005. "Local Tax System, Intergovernmental Transfers and China's Local Fiscal Disparities," *Journal of Comparative Economics*, 33 (1): 173–196, March.

Wan, Guanghua, Ming Lu, and Zhao Chen, 2003. "Globalization and Regional Inequality in China," World Institute of Development Economic Research (WIDER) working paper, http://www.wider.unu.edu/conference/conference-2003-3/conference-2003-3-papers/wan-chen-3-9-03.pdf.

West, Loraine A. and Christine Wong, 1995. "Fiscal Decentralization and Growing Regional Disparities in Rural China: Some Evidence in the Provision of Social Services," *Oxford Review of Economic Policy*, 11 (4): 70–84.

World Bank, 2002. *China National Development and Sub-national Finance: A Review of Provincial Expenditures*. Washington DC: World Bank.

Xu Yong, 2003. "Xiangcun zhili jiegou gaige de zouxiang" (Direction of Reforms on Rural Governance), *Zhanluo Yu Guanli (Strategy and Management)*, 4: 90–97.

Zhang, Le-Yin, 1999. "Chinese Central-Provincial Fiscal Relationships, Budgetary Decline and the Impact of the 1994 Fiscal Reform: An Evaluation." *China Quarterly*, 157: 115–141, May.

Zhang, Tao, and Heng-fu Zou, 1998. "Fiscal Decentralization, Public Spending and Economic Growth in China," *Journal of Public Economics*, 67: 221–240.

Zhang, Xiaobo, 2007. "Assymetric Property Rights in China's Economic Growth," *William Mitchell Law Review*, 33 (2): 101–116.

Zhang, Xiaobo and Shenggen Fan, 2004. "Public Investment and Regional Inequality in Rural China," *Agricultural Economics*, 30 (2): 89–100.

14 Social entitlement exchange and balanced economic growth

Xiaopeng Luo and Xiaobo Zhang

Abstract

In China, the government replicates itself from the central to the local level. The structure and size of governments at the lower levels are closely related to those in the upper levels, and have little to do with local economic development. As a result, under fiscal decentralization, the regional fiscal burdens to carry out various central mandates and regulations have become increasingly uneven. This has led to the underprovision of public goods in both less developed and developed regions, thereby widening inequality. We argue that the large regional differences also imply opportunities for regions to trade social entitlements so as to increase both efficiency and equity. The latest innovations in land development right transfers in the coastal provinces and the use of police officers from the same regions as the local migrants to fight crime in the coastal provinces show the feasibility of social entitlement exchanges.

Since the start of economic reforms in the late 1970s, China has achieved remarkable success in its economic development. However, these achievements have not come without costs. One of the most serious consequences is rising inequality. Presently China's income inequality within communities, between urban and rural areas as well as among regions, has rapidly widened. Rising inequality has become one of the most pressing social issues and has drawn wide attention (Gustafsson and Shi, 2002; Kanbur and Zhang, 2005; Xing et al., 2009).

Due to the decentralized fiscal arrangement and the centralized governance structure (Zhang, 2006a), the large differences in initial economic structures and revenue bases have resulted in fiscal burdens to support the functioning of local government which vary significantly across jurisdictions. Regions where agriculture is the major economic activity have little resources left for public investment after paying for the bureaucracy. Therefore, public goods are underprovided in less developed western regions. In turn, this greatly reduces the opportunities to develop modern agriculture and non-farm industries and lowers the opportunity costs of farmers to leave their native regions for jobs in coastal areas. In contrast, because of its booming economy, coastal regions have attracted a large number of migrant workers from interior regions. Despite the large number of migrants, the size of local governments usually do not change accordingly as it is determined by the upper level government primarily based upon the number of registered residents under the *Hukou* (household registration) system. As a result, some public goods and services, such as public security and schools for the children of migrants, may be underprovided, increasing the private and social costs of peasants becoming urban citizens. Consequently, the under-provision of goods in both areas not only widens rural–urban and regional disparities, but also increases the risk of social unrest in rural China. With increasing inter-provincial migration, the imbalance between the decentralized economic structure and centralized administrative controls will become more pronounced. This paper aims to illuminate the causes of widening disparities in China over the past several decades from the perspective of institutional reform. It also suggests entitlement exchange as a means of reducing regional disparities and promoting balanced growth.

14.1 Institutionalized hierarchy of property rights combined with hierarchy of social status – an important feature in China's governing structure

China's present governing structure is a replicate hierarchy (Luo, 1995; Zhang, 2006a). In order to carry out central mandates, such as family planning, a replicate governance structure has been set up. The structure of local governments closely maps that in the upper level government. Under this organizational structure, the central government can delegate some central tasks to local governments. There are several salient features to this type of governance structure:

(1) The higher a unit in the replicate hierarchy is, the more privileges it possesses in accessing public resources, and the more economic safeguards its members will enjoy. However, government units at the upper level face more restrictions in terms of day to day decision-making in productive activities. The lower-level units in the replicate hierarchy possess few rights in accessing and using resources but have more freedom in making independent economic decisions. Compared to higher-level units, the income of lower-level units is more directly related to the performance of the local economy.

(2) Before economic reforms, migration was largely restricted. The governance structure not only created hierarchical property rights, but also hierarchical social status for people working in different units. People working in upper level units in the structure enjoyed greater social welfare than those at the lower levels, thereby creating a rigid social class system. The most vivid division of social status was the gap between urban and rural residents. However, even within urban residents, there were significant differences in

terms of social welfare between the ranks of central and government agencies and between state and collective enterprises.

(3) The size of government is highly related to that of population. In principle, the size of governments at various levels is authorized by the Staffing Control Office in the upper-level government. From the county-level data shown on Figure 14.1, we can see that the overall scale of fiscally supported staff at the county level is not related to the level of local economic

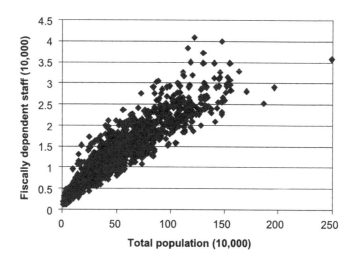

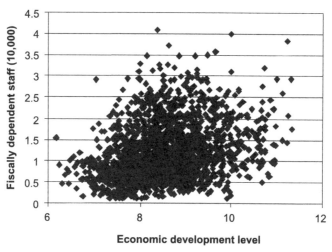

Figure 14.1 Fiscally supported staff/size of population and level of economic development (2000).

Source: China Statistical Yearbook on County-level Finance.

Note: Economic development level is defined as per capita gross output value of industry and agriculture in logarithm.

development but rather to the size of the population. In a self-governed democratic society, the size of local governments should be related to both the size of population and the level of economic development. This contrasts with China where there is almost zero elasticity between the size of local governments and the level of economic development.

(4) The central government usually adopts an "across-the-board" approach in issuing mandates related to policy, giving local governments little discretionary power to adjust for local conditions. Under such an organizational structure, information asymmetries and moral hazards are so serious that the central government is neither willing to nor secure enough to give much autonomy to local governments. The central government often adopts "one-size-fits-all" types of policies for significant issues, such as family planning and land acquisitions, so as to execute top-to-bottom controls. However, since local conditions vary greatly across regions in China, the "one-size-fits-all" approach inevitably results in uneven costs for the implementation of the same set of central mandates.

(5) The strict and unified hierarchy possesses tremendous capacity for organization and mobilization. When carrying out some central mandates or during emergencies, China can act swiftly with a determination unlike some democratic countries, such as India, where collective actions are hard to put in place. One typical example was the Chinese Government acting swiftly to prevent the spread of SARS in 2004.

14.2 China's reform strategy: expanding market entitlements within existing social entitlements

Different entitlement systems may evolve in different societies during the course of development. Sen (1981) put forth the concepts of "entitlement" and "exchange of entitlement" in his study on the cause of famines. According to Sen, an entitlement system consists of two subsystems. One is a market entitlement subsystem, equivalent to property rights, while the other refers to the social entitlement subsystem, such as employment rights and other social rights in modern society. Social entitlements are often dependent upon the underlying institutional arrangements and cultural background. In common Chinese, social entitlements can be called "*mingfen.*" These are rights based on social status or titles rather than on the ownership of property. Social entitlements include not only those explicitly stipulated and legally protected, but also those determined by means of established rules and customs. Most social entitlements are financed and enforced through state power.

To change old institutional arrangements, reformers must face the existing "rent claim rights" arising from established social arrangements. "Revolutions" are distinguished from "reformations" in that the former totally deny established entitlement systems. The latter, for the purpose of peaceful transformation, recognize a variety of historically formed social entitlements before reforming some obsolete ones which have become obstacles to the desired social changes. In the era of planned economy, independent property rights did not exist and individual economic freedom was mostly constrained. People were organized into one uniform replicate hierarchy structure and therefore lacked the incentives for productive activities. In order to increase the incentives of individuals and local governments, over the course of several decades, the Chinese government has carried out the following reforms.

First, the government dissolved collective farming by making production contracts with individual rural households. Initiated by peasants and promoted by governments, the radical reform came into place in the Chuxian prefecture, Anhui Province, and rapidly spread nationwide as the basic operational mode in Chinese agriculture. The principle of the household responsibility system (HRS) is: that "[a]fter individual households have handed in the grain quota to both the state and collective units, they can retain the remnants." Under this arrangement, the rent claim rights on agriculture products belong to peasants. The key condition is that farmers must meet the compulsory quota to the state before selling the extra production to the market.

Because peasants could possess all remnants after fulfilling the state quota, their enthusiasm for production dramatically increased. The improved incentive system immediately resulted in the full utilization of the long-term investments by the state in agricultural research and development, irrigation, and other infrastructure. As a result, agricultural production efficiency has increased rapidly (Fan, 1991; Lin, 1992). The adoption of the agricultural HRS weakened the hierarchy property rights system and revitalized individual property rights.

Secondly, the central government took a critical step to carry out fiscal decentralization. Contracts on revenue sharing between the central and local governments were negotiated to encourage local governments to obtain more revenues through the development of the local economy. Once again, by keeping the existing hierarchical property rights and social entitlements intact, the contracts expanded market entitlements for local governments by allowing them to share marginal tax revenues with the central government. Under such contracts, local governments obtained more financial autonomy, tied their expenditures with revenues, and linked their financial interests with the development of the local economy. Meanwhile, the upper-level government received greater revenues as the economy grew. Fiscal decentralization also intensified the competition between local governments to attract the limited available mobile capital. As a result, while initially opposed, many local government officials began to support a private economy and to protect property rights. The fiscal competition prompted local governments to continuously adjust local institutional arrangements in order to generate more revenues. Consequently regional competition has become a driving force behind economic reforms (Luo, 1995; Qian and Roland, 1998; Zhang, 2006b).

Thirdly, the central government implemented the dual pricing system as another critical reform measure (Lau, Qian, and Roland, 1997). Prior to reform, in the hierarchical property right and entitlement system, urban sectors, particularly state-owned enterprises (SOEs) under the control of the central, provincial, and municipal governments, enjoyed privileged access to a variety of scarce materials and capital goods through quotas. There were few quotas, however, for other lower-level state-owned enterprises and even fewer for collectively-owned enterprises. The dual pricing system allowed state-owned enterprises to sell unused input quota at market price to township and village enterprises (TVEs) which were outside the command economy. Such exchanges not only protect the original privileges of higher ranking entitlements, but also present TVEs with opportunities to access industrial inputs via market channels and to participate in the market economy. In other words, the dual pricing system provided a functional pricing mechanism for rent sharing through both hierarchical and market systems.

Overall, the Chinese economic reforms have been marked by effective strategies in improving exchanges within the existing entitlement system. Undoubtedly these reforms greatly enhanced the incentives of individuals and local governments, and promoted economic development. However, as discussed in the next section, because of a large regional difference in initial conditions, the reform has caused increasing imbalances between the underlying decentralized economic structure and the centralized governance structure.

14.3 Imbalance between the economic and governance structures

14.3.1 Less developed regions: high effective tax rates and the expansion of government employment

Although fiscal decentralization prompts local governments to increase revenues, the contract system on revenue and expenditure does not change the rent claim privileges of government employees. The government payroll receives top priority among public expenditure allocations. However, the fiscal burden to support the bureaucracy is unevenly divided across regions with governments in less developed regions facing much larger pressures.

In less developed regions, there are few nonfarm enterprises to add to local revenues. Since the size of local governments in China is rather fixed, after paying the public payroll, local governments in poor regions often have little resources for remaining public investments. Consequently, existing firms are more likely to be the predatory targets of their local government's excessive taxes and fees. This creates an implicitly higher industrial tax rate, hampering the growth in the nonfarm sector over the long run. Furthermore, low levels and quality of public infrastructure and service often result in an unfavorable investment environment. As shown in Figure 14.2, the effective industrial tax rate is regressive across regions. Unsurprisingly, large amounts of capital flowed from inland regions to coastal regions, further exacerbating

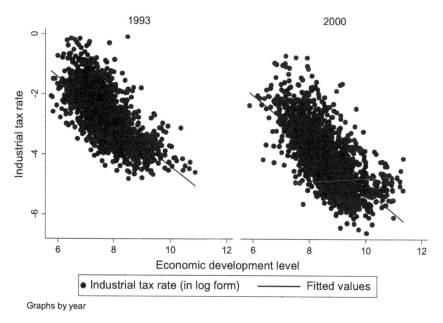

Figure 14.2 Effective industrial tax rate and economic size (2000).

Source: China Statistical Yearbook on County-level Finance, adapted from Zhang (2006a).

Note: Industrial tax rate and per capita gross output value of industry and agriculture in logarithmic form.

regional inequality (Zhang, 2006a). Along with increases in wages and land rent in coastal areas, capital would be expected to move to interior regions where factor prices are lower. However, the flow is rather limited and may even be reversed. As capital moved out of less developed regions, the lack of local employment opportunities impels peasants to leave their native regions in search of jobs. Therefore, a vicious cycle would be formed in the economy of less developed regions: the poorer the region, the heavier the burden of state employees, the higher the effective tax rate, the less favorable the investment environment, and the less sufficient the development opportunities.

The abolishment of agricultural taxes is another factor which aggravated regional disparity in per capita financial capacity. Agricultural taxes were one of the major tax revenue sources in less developed regions, resulting in increased financial pressure for local governments when agricultural taxes were removed. After paying salaries on the public payroll, many agencies which are not vertically administered, such as agricultural extension services, possess limited operational budgets. According to our survey, in some agricultural extension service stations at the township level in Guizhou, per capita monthly operational expenses amounted to only five RMB. Therefore, it is hard for the extension agents to assist farmers. Among the nine townships surveyed in Gansu, the average debt was nearly one million RMB.

Differences in regional financial capabilities also lead to disparities in the salary levels of public servants across regions. In principle, after controlling for skills, qualifications, and years of service, civil servants in different areas and departments should receive roughly the same salaries. The widening gap in salary levels results in many civil servants in less developed regions feeling dissatisfied. As civil servants play an important role in reporting social conditions, implementing central mandates and maintaining order, their dissatisfaction over pay may lead to increasing instability. This is why there is a strong call to even salaries of civil servants across regions. However, given the increasing rural–urban gap and stagnant poverty levels, raising the salaries of civil servants in poor regions may not be a popular decision as it will cause more hatred from ordinary people, in particular those lagging behind in the reform process.

Recently, the central government also decided in the next several years to exempt the incidental expenses of middle and primary school students. Some rich areas, such as Suzhou with strong fiscal capacity, have already taken the lead in enacting nine-year compulsory education.[1] However, the financial revenues of many interior counties are only tens of million RMB, insufficient to foot the bill of government payroll. With limited local revenues, the exemption of incidental expenses of school students would further pressure already tight local finances if central transfers are not put in place. Yet, increasing transfers may result in aid dependency: civil servants devote energy to seeking transfers rather than to developing the local economy.

14.3.2 *Developed regions: low tax rate and limited urbanization*

In developed coastal regions, rapid industrialization has dramatically increased demand for land for industrial and commercial use. However, the central government has adopted an across-the-board approach in issuing land permits. Given the insufficient number of land permits, enterprises try any means to please land administrators resulting in corruption. Since coastal regions have more job opportunities than the hinterland, a large number of workers flow into coastal towns leading to actual population sizes that far exceed those reported in statistics. In some townships in Zhejiang Province, there are two times as many migrants as local residents.

In coastal regions with many enterprises, the limited number of tax collectors tends to result in lump sum taxes from small enterprises, thus greatly lowering the effective tax rate. In turn, the low effective tax rate attracts more entrepreneurs to make investments and create jobs. A larger number of rural industrial clusters have emerged in the eastern region. For example, in 2004, in the sweater cluster in Puyuan Township, Tongxiang County, Zhejiang Province, there were more than 10,000 market entities, such as manufacturing enterprises, family workshops, and dealers, making it one of the largest sweater production centers (Ruan and Zhang, 2009). Yet, the number of tax collectors in this township does not match this. Despite the very low tax rate, the tax revenue generated from this township far exceeds that of many counties in the western regions. However, under the current policy, it is extremely difficult to move from town to city status, a move which would bestow more permits for land use and a larger government size.

Therefore, unlike western regions, the size of governments for some industrial centers in the eastern rural areas is actually very small relative to the total number of residents. As a result, there are shortages of many public services, such as policy officers, education, health, and environmental protection. Not surprisingly, many reports attribute the deterioration of public security to the massive inflow of migrants (Shi Jinping and You Tao, 2002).[2] Many local residents wish to have a secure social and economic environment. The unmet need for public service leads some rich people to transfer money abroad or to send their children overseas for education. While local residents have access to crowded school facilities, there are very few schools for the children of migrant workers. As a result, it is hard for migrants to settle permanently in coastal regions.

To sum up, the rapid economic development in coastal regions has boosted land prices and attracted a large number of migrant workers. However, the unified national policy and inflexible government size have intensified the binding constraints of land and public good provision in the rural coastal areas thereby limiting local economic development.

14.4 Expanding social entitlement exchanges

The question on how to handle historically formed social entitlements is a challenge to reformers. The success of further reforms in China will also depend on whether an ingenious method, such as the dual pricing system in the eighties, can transform the existing entitlement and make it exchangeable. The rigid governmental organization and land development rights, which originated from the command economy system, did not adapt to the rapid changes resulting from the economic reform. The large regional differences in economic development have led to great regional variation in the cost of implementing across-the-board central mandates. For example, in coastal regions there are sharp shortages of land permits for industrial and urban development, while some inland regions cannot use them all. In other words, the shadow prices of land greatly vary across regions. If these entitlements could be exchanged, each side would benefit and achieve a Pareto improvement. Moreover, social entitlement exchanges may help reduce regional inequality.

The concept of entitlement exchange is not new. Some developed countries have already established markets for pollution emission permits.[3] Under the framework of the *Kyoto Protocol*, a market for the trading of pollution discharge permits on CO_2 and other substances has already been established in EU countries. Moreover, a worldwide trade market is also under preparation.[4]

In so doing, countries which generate less pollution discharges than their permits allow, sell the extra permits to other countries.

As a matter of fact, permit exchanges have occurred in China. For example, local governments have exchanged land development rights in a few developed provinces. According to reports from Xinhua News Agency, both Jiangsu and Zhejiang Provinces have traded land development rights within their provinces.[5] In Jiangsu, the more developed southern areas purchased land development rights from the less developed northern areas. In 2002, the capital city of Zhejiang Province, Hangzhou, purchased the development rights of 3,000 *mu* of lands, at a price of 60,000 RMB Yuan per *mu*, from Haining City, a less developed region in Zhejiang Province. Land development rights trading were high at 68 percent, 57 percent, 78 percent and 78.3 percent for industrial parks in Hangzhou, Ningbo, Wenzhou, and Shaoxing, respectively.[6] In 2003, the Department of Land Resource Administration of Shandong also promulgated the "*Opinion Concerning Implementation of Land Rights Trading for Industrial and Agricultural Use*" to encourage exchanges of land permits within the province.[7]

Apart from land development right transfers, a case of borrowing police officers from elsewhere also recently emerged. According to the Workers Daily (2006),[8] there are more than 40,000 migrant laborers in Diankou Township, Zhuji City, Zhejiang, among which 14,000 are from Guizhou Province. With the rapid inflow of migrant workers, public security had become a major problem. Facing the challenges of fighting crime related to the floating population, since 2004, Zhuji City has borrowed two police officers from Zunyi County, Guizhou Province, to take charge of public security issues related to migrant workers from Guizhou working at Diankou Township. After its implementation, there has been a clear improvement of public security in this town. Because Zhuji City pays these two police officers according to the same level as local officers, they earn significantly more than in Zunyi County. Moreover, the police force in Zunyi had become relatively large after the enormous outflow of migrant workers to the coastal areas. The exchange helped to reduce the pressure on the payroll in Zunyi. Such an exchange is a win-win strategy. The Ministry of Public Security recently held a conference in Zhuji City to promote the Zhuji model, namely "borrowing police officers from the origin of migrants."

This exchange not only supports the idea that the size of inland governments is too large while that of coastal governments is too small, but also shows that the principle of social entitlement exchange can be applied to many problems in different forms. The case of police officer exchange involves only bilateral agreements between low-level local governments and the land development right exchange is also restricted to within a province.

In this paper, we propose an expansion of the concept of social entitlement exchange and the creation of a nationwide market system for social entitlement exchange. A nationwide trading system will greatly improve the efficiency of bi-literal trade. With a control on the total scale of land conversion, land development rights should be auctioned. Capital raised from the auctions can be used to establish a fund for reform. The fund can help inland local governments cut redundant government payrolls. Specifically, the entitlement of state employees can be bought out. Based upon our research, a potential market exists. At the township level in Guizhou Province, per capita salary averages only 1,000 to 1,500 RMB Yuan. The cost of buying out one civil servant is approximately ten times his salary. Conservatively speaking, one million yuan should buy out six government employees.

The potential benefits of social entitlement exchange are evident. First, government employees who are bought out acquire a startup fund which overcomes the credit constraints plaguing many entrepreneurs in the inland regions. Second, given limited local revenues, a reduction in government employees may help improve the salary level of the remaining civil servants and alleviate their dissatisfaction about low pay. Third, smaller government will result in larger fiscal revenues for increased and better quality public service, thereby enhancing investment environments. Fourth, regional disparities can be effectively reduced. The trade enables less developed regions to trim redundant government size and provide more public services, and helps more developed regions overcome bottlenecks of land and public services, create more employment opportunities, and attract more migrants. In doing so, the rent from rising land value can be more effectively utilized to promote balanced growth.

Expanding social entitlement trading will not affect the legitimacy of the central government. A broad trading system requires the central government to act as a designer, arbitrator and enforcer in the social entitlement market. Under a well designed system, social entitlement exchange is a Pareto improvement. With its great leverage, the central government can also help improve efficiency and equity through targeted subsidies.

Expanding social entitlement exchanges bears particular significance on China's economic development. With its vast size and prominent regional disparities, China has maintained a highly concentrated political authority. With rapid economic growth, the regional imbalance between the economic and governance structures has become more evident. Nonetheless, the large regional gap also suggests potential efficiency gains from further social entitlement exchanges. Past reforms show that social entitlement exchange is an effective strategy in ensuring a stable transition from a planned to a market economy.

Notes

1 http://news.xinhuanet.com/edu/2005–09/08/content_3460247.htm.
2 E.g., one striking title of a report in Beijing Youth (2005) reads, "Five Crime Peaks after Founding of P.R.C., Focus on Crimes Committed by Immigrants" (http://news.sohu.com/20051122/n227560585.shtml).
3 E.g., http://www.emissionstrading.com/.

4 E.g., exchange system of atmospheric emission in EU, http://ec.europa.eu/comm/environment/climat/emission.htm.
5 http://news.xinhuanet.com/edu/2004–09/08/content_3460247.htm.
6 www.cq.cei.gov.cn/content.asp?fcode=34880–3k.
7 http://www.sd-china.com/law/zdu/02.htm.
8 http://www.zjrb.cn/news/2006–4/20/content_81982.htm.

References

Fan, Shenggen, 1991. "Effects of Technological Change and Institutional Reform on Production: Growth in Chinese Agriculture," *American Journal of Agricultural Economics*, 73: 266–275.

Gustafsson, Björn and Li Shi, 2002. "Income inequality within and across counties in rural China 1988 and 1995," *Journal of Development Economics* 69: 179–204.

Kanbur, Ravi and Xiaobo Zhang, 2005. "Fifty Years of Regional Inequality in China: A Journey Through Central Planning, Reform and Openness," *Review of Development Economics* 9(1): 87–106.

Lau, Lawrence J., Yingyi Qian, and Gerard Roland, 1997. "Pareto-improving Economic Reforms through Dual-track Liberalization," *Economics Letters*, 55(2), 285–292.

Lin, Justin Y., 1992. "Rural Reforms and Agricultural Growth in China," *American Economic Review*, 82 (1), 34–51.

Luo, Xiaopeng, 1995. "Regional Competition and Property Rights: The Logic of Chinese Economic Reform," *Modern China Research*, 2: 1–16.

Qian, Yingyi and Gerard Roland, 1998. "Federalism and the Soft Budget Constraint," *American Economic Review*, 88 (5): 1143–1162.

Ruan, Jianqing and Xiaobo Zhang, 2009. "Finance and Cluster-based Industrial Development in China," Economic Development and Cultural Change, forthcoming.

Sen, Amartya, 1981. *Poverty and Famines: An Essay on Entitlement and Deprivation.* Oxford: Oxford University Press.

Shi Jinping and You Tao, 2002. "Crimes Committed by Immigrants: One Topic Drawing Much Attention," *Beijing Statistics*, 7: 22–23.

Xing, Li, Shenggen Fan, Xiaopeng Luo, and Xiaobo Zhang, 2009. "Community Poverty and Inequality in Western China: A Tale of Three Villages in Guizhou Province," China Economic Review, forthcoming.

Zhang, Xiaobo, 2006a. "Fiscal Decentralization and Political Centralization in China: Implications for Growth and Regional Inequality," forthcoming in *Journal of Comparative Economics*, 34 (4): 713–726.

Zhang, Xiaobo, 2006b. "Asymmetric Property Rights in China's Economic Growth," International Food Policy Research Institute (IFPRI) Development Strategy and Governance Division Discussion Paper No. 28.

Index